# The Golden Era of
# Major League Baseball

# The Golden Era of Major League Baseball

## A Time of Transition and Integration

Bryan Soderholm-Difatte

ROWMAN & LITTLEFIELD
Lanham • Boulder • New York • London

Published by Rowman & Littlefield
A wholly owned subsidary of The Rowman & Littlefield Publishing Group, Inc.
4501 Forbes Boulevard, Suite 200, Lanham, Maryland 20706
www.rowman.com

Unit A, Whitacre Mews, 26-34 Stannary Street, London SE11 4AB

British Library Cataloguing in Publication Information Available

**Library of Congress Cataloging-in-Publication Data**

Soderholm-Difatte, Bryan.
The golden era of major league baseball : a time of transition and integration / Bryan Soderholm-
Difatte.
pages cm
Includes bibliographical references and index.
ISBN 978-1-4422-5221-9 (hardcover : alk. paper) — ISBN 978-1-4422-5222-6 (ebook) 1. Base-
ball—United States—History—20th century. 2. Baseball—Social aspects—United States. I. Title.
GV863.A1S688 2015
796.357'64—dc23
2015016289

Printed in the United States of America

*To my dad.*
*Thanks for hitting me all those ground balls when I was aspiring to be*
*Phil Rizzuto.*

# Contents

# Acknowledgments

The focus of my baseball research and writing over the years has been on identifying the underlying factors that provide context and insight to what happened and why. I have been particularly interested in considering key events and broader developments from perspectives that are different from the standard narratives about them. This is not, however, an intent to interpret any sort of "revisionist" history but rather to elucidate a better understanding of the history that did happen.

As such, perhaps my most important acknowledgment should be to the indispensable websites www.baseball-reference.com and www.retrosheet.org, from which derives the statistical data that underlies many of the judgments made in this book. Membership in the Society for American Baseball Research, including its journals, newsletters, and annual conferences, has provided the invaluable benefit of intellectual engagement with men and women devoted to the study of the game's history and statistical analysis.

Individually, I am most indebted to Fred Claire, professors Mary Corey (the College at Brockport, State University of New York) and Steven Wisensale (University of Connecticut), and peer reviewers for the Society for American Baseball Research (SABR) for insightful feedback and suggestions, particularly on the issue of major-league integration, that helped me to identify angles I had not considered and to clarify my analysis and writing.

Finally, special thanks to Jodi, who supported my decision to retire from working in the real world so I could pursue my passion for researching and writing about baseball. She has been endlessly encouraging about this project.

# Introduction

Batting seventh for the St. Louis Browns, number 7, second baseman Hank Thompson.

So it was on July 17, 1947, that Hank Thompson made his debut as the third black man to play in the major leagues, less than two weeks after Larry Doby made his with the Cleveland Indians on July 5. Doby is recognized as the first black player to integrate the American League, but the reality is that Hank Thompson and his teammate Willard Brown, whose first big-league game was two days later, had far more playing time and were far more consequential in that first year of major-league integration in 1947. Larry Doby started only 1 of the 29 games he played that season and appeared in the field in only 5 others. Used primarily as a pinch hitter, Doby hit a woeful .156 while striking out in a third of his plate appearances. Thompson started 18 games at second base for the Browns and hit .256, while Brown started 18 games in the outfield, with a batting average of only .179. By the end of August, both players were deemed major-league busts by the Browns and returned to the Negro League Kansas City Monarchs, from whence they had come.

Meanwhile, back East, east of the East River in Brooklyn, Jackie Robinson was shivering the timbers of major-league baseball's segregationist pillars. . . .

\* \* \*

The 1950s in major-league baseball. They call it the Golden Age. There were two "America's teams," both in New York, America's most vibrant and commercially significant city. One was the New York Yankees, representative of American drive and industry in the pursuit of excellence—efficient, resilient, resourceful, goal-oriented, and relentless to be the best every year. They had the golden boys, Mickey Mantle and Whitey Ford, to worship in American sports' most elegant and imposing cathedral, the Yankee Stadium. They were a team respected, admired, even feared nationwide, although not necessarily loved.

And there were the Brooklyn Dodgers, representative of the more populist and melting-pot strain in American society (the concepts of "multicultural" and "diversity" were yet to be had)—dynamic, reliable, stable, morally centered, forever optimistic about "next year" if this year was disappointing. They had the Boys of Summer, guys known familiarly as Jackie, Campy, Newk, and the Duke, Oisk, and Pee Wee, to see play in a bandbox that was close to being a dump, Ebbets Field. They too were a team respected, admired, and even feared nationwide but had more of a following and were more beloved across the land because of who they were.

There were perhaps an unprecedented number of great players in the major leagues in the 1950s, no doubt in large part because blacks were now able to play. *Hank Aaron*, Luis Aparicio, Richie Ashburn, *Ernie Banks*, Yogi Berra, Jim Bunning, *Roy Campanella*, *Orlando Cepeda*, *Roberto Clemente*, *Larry Doby*, Don Drysdale, Whitey Ford, Nellie Fox, *Monte Irvin*, Al Kaline, George Kell, Harmon Killebrew, Ralph Kiner, Sandy Koufax, Bob Lemon, Mickey Mantle, Eddie Mathews, *Willie Mays*, Bill Mazeroski, *Willie McCovey*, Stan Musial, Pee Wee Reese, Phil Rizzuto, Robin Roberts, Brooks Robinson, *Frank Robinson*, *Jackie Robinson*, Red Schoendienst, Duke Snider, Warren Spahn, Hoyt Wilhelm, Ted Williams, and Early Wynn are all Hall of Fame players whose best years included the 1950s, whose careers were centered on the 1950s, or who broke in late in the decade already showing what great players they would become. The 11 players whose names are in italics are black, because of which they would not have played in the major leagues had organized baseball's segregationist policies not been upended by the conviction of Branch Rickey and the courage of Jackie Robinson.

That list of names doesn't include Cooperstown immortals like Joe DiMaggio, Bob Feller, Johnny Mize, Hal Newhouser, and Country Slaughter, who had their moments in baseball's Golden Age but were at or near the end of their careers. And that's also not mentioning Hall of Fame managers Walt Alston, Leo Durocher, Al Lopez, and Casey Stengel.

\* \* \*

But this book isn't about the players. There will be little recounting of their exploits or personal anecdotes about their careers. It's about the 1950s being a decade of transition for major-league baseball.

Integration is the foremost legacy of the Golden Age. Even as the country was grappling with the volatile issues of equality (remember separate but equal?) and civil rights (Jim Crow, the right to vote, vigilante injustice) in American society, major-league baseball, mired in tradition and disdainful of "revolutionary" changes, found itself ironically at the leading edge of profound social change in the United States, although not without powerful resistance from within.

And there was a powerful impetus for expanding the geographic reach of the major leagues, leading inexorably toward expansion and a change in the status quo of the basic structure of the game that had been in place since the turn of the century. The United States, after all, had won a world war and was now the indispensible power in the new global fight against the evils of Soviet ideology and threat of Communist expansion. And even though facing up to that challenge meant fighting another bloody war, in Korea, in the early 1950s, the U.S. economy was booming, as was the country's population. The post–World War II "baby boom" was the biggest sustained surge in U.S. population since the period from the end of the Civil War to the turn of the century, and back then, the United States was fulfilling its Manifest Destiny of westward expansion by growing from 36 to 45 states. Consumerism and mobility became part of the American ethic, and there seemed no limits to growth. But if major-league baseball was at the forefront of change on societal issues, here baseball was behind the pace of change.

Then there was the game itself. If there has been nostalgia for the 1950s as a time of relative stability in American society, a simpler time when mainstream norms and values were not much questioned, still less assaulted, with the vigor of the counterculture generation that came of age in the sixties, the same seemed true for baseball. Baseball still had pride of place as the national pastime in its Golden Age, but, as the term itself implies—"golden age"—for all the dynamism of its new generation of star players, baseball was said to be more conservative on the field of play, less exciting, than in earlier generations. Part of that may have been because baseball always seemed to be about New York.

But just as there was considerable tumult about some of the particulars of American society, most notably segregation but also the excesses of McCarthyism, there were underlying currents in how the game was played that belied its depiction as rote and dull. In particular, position-player platoons in starting lineups and substitutions for a "platoon" advantage in batter–pitcher matchups at key moments that might affect the outcome of the game became more of an art; the structuring and managing of pitching staffs, especially relievers, was becoming more sophisticated, even though there was still no official statistic for "save"—(consequently, the "save" statistics used in this narrative were awarded to pitchers retroactively after major-league baseball first adopted saves as an official stat in 1969); and the excitement of the speed game, while lost in an era of unprecedented home runs, rising strikeouts, and fewer stolen bases and sacrifice bunts than in previous decades, was still there to be had and, by the end of the decade, was gaining momentum.

Finally, although not so much appreciated at the time, because it was mostly in-house, this was also an era when baseball statistical analysis was becoming more sophisticated. It had long been understood by insiders, including the writers who covered baseball, and anecdotally by savvy fans, that player performances should be judged by more than reliance on longstanding traditional box-score statistics like batting average, home runs, runs batted in, even won–lost record for pitchers. There was an appreciation that some statistics could misleadingly inflate or understate perceptions of a player's value, hence, Leo Durocher's famous words about scrappy second baseman Eddie Stanky—whose lifetime batting average was only .268 and whose .410 on-base percentage was below the radar and not on the back of baseball cards—"can't hit, can't run, can't field . . . all [he] can do is win," and, likewise, the argument that Joe DiMaggio was a better ballplayer in the aggregate—and the one you'd rather have on your team—than Ted Williams, who had the far more gaudy offensive statistics.

The unsung hero of this era whose life's work lurks behind the scenes of this narrative was not a ballplayer, a manager, or a team executive. He was Alan Roth, who pioneered the analysis of player performance beyond the box-score statistics. Hired by Branch Rickey, Roth took scoring a game to a new level by keeping track of the minute specifics of every pitch, every play, and every game situation that allowed him to present to the Dodgers detailed breakdowns on players' overall tendencies, how they did against specific pitchers or batters, and their ability to execute in particular situations. The specificity of his data was so unusual for the time that after Rickey left Brooklyn neither Dodger owner Walter O'Malley nor manager Charlie Dressen was much inclined to use them. But in fact, his data splits were a reliable, quantifiable check on the notes many players and managers were keeping in little black books or called on from memory and observation.

Roth's splits data and statistical analysis were still a very long way from today's advanced metrics to assess player performance and player value—such as the "win shares" metric developed by Bill James, a founding guru of modern statistical analysis, and the "wins above replacement" (WAR) metric used in the indispensible Baseball-Reference website. But they were the start. Wins above replacement—which measures a player's value by the number of wins he adds to his team above what would be expected of a replacement player from Triple-A—is the metric relied on for comparative purposes in this account of major-league baseball in mid-century transition.

\* \* \*

Three central characters are in this narrative—the visionary Branch Rickey, the eccentric-genius "Perfessor" Casey Stengel, and the brash, ethically challenged, do-whatever-it-takes-to-win Leo Durocher—and a fourth, Jackie Robinson, whose career animates the Golden Age, even if it is not the focus of attention here. And there is arguably a fifth—a player who was emblematic of baseball's challenge, once Jackie Robinson had broken the color barrier, to consolidate integration so that *any* black player with major-league ability, not just those like Robinson with superior skills, would have the same opportunities as white players of comparable ability to realistically compete for regular positions on major-league teams. That player's name is the aforementioned Hank Thompson.

# ONE

## The Arc of Integration

The story of the integration of major-league baseball is often presented as a triumph of the spirit and the ideals inherent in the idea of the United States of America at a time of narrow-minded widespread acceptance of segregation in American society even after the country had just fought a world war in the name of liberty, freedom, and justice for all. Part of what makes that narrative so compelling was not just the courageous forbearance and tremendous grace under pressure of Jackie Robinson on the field of play but also Branch Rickey's determination to press ahead with his "great experiment," as he called it, in the face of overwhelming opposition from his fellow owners. Rickey was guided by the courage of his convictions, informed by both his religious and political beliefs, that giving blacks the opportunity to compete in the major leagues was not just a moral imperative but also was sure to benefit the team for which he was part-owner and general manager—the Brooklyn Dodgers.

Two teams stood out in following the Brooklyn Dodgers down the road to integration in 1947—the Cleveland Indians and St. Louis Browns, both in the American League—but they did so without the careful preparation that Rickey considered essential to success. Rickey had put himself out on a limb in opposition to nearly all of the organized (white) baseball establishment with his intention to bring a black player into the major leagues and so did everything he could to minimize the chance of failure. Rickey intuitively knew that, had his social-engineering gambit failed, eventually there would have been integration, but it likely would not have been until well into the 1950s before another owner would have taken the chance.

In addition to carefully selecting a Negro League star with major-league-level skills and satisfying himself that he had the mental discipline and emotional fortitude to withstand the horrid racist treatment he

1

was bound to get, Rickey made sure to prepare the way by requiring that Robinson first spend a year of seasoning in the minor leagues at the Triple-A level. Of equal importance, although lost in the drama of the Jackie Robinson story, Rickey also signed two other Negro League players to minor-league contracts in 1946, catcher Roy Campanella and pitcher Don Newcombe, sending both to Brooklyn's B-level affiliate in Nashua, New Hampshire. He was building for the future, both to improve the Brooklyn Dodgers at the big-league level and to reinforce to fellow owners that Jackie Robinson was not a test case, that he was not going to back down from signing black players and promoting them to Brooklyn when they were major-league ready, that it was in the competitive interests of big-league teams to employ the best players they could find, regardless of race, and, moreover, that excluding blacks from America's national pastime was counterproductive from a business perspective and morally untenable.

Even as Robinson was tearing up the International League with Montreal in 1946, which made it obvious that Rickey was going to put him on Brooklyn's roster sooner than later, and Campanella and Newcombe were succeeding in Nashua, no other major-league team made a move to sign a black player and assign him to one of their minor-league teams. When Jackie Robinson made it to Ebbets Field on opening day in 1947, Brooklyn was the one and only major-league team with black players anywhere in its organization.

Needless to say, then, when the Indians and Browns decided to integrate their teams in the summer of 1947 after watching Jackie make good in his Brooklyn debut, they had no black players in their minor-league systems to call upon. Instead of providing them any seasoning with a Triple-A affiliate, both clubs assigned the black players whose contracts they had just purchased from Negro League teams directly onto their major-league roster. As a result, neither the Cleveland's Larry Doby nor the Browns' Hank Thompson and Willard Brown, good as they were in the Negro Leagues and clearly capable of playing in the majors, had the advantage of Robinson's acclimatization in the minor leagues to prepare for the challenges of being the first black players on their teams.

The Indians, however, handled the situation far better than the Browns. Becoming the second black to play in a major-league game when he appeared as a pinch hitter on July 5, 1947, Larry Doby did not break into the starting lineup in his rookie season. Not only was there no position for him to move to, because he was a second baseman and Cleveland was well set in the middle infield with Lou Boudreau at short and Joe Gordon at second, but also Doby was hopelessly overmatched at the plate, accruing only four singles, a double, and a walk in 33 plate appearances.

With such a dismal record of performance, Doby could have been deemed a bust—his inability to hit big-league pitching cited as evidence that, Jackie Robinson aside, Negro League players were just not up to major-league snuff—so no point in giving him another chance. But Cleveland's maverick owner, Bill Veeck, remained committed to Doby, boosting his opportunity to succeed by switching him from the middle infield to the outfield. Veeck acknowledged in his 1967 look back at his baseball life, *Veeck as in Wreck*, that he had not done due diligence in selecting and preparing the 23-year-old for the experience, which in retrospect he considered a mistake because Doby had not faced hard-edged prejudice in real life.

Unlike the Dodgers' careful preparation of Robinson and the Indians making it possible for Doby to succeed, the Browns' effort at integration was ill-considered, poorly planned, and virtually guaranteed to fail. The St. Louis Browns, in fact, were the poster team for how *not* to integrate. They became the third major-league team with a black player on their roster on July 17, 1947, when they purchased the contracts of Thompson and Brown from the Negro League Kansas City Monarchs, whose home base was across the state in Missouri. Both were major-league-quality players, Willard Brown in particular. An accomplished 13-year veteran of Negro League baseball, Brown was one of the best players in its history.

In giving them a chance to play major-league baseball, however, Browns' front-office executives were motivated less by the spirit of gaining a competitive advantage for a team mired in last place since only the 17th game of the season, after finishing seventh the year before, than by the desire to capitalize on the novelty of integration in hopes that having black players would boost their woeful attendance in a city with a large black population. At the time they were signed, the Browns were averaging less than 5,900 fans per game, by far the worst attendance in major-league baseball. While every other team was still benefiting from the postwar surge of attendance at big-league games—the number of fans who watched the action in 1947 surpassed the record set the previous year by 1.3 million—the Browns were drawing fewer people to their home field than they had in 1943. No other team had to endure such an indignity.

Hank Thompson and Willard Brown were perhaps not the right players to break the color barrier in the farthest south of all major-league cities. Thompson had neither the talent nor the temperament of either Jackie Robinson or Larry Doby and had problems with alcohol and trouble with the law. Brown was now at least 32 years old and more likely 4 years older. Moreover, notwithstanding his excellence, Brown lacked Robinson's drive and work ethic, according to accounts by contemporaries like Monte Irvin. Thompson and Brown, like Doby, went directly from the Negro Leagues one day to the major leagues the next.

Unlike Doby in Cleveland, however, both were immediately put into the starting lineup. Thompson started 18 of the 27 games he played for St. Louis, but in a platoon role; a left-handed batter, he started not once against southpaws, and only 3 of his 89 plate appearances were facing a lefty on the mound. Brown also started 18 games and appeared in 3 others as a pinch hitter. Thrust into the major leagues in a hostile clubhouse environment, both struggled to get untracked, and neither met whatever expectations the Browns had. Five weeks after being signed, both players were let go, their presence having made little impact on either the standings or attendance.

Neither was given a fair shot, although both went out on a high note. Thompson hit .333 with hits in eight of the last nine games he played for the Browns before being released. Brown had only three hits in his last 29 at bats before he was sent packing, but his last hit in the major leagues was a pinch-hit two-run eighth-inning game-winning home run off Detroit Tigers ace Hal Newhouser, a Hall of Fame pitcher still in his prime. That earned Willard Brown but one more start (the next day) and another pinch-hitting appearance before he and Thompson were back with the Monarchs.

* * *

Because integration was a revolutionary idea in major-league baseball, its success was dependent not only on the talent, courage, and relentless will of the black players breaking the color barrier for the teams willing to make history but also on the support of their manager. The role of one manager in particular—Leo Durocher—should not be overlooked, either with the Dodgers or the Giants.

As early as 1942, in only his fourth year as Brooklyn manager, Durocher had been called on the commissioner's carpet for insinuating that black players were being barred from major-league baseball. It certainly didn't help his case with the commissioner, Judge Kenesaw Mountain Landis, that Durocher made his comments to a Communist Party newspaper, the *Daily Worker*, which, like other New York City dailies at the time, covered sports—particularly baseball—in addition to its focus on labor issues and politics. If certainly impolitic regardless of which media outlet he might have chosen, Durocher was correct on substance; Commissioner Landis and the most influential owners around him refused to entertain such a notion as the integration of black players into the major leagues.

It was Durocher who welcomed Jackie Robinson in the spring of 1947 and who had to navigate the opposition of key Dodger veterans to the unprecedented presence of a black player in a big-league clubhouse. Though this was Branch Rickey's initiative and he worked for Mr. Rickey (and, therefore, he could go along or move on along to somewhere else), Durocher genuinely recognized Robinson to be an outstanding player who could only help Brooklyn's pennant chances, particularly in the year after the Dodgers had finished the scheduled season in a first-place tie only to lose the pennant to the St. Louis Cardinals in a playoff series. It was Durocher who, in the strongest terms, warned the Dodgers' mostly Southern insurrectionists threatening to refuse to play with a black man that, if they didn't like it, well, then *they* were expendable.

Durocher did not get to manage Robinson in his rookie year because of his suspension by new the commissioner, former U.S. senator A. B. "Happy" Chandler, for conduct—including his tempestuous personal life and associations with Hollywood high rollers and gamblers—deemed detrimental to the best interests of baseball. Returning to the Dodger dugout in 1948, Durocher stood by his beleaguered player after antagonizing Robinson by criticizing and hounding him for coming to spring training overweight and out of shape. Durocher also wanted Roy Campanella to be the Dodgers' starting catcher when the season opened, was overruled by Rickey's decision to send the aspiring major leaguer back to Triple-A, but wasted no time inserting Campy into the daily lineup when he was recalled to Brooklyn at the beginning of July. By mid-July, however, Durocher had worn out his welcome with Mr. Rickey, who arranged an offer for him to manage the archrival New York Giants, much to the amazement and chagrin of the Brooklyn faithful.

The team Durocher inherited at the Polo Grounds was not his kind of team. The Giants had considerable power in their lineup, but he was unhappy with the lack of team speed because it limited him to a one-dimensional offense. It being that the Giants had not been a factor in any pennant race since the late 1930s, Durocher demanded a makeover and, having seen Robinson and Campanella and knowing all about Newcombe, insisted that owner Horace Stoneham follow the Dodgers' lead and recruit major-league-level players from the Negro Leagues. As the 1949 season was about to get underway, the Giants acquired the rights of future Hall of Famer Monte Irvin and Hank Thompson, who had already "failed" his trial run with the Browns two years before. Both were assigned to the Giants' Triple-A affiliate in Jersey City in preparation for being called up to New York.

With the quite rational baseball philosophy of "as long as you can play good baseball, you can play for this team," as he was quoted by Irvin, Durocher that year helped ease the major-league transitions of Irvin and Thompson and of Willie Mays in 1951. Thompson, given a second chance by Durocher despite not being an elite player, and Mays, who Durocher famously carefully nurtured and protected through his early struggles, were excellent examples of the difference a supportive manager made to the success of black players coming into the historically closed society that was major-league baseball. Leo Durocher was instrumental in Hank Thompson's being the first black player who was not a potential superstar to become a long-term regular in the starting lineup of a major-league team. Willie Mays, of course, had more potential as an unproven player than Thompson, but it is conceivable that his resplendent career might never have taken off were it not for Durocher's patience and refusal to give up on Mays when he was struggling badly after being called up as a 20-year-old rookie in late May 1951.

\* \* \*

In Cleveland, meanwhile, player-manager Lou Boudreau was sufficiently farsighted that he did not give up on Larry Doby when the young player failed to get traction after being thrown into a major-league uniform in July 1947 with no preparation for the experience. As manager, Boudreau could have resisted owner Bill Veeck's refusal to follow the Browns' lead and release his first black player for not making the grade, and he would have had Doby's paltry numbers to back him up. Instead, Boudreau did his best to make Doby feel welcome, encouraged him in his shift from the infield to the outfield, and presided over Larry Doby having a breakout season in 1948 that helped the Indians win a tight three-team pennant race and the World Series on his way to a major-league Hall of Fame career. Doby's .375 batting down the stretch was the best on the team as the Indians won 22 of their final 30 games to win the pennant. He also hit for the highest average among Cleveland's starting position players in their six-game World Series dismantling of the Boston Braves. His home run off 24-game winner Johnny Sain was the difference in Game 4, which gave the Indians a decisive three-games-to-one lead in the Series.

Whatever his attributes as a player-manager—and he was not widely considered to be one of baseball's better managers at the time—Lou Boudreau earned considerable respect among black players that carried well into the 1950s for his giving blacks the opportunity to succeed. After Veeck signed veteran Negro League pitching star Satchel Paige, of indeterminate age but at least already in his early to mid-40s, almost a year to the day after Doby was acquired, Boudreau immediately thrust him into the heat of the 1948 pennant chase. Paige was used mostly in relief but won four of his five starts in August, with a no decision, as the Indians took a short-lived lead in the pennant race. The first shutout of his career in only his second start in the big leagues put the Indians into first place at the time. Two years later, Boudreau stuck with 34-year-old slugging first baseman Luke Easter despite his early struggles against big-league pitching.

After he left Cleveland, Boudreau's reputation was only enhanced by the perceptions of the team's black players that his successor, Al Lopez, treated them unfairly. Lopez was considered too quick to sideline black players if they struggled, including Easter, who Lopez soured on because of his age, injuries, and defensive deficiencies. Doby, Easter, and outfielder Al Smith were nonetheless cornerstone position players without whom Lopez's Indians would not have been competed in close pennant races with the Yankees in the first half of the 1950s.

\* \* \*

The biggest mistake made by the St. Louis Browns in their ill-fated and aborted effort at integration in 1947 was failing to get their manager's buy-in, which assured there would be no time for manager Muddy Ruel to prepare his clubhouse for the arrival and playing time of Hank Thompson and Willard Brown. Whatever credit Browns' front-office executives deserved for making an effort more venal than righteous to integrate the team, it was undermined by the fact that Ruel—who was himself from St. Louis—was not supportive of the move and did little to create a clubhouse environment where Thompson and Brown could feel like accepted members of the team. As was the case in the Brooklyn clubhouse when Jackie Robinson was breaking in, there was considerable hostility by the white Browns toward their new black teammates.

But Muddy Ruel was no Leo Durocher. Instead of upbraiding Browns players who objected to blacks on the team and making clear his full support for Thompson and Brown, as Durocher did for Robinson to stymie the incipient rebellion by members of the Dodgers' Southern contingent in spring training 1947, Ruel did nothing but implicitly show his contempt for their presence by maintaining a studious passivity, both in the clubhouse and with the media. One player who quit the team in protest at having to play with blacks was reinstated a few days later after he thought better about the loss of income. When the two players were returned to their Negro League team after five weeks in the big leagues, Ruel said they had received a "fair trial" but lacked major-league talent, and Browns' general manager Bill DeWitt proclaimed that they "had failed to reach major league standards." These were precisely the sentiments that most in (white) organized baseball were inclined to believe about black players and were not displeased to see seemingly validated.

Thompson certainly would have benefited from at least a year of preparation in the minor leagues but would not have been a great player on the order of either Robinson or Doby. The more damning indictment is that had Ruel and the Browns shown the patience and support for Willard Brown during his brief tenure in 1947 that Durocher and the Giants did when Mays struggled when he was first called up, he might have been as formidable a player in the major leagues as would have been possible for someone already at least 32 years old. Just as Mays broke out of a debilitating and demoralizing slump at the start of his career by hitting his first career home run off a future Hall of Fame pitcher, Warren Spahn, perhaps Brown's first (and only) big-league home run off a future Hall of Fame pitcher, Hal Newhouser, might have jump-started his career—if he had been given more of a chance. As it was, Willard Brown resumed a starring role in the Negro Leagues after his brief major-league trial, winning a batting title in 1951, and in 2006, he was elected to the Hall of Fame for the excellence of his Negro League career.

* * *

Once the immediate competitive success of Brooklyn and Cleveland with black players in starring roles assured that integration was a fait accompli, at least as far as *outstanding* players were concerned, other teams began scouting and signing black players for the minor leagues. Few teams, however, had in mind to promote them to their big-league roster any time soon, and those that did gave much less thought to the importance of the manager in helping to shepherd black players through the ordeals of breaking the color barrier in the clubhouse, where white players were still generally unsupportive if not outright hostile, while simultaneously breaking into the league. Through most of the 1950s, many managers, all of whose baseball careers had been when the major leagues were staunchly segregationist, betrayed a casual racism in their clubhouse interactions even while they valued the presence of black players on their roster and their performance on the field.

The Boston-to-Milwaukee Braves were the fourth major-league team to integrate their roster and not take a step back, as the Browns did in giving up on Thompson and the veteran Brown after only five weeks in 1947 and not having another black player on their roster until Satchel Paige in 1951. Despite the Braves being a franchise committed to integration, their managers were complicit in attitudes perceived as demeaning by their black players.

When Sam Jethroe, a promising prospect acquired from the Dodgers' organization, took his place in center field on April 18, 1950, the Braves were one of only four major-league teams to open that season with at least one black player. But they did little to ease his transition into the major leagues. Old-school manager Billy Southworth, who by now had alienated most of his team since winning the 1948 pennant, was not encouraging of Jethroe in his rookie year and was prone to using racial slurs to criticize (or perhaps motivate?) his lone black player. When he struggled after getting off to a hot start, and again in the final month, the Braves did little to publicly support Jethroe in the face of hypercritical Boston press coverage. It being that he nonetheless led the league in steals and was voted NL Rookie of the Year, Jethroe deserved better.

During his three years in Boston, where he grappled with loneliness and problems with his eyesight, the Braves were unsympathetic to Jethroe's struggles and bemoaned his underachievement. In 1952, in the midst of striking out a horrendous (especially for the era) 112 times in 687 plate appearances hitting primarily in the leadoff spot, Jethroe clashed with new manager Charlie Grimm, ultimately sealing his fate with the Braves. Rather than give Jethroe the opportunity to seek appropriate attention and rehabilitation for his lack of visual acuity, Grimm played him in all but four of the Braves' games. Jethroe did not accompany the Braves to their new home in Milwaukee in 1953 but had a terrific season with their Triple-A affiliate, including 27 steals, 28 home runs, and a .309 batting average—none of which was enough to get him another look in a Braves uniform.

Whatever their feelings about Jethroe, Braves executives—in particular, General Manager John Quinn—remained committed to scouting and promoting black players as part of a long-term strategy to improve the team, which included the move from Boston to Milwaukee. Outfielders Hank Aaron, Bill Bruton, and Wes Covington were products of this strategy, which paid off in helping make the Milwaukee Braves the National League's best team in the latter half of the decade.

Despite the instrumental role of their black teammates in the Braves becoming pennant contenders, and indicative of the time, there remained an undercurrent of cultural insensitivity at best, or racial prejudice at worst, in the clubhouse that Grimm, likely without malice, played into even though he was manager. An astute judge of talent, Grimm on the one hand was proactive in giving talented black players who could improve his team the opportunity to play regularly. In 1954, for example, Grimm insisted on promoting Aaron to the big-league club a year earlier than the Braves had planned, and the previous year he made the far less talented Bruton his center fielder, replacing Jethroe. On the other hand, rather than using his authority to transform the clubhouse culture, Grimm—widely known as a players' manager who liked to be one of the guys (who were predominantly white)—participated in clubhouse razzing of his team's black players, including referring to Aaron by demeaning names associated with minstrel shows.

\* \* \*

The aging patriarchs of the American League fought a passive-aggressive rear-guard action to impede integration. As early as 1950, they must have recognized that the Dodgers' and Indians' competitive success with black stars meant there was no returning to segregated major-league baseball but probably hoped to limit the crossover of blacks. Connie Mack, who both owned and managed the Philadelphia Athletics, Clark Griffith (and his nephew, who was like a son) of the Washington Senators, and Walter Briggs (and his son) of the Detroit Tigers, as well as the younger owners of the Boston Red Sox (Tom Yawkey) and the New York Yankees, whose ownership group in 1946 and 1947 included Larry MacPhail, were adamantly opposed to Branch Rickey's "great experiment" and held out against the integration of their own teams for as long as they could or until the shame of doing so forced their hand.

Even as the Dodgers and Indians immediately reaped competitive benefits from integration, Mack, Griffith, Briggs, Yawkey, and the Yankees held to the notion that the purity of the game demanded segregation. Seeing themselves as defenders of the traditions and sanctity of the game, they believed major-league baseball, because it had always been segregated, should remain so. Moreover, blacks had their own "major leagues"—the Negro Leagues—which, in any event, according to them, did not really play up to "major league" standards. They argued that segregation in major-league baseball was a good thing because it protected the viability of the Negro Leagues, giving blacks the opportunity to play baseball for a decent living. This was, of course, an insincere paternalistic plantation mentality that should have been long discredited since the Civil War.

These attitudes reflected the consensus of a report addressing fundamental issues facing major-league baseball, including the "race question," that was prepared for Commissioner Chandler in August 1946 by an owners' subcommittee that included both league presidents, MacPhail and Yawkey from the American League, and Phil Wrigley, owner of the Chicago Cubs, and St. Louis Cardinals' owner Sam Breadon from the National League. The "MacPhail Report," as it came to be known, tackled head-on the "people who charge that baseball is flying a Jim Crow flag at its masthead—or think that racial discrimination is the basic reason for failure of the major leagues to give employment to Negroes" by accusing them of "simply talking through their individual or collective hats."

The report set as its foundation premise in addressing the "race question" that "professional baseball is a private business enterprise [that] depends on profits for its existence, just like any other business." Written in the year Branch Rickey had integrated organized (white) baseball by assigning Jackie Robinson to the Dodgers' Triple-A team in Montreal, where he was excelling in all aspects of the game on his way to the International League batting title, the report observed that there was a tremendous increase of black fans at all the games in which he played, and in two Triple-A cities—Newark and Baltimore—blacks accounted for more than half the attendance when Robinson's team played there. As paying spectators, they were surely contributing to club coffers, but the report warned that such levels of black attendance at Yankee Stadium and the Polo Grounds in New York City and Comiskey Park, home of the White Sox in Chicago, "could conceivably threaten the value of the Major League franchises owned by these clubs." The report did not specify Ebbets Field, which all concerned knew was Jackie's ultimate destination.

Once that very pregnant point was made—and it was certainly one that motivated the Yankees well into the integration era—the MacPhail Report went on to assert that very few blacks in the Negro Leagues had "the technique, the coordination, the competitive aptitude, and the discipline" to compete at the major-league level and that the Negro Leagues were not developing black players with those attributes. Furthermore, if the best black players left to play in the major leagues, then the "Negro leagues will eventually fold up—the investments of their club owners will be wiped out—and a lot of professional Negro players will lose their jobs." And finally, back to the issue of money, major-league teams would lose out on substantial revenue from renting out their stadiums to Negro League teams with star players. All of this "is not racial discrimination," the committee concluded. "It's simply respecting the contractual relationship between the Negro leagues and their players." The MacPhail Report made no specific recommendations but went "on record" asserting that the problem "vitally affects each and every one of us" and that any "fair and just solution" should be "compatible with good business judgment and the principles of good sportsmanship."

While these patriarchs of the game all almost certainly harbored racially prejudiced attitudes toward blacks as inferior to whites, their mindset was consistent with the large segregationist sentiment in broader American society. To be fair, however, they may have been racially prejudiced more by acculturation and habit than from any overt Jim Crow mentality, giving little critical thought to the basis of their attitudes. Either way, they feared the consequences of integration, and they may genuinely have believed Branch Rickey's and Bill Veeck's social engineering contained the seeds of the game's destruction.

They may have opposed integrating major-league baseball because they believed in segregation—separate but equal—between races, with its foundation prejudice of white superiority. Or they may have been opposed to such a revolutionary change for practical and economic reasons, concerned that integration would undermine the structure of America's "national pastime" by alienating players and especially a fan base that believed in a segregated society. Or they may have been boxed in by decades of their own rhetoric to justify (white) organized baseball's no-blacks-allowed policy and did not want to admit—even to themselves—that they may have been wrong in asserting blacks could not play up to major-league standards. For any of these reasons, following the lead of Rickey and Veeck would have forced them to confront the reality—and worse, to publicly do so—that they had perpetrated both an evil and a fraud on the game by having so long denied blacks the opportunity, and the right, to play major-league baseball.

Many of the teams that held fast against major-league integration nonetheless signed black players for their minor-league affiliates, if for no other reason than appearances' sake. Doing so allowed them to rationalize, as the Yankees famously did, that not integrating their teams had nothing to do with discrimination. Rather, they had yet to find "the right Negro player" and would not in the meantime be pressured or intimidated into promoting black players who did not have the skills to play in the major leagues.

Blacks were playing in the Yankees' minor-league system as early as 1949, but it would not be until six years later that their dugout at Yankee Stadium was integrated. The Red Sox signed Negro League star infielder Piper Davis in 1950, released him because of "economic conditions" once the season was over, did not sign another black player until 1953, and waited another six years before integrating their dugout at Fenway Park. The Athletics did not sign a black player until 1951, after Mack, approaching 90, finally retired as owner as well as manager, and did not promote a black onto their big-league roster for another two years. Griffith's Senators signed their first black players in 1952, but they were from Cuba, where the team had recruited non-black Latin players since the 1930s. It was a player from Cuba who integrated the Senators in September 1954, and it was not until late in the 1957 season, after Griffith had died, that Washington had an African American in their Griffith Stadium dugout. Detroit did not sign a black player until 1953, after the elder Briggs died. They were the next-to-last major-league team to integrate five years after that.

That these teams were able to hold out on integration for as long as they did was entirely attributable to the New York Yankees being enormously successful in the early 1950s without having an integrated roster. Yankee owners Dan Topping and Del Webb—MacPhail left the ownership group after the 1947 World Series—were first opposed, then resistant, and ultimately very slow to embrace racial diversity. They could afford to be because of the depth of their "white" talent at both the major-league and minor-league levels. Even when they had a black player who not only played extremely well for their highest minor-league affiliate but also played a position—first base—where the Yankees had been platooning since 1948, it was not enough for them to bring him up to the Bronx. Despite hitting .340 in 1952 and 1953 for Triple-A Kansas City, and winning the batting title the second year, Vic Power never got to play in New York pinstripes; he was traded to the Athletics instead.

The Yankees did not integrate until Elston Howard made the roster in 1955 as the backup catcher to Yogi Berra because he was versatile enough to also play the outfield and corner infield positions, even though he was not—apparently to manager Casey Stengel's chagrin—very fast. Despite his lack of speed, Howard quickly proved valuable as a role player in Stengel's scheme of constantly shuffling his lineup, but he was the Yankees' only black player until outfielder Harry Simpson was acquired in a trade from Kansas City during the 1957 season.

Indicative of American League teams' dragging their heels on integration, in 1956—10 years into the Jackie Robinson era—only 7 of the 21 black players who were regulars played in the junior circuit. Three of them (Power, Simpson, and Hector Lopez) played for one team alone, the downtrodden Kansas City Athletics. Three others played for the Indians (Al Smith) and White Sox (Larry Doby and Minnie Miñoso), the two earliest AL teams to fully embrace integration. By the end of the 1959 season, when the major league's last holdout team against integration—the Boston Red Sox—finally fielded a black player, 41 blacks had played in the American League, less than half the number (89) who had worn the uniforms of National League teams, according to Rick Swaine's count in his 2006 book, *The Black Stars Who Made Baseball Whole*. And only 5 of those 41—in order of appearance, Doby, Miñoso, Smith, Power, and Lopez—were regulars for as many as five years between 1947 and 1960.

Not counted among those five is Elston Howard, a key utility player for the Yankees who reached as many as 400 plate appearances only twice between his rookie year of 1955 and 1960. Until he finally became the Yankees' regular catcher in 1961 at the age of 32, Howard had started as many as 100 games only once—in 1959, divided between first base, catcher, and the outfield. In 1963, 16 years after Doby integrated the league, Howard became the first black player to be named Most Valuable Player in the American League. The National League in those 16 years had 8 different black players win a total of 11 MVP Awards.

The hardheadedness (and hardheartedness) of the Athletics, the Senators, the Tigers, the Red Sox (who were hardheaded and hardhearted longer than any other franchise), and especially the New York Yankees—the league's flagship team—condemned the American League to being slower to accept blacks as bona fide major leaguers, to its shame—and its detriment—because black players helped make the National League the more exciting and dominant league over the next two decades, especially as measured by the outcome of annual All-Star Games but also as measured by attendance.

\* \* \*

Fortunately for the legacy of major-league baseball being ahead of the curve on the issue of racial equality in postwar America, Branch Rickey ignored his fellow owners' concerns about the consequences of integration, including the "bad for business" rationale articulated in the Mac-Phail Report, and did not hesitate to promote Jackie Robinson to the Brooklyn club in 1947. The wisdom and righteousness of Rickey's cause was validated by the fact that every pennant-winning team in the National League between 1949 and 1960 included multiple black players in starting roles except for one—the all-white 1950 Philadelphia Phillies, a franchise whose attitude toward integration was as reprehensible as any in the American League.

# TWO

## Boston's Postwar Dynasty That Wasn't

It took a world war to end the New York Yankees' dominance of the American League.

From 1936, when Joe DiMaggio burst onto the scene as a rookie, through 1942, major-league baseball's last year of normality before wartime exigencies stripped many players from their teams to serve in the armed forces of the United States, the Yankees won six pennants and five World Series in seven years. And they did so in dominating fashion. The Yankees won 100 games 5 times and just missed out with 99 wins in 1938 when 2 games that had been rained out were not made up. In all 6 of their pennants, the Yankees finished at least 9 games ahead of the runner-up, including 3 by 17 games or more. So dominant were the Yankees in winning their six pennants that they were not seriously threatened after July in any of those seasons. They dominated the league offensively, leading the American League, indeed both major leagues, in scoring five times. And they dominated the league in pitching and defense, allowing the fewest runs of any American League team in all six of their pennants.

The Boston Red Sox were the Yankees' only real rival in the first seven years of DiMaggio's career. Boston owner Tom Yawkey's lavish spending in the mid-1930s on veteran great players like Lefty Grove, Joe Cronin, and Jimmie Foxx and young up-and-comers including Ted Williams paid off with the Red Sox finishing second in four of the five years up to 1942. But Boston never seriously threatened New York's stranglehold on first place. The one year the Yankees failed to win the pennant in 1940, when they finished a close third, the Red Sox failed to take advantage by having their own bad season, ending up tied in fourth place.

The two teams were poised to battle for supremacy when America's wartime manpower needs began decimating their rosters. Two-thirds of

the 1942 Yankees' starting outfield—DiMaggio and Tommy Henrich—
and shortstop Phil Rizzuto were called into service for three wartime
years beginning in 1943, as was two-thirds of Boston's starting outfield—
Williams and Dom DiMaggio—and their shortstop, Johnny Pesky. In
1944, the Yankees lost five more of their players to the world at war—left
fielder Charlie Keller, second baseman Joe Gordon, catcher Bill Dickey,
starting pitchers Spud Chandler and Marius Russo, and ace reliever Johnny Murphy. Boston's star second baseman, Bobby Doerr, joined them in
late 1944 and was missing from baseball action in all of 1945, and Red Sox
pitching ace Tex Hughson was called up in 1945.

There is every reason to suppose the Red Sox would have given the
Yankees a run for their pennant money through the mid-1940s had there
been no war and both teams' rosters stayed intact. When their star
players returned from the war in 1946—most prominently, Joe DiMaggio,
Dickey, Gordon, Henrich, and Rizzuto for the Yankees and Williams,
Doerr, Pesky, and Dom DiMaggio for the Red Sox—the two teams were
primed to resume their rivalry.

But war or no war, the Red Sox—and not the Yankees—would have
won the American League in 1946, so dominant was Boston that year.
With a 104–50 record, the Red Sox were in command all season long,
eventually winning the pennant by 12 games over the Detroit Tigers, the
defending World Series champions. The only day the entire season Boston was not in first place was nine games into the schedule. The Yankees
held first place that day, but they were never a factor in the pennant race,
finishing 17 games behind in third. Although they lost a compelling
seven-game World Series to the St. Louis Cardinals, which was just what
America needed after four years of fighting a world war, their 1946 pennant seemed to set the table for them to displace the New York Yankees
as the likely next dynasty in major-league baseball.

Times were changing in New York and not just because Boston now
had a team that seemed as enduringly formidable as the Yankees had
been. The Yankees had a new ownership group led by mercurial team
president Larry MacPhail, who made it clear that Joe McCarthy was no
longer welcome as manager despite the enormous role he played in
building the dynastic brand the Yankees had become. MacPhail thought
McCarthy, now 59 years old, was too insular and inflexible, behind the
times, and made much of his drinking habits (although MacPhail himself
often behaved outrageously under the influence). McCarthy, for his part,
resented MacPhail's meddling.

Thirty-five games into the 1946 season, McCarthy was gone as manager—even though the Yankees were in second place with a 22–13 record,
on pace for 97 wins over a 154-game schedule. With MacPhail engaging
in some less-than-subtle character assassination about his having lost his
edge and drinking to excess, McCarthy's departure from the Bronx was
less than celebratory, especially for a manager with his record of accom-

plishment. Nobody was going to catch the 1946 Red Sox, but the Yankees did not play nearly as well after McCarthy "resigned" as their manager.

The two teams' fortunes were reversed in 1947. The Red Sox put up little fight in their defense of AL bragging rights. This time it was the Yankees winning the pennant by 12 games, the Tigers were again caught in the middle, and it was the Red Sox who were far behind in third place, 14 games off pace. Now managed by Bucky Harris, whose long-time managerial pedigree dated to when he guided the previously woeful Washington Senators to back-to-back American League pennants as a player-manager in 1924 and 1925, the team in the Bronx won in what had become the traditional Yankee way by taking virtually unassailable charge of the pennant race by mid-season. From mid-June to mid-July, 31 wins in 34 games, including 19 straight at one point, allowed the Yankees to open an insurmountable 11½-game lead by the end of July.

Following Boston's competitive collapse in 1947, Joe Cronin, their long-time manager, stepped out of the dugout to move onto Yawkey's executive staff as general manager. Cronin had been managing in Boston since 1935, but his time had come and gone with only the 1946 pennant to show for his efforts and a deflating aftermath to that crown. There was a perspective among Boston baseball writers that Cronin, perhaps because he was a player-manager until 1941 (and when necessary during the war years), was too relaxed as manager, that he lacked a killer instinct in command. This is not to say Cronin didn't want to win as badly as any other manager, only that he did not pay as much attention to preparation as he might have to ensure that his players instinctively knew what to do in any circumstance on the ball field and never let up no matter how lost-cause the season might seem.

These were not faults that could be attributed to Joe McCarthy. Relentless preparation, attention to detail, and sustained intensity were the strengths that made him such a great manager with the Yankees, who McCarthy guided to eight pennants and seven World Series titles in his fifteen years in the Bronx.

The Red Sox were clearly thought to have underachieved, and the now-retired McCarthy was seen as just the manager needed to return them to first place. When Yawkey and Cronin offered him the manager's spot in the Fenway dugout, it probably occurred to McCarthy that beating out the Yankees for the pennant would be a validation that he could still manage in the big leagues and prove that MacPhail was wrong about his having lost his edge. And the Red Sox, with the strength of their roster—and a veteran roster at that—seemed a good bet, under his command, to displace the Yankees for some years to come as the best team in baseball.

Aside from the new level of discipline, intensity, and work ethic that McCarthy brought to Boston, the 1948 Red Sox were much improved on the field. They added star, power-hitting shortstop Vern Stephens and pitchers Jack Kramer and Ellis Kinder in a lopsided trade with the St. Louis Browns. Versatile rookie Billy Goodman was on board to play first base. Southpaw Mel Parnell was ready to move into the starting rotation after only 15 games and 51 innings pitched in 1947.

McCarthy mystified some by his controversial decision to shift short-stop Johnny Pesky over to third to make room for Stephens. Pesky was perceived as the better defensive shortstop, had starred at the position for Boston since his rookie season of 1942 (not including three years of World War II service), and was a Fenway fan favorite, but McCarthy considered Pesky better suited to third base than Stephens because of his superior agility and quickness.

* * *

McCarthy managed in Boston for only two full seasons—1948 and 1949— and turn around the Red Sox he surely did in two of baseball's pennant races for the ages. Both years the Red Sox got off to sluggish starts. Both years McCarthy drove his team from the middle of the pack in midsummer into contention for the pennant. Both years his team outpaced their rivals in the second half of the season. Both years the Red Sox entered the final day of the season tied for first place. And both years ended bitterly for McCarthy, with his Red Sox losing the final game that meant everything because of pitching decisions he made that backfired, were much second-guessed at the time, and remain second-guessed for all time.

Shades of the previous year, the 1948 Red Sox started off slowly and were no better than even at 32–32 when they took the field on Independence Day. But a 25–9 record in July thrust them into the heart of what became a ferocious three-team pennant race that included the Cleveland Indians, who spent most of the summer on top, and the Yankees, of course, who spent only two days in first place the entire season but were never far from the top.

The 1948 Red Sox had an imposing offense. Batting leadoff, Dom Di-Maggio got on base nearly 40 percent of the time, and his 127 runs were second in the league. Ted Williams, the best offensive player in the league, got on base almost exactly half the time he came to bat, hit .359 to lead the league in batting, knocked out 25 home runs, and drove in 127 runs. Taking advantage of home-field Fenway Park's close-in left-field wall—not yet globally famous as the Green Monster—Stephens hit a new career-high 29 home runs, and his 137 RBIs led the team and were second in the league. Bobby Doerr knocked out 27 home runs and had 111 RBIs. Pesky made a successful transition at third. The 907 runs scored by Boston were the most by any team since the 1939 Yankees.

For most of September, Boston held serve in first place, their rivals not far behind. On September 22, Cleveland ace Bob Feller beat the Red Sox, and the two teams now shared the top of the standings. Two days later, after the Yankees beat the Red Sox, all three teams were tied for first, each with seven games left on their schedules. While the Red Sox eliminated the Yankees on the next-to-last day of the season, they still trailed the Indians by one game. To finish the season with identical records to force a playoff for the pennant, Boston needed to beat New York again *and* for Cleveland's indomitable Feller to lose. Both things happened.

The 1948 American League pennant was only the second in major-league history to be decided by a playoff, coming just two years after the Cardinals and Dodgers finished the 1946 National League schedule in a flat-footed tie. Unlike the three-game playoff that was the National League format if 154 games were not enough to determine the pennant winner, the American League format called for just one game.

This was a pivotal moment in Boston Red Sox history and not just because a pennant was at stake. Win and, especially with their imposing lineup, the Red Sox were poised to become one of the best teams in history. Lose and they might be remembered for squandering greatness.

With the pennant race having come down to a single-game playoff to decide the outcome, and the game to be played at home in Fenway Park, McCarthy had his best pitcher, 15-game winner Mel Parnell, available with three days' rest—which was typical for starting pitchers at the time. McCarthy instead chose to start little-used Denny Galehouse.

Who?

Galehouse was a veteran journeyman 36-year-old pitcher nearing the end of the road. (He would in fact pitch only two more games in the major leagues after this one.) He had lost more than he won, with a career 109–117 record coming into this game. And he was not a regular among McCarthy's core of Boston starting pitchers. But he did have experience pitching in games with the highest of stakes. Pitching for the 1944 St. Louis Browns, who had never in their entire American League history won a pennant, Galehouse shut out the Yankees on five hits on the next-to-last day of the season to ensure the Browns went into the final day tied for first with Detroit. The Browns won the next day, the Tigers lost their game, and major-league baseball had the first and only World Series played exclusively in St. Louis, as the Browns took on the National League–champion Cardinals. Galehouse won the opening game of the Series, 2–1, beating Cardinals' ace Mort Cooper, but lost to Cooper, 2–0, in Game 5, surrendering two home runs while pitching another complete game. The Browns lost the only World Series they played the next day.

Other than the specific choice of Galehouse, however, McCarthy's decision not to pitch Parnell had a certain logic. Cleveland's most danger-ous hitters and run-producers—shortstop (and manager) Lou Boudreau, second baseman Joe Gordon (who had starred for McCarthy with the Yankees), and third baseman Ken Keltner, batting third, fourth, and fifth—were all right-handed hitters, and Parnell was both a southpaw *and* a rookie pitching at Fenway Park, where that close-in monster wall was an inviting target for right-handed batters. Moreover, Parnell started most often on four days' rest that year and had made only one start with three days of rest since early August, which was his last start in Boston's third-to-last game of the scheduled season. On the other hand, 8 of Parnell's 15 victories came at Fenway Park, and he had beaten Cleveland three times, including twice in Boston.

But why Galehouse, who had started only 14 games, had appeared in 26 games total, and had but 8 wins on the season? One of his wins, however, was against the Indians in Cleveland, back in July in extended relief of Parnell, who had been battered for seven runs in the first inning. Two of McCarthy's other right-handed starters, Jack Kramer (18–5 for the year) and Joe Dobson (16–10), were spent, having pitched in must-win games against the Yankees the two previous days, but McCarthy also had Ellis Kinder available with sufficient rest. Although the right-hander Kinder was 10–7 and pitching well, he was not in McCarthy's starting rotation when the season began, most of his starts were against second-rate teams, and his pitching performance against the Indians hardly inspired confidence. Of Kinder's 10 wins in 1948, his only victory against either of the two other top teams in the league was at the expense of the Yankees, and he had been battered the three times he faced the Indians, two of them starts, giving up 22 hits, 9 walks, and 16 earned runs in 14⅓ innings.

In deciding to start Galehouse, McCarthy was perhaps remembering back to Game 1 of the 1929 World Series, when he was managing the Chicago Cubs. In only his fourth year as a big-league manager, McCarthy was up against the most highly respected manager in the game, the Philadelphia Athletics' Connie Mack. The Athletics completely dominated the American League that year, and Mack had any of three aces he could have used to get the World Series off to a great start for his team. There was Lefty Grove, whose 20–6 record gave him the best winning percentage among American League pitchers, who led the league in earned run average for the first of four consecutive seasons, and who led the league in strikeouts for the fifth-straight year. Or Mack could have started right-hander George Earnshaw, another power arm, with a 24–8 record. Southpaw Rube Walberg, with an 18–11 record, was a third possible option. All three were sufficiently well rested. Instead, Mack went with 35-year-old has-been Howard Ehmke.

Ehmke was at the end of a respectable career that took off after World War I. His career record stood at 166–165, and he would have only one more regular-season decision in his big-league career—a loss in three games the next year. But Ehmke had pitched in only 11 games all year and only three times, accounting for 13 innings, since the end of July. With McCarthy's Cubs running away with the National League pennant, Mack sent Ehmke on a mission to scout their games in August. Since McCarthy's lineup was stacked with dangerous right-handed batters,

Mack apparently decided Ehmke's slow stuff was just the thing to throw off their timing and gain a quick advantage in the World Series. It proved to be a brilliant maneuver to start him in Game 1 as Ehmke set a new World Series record by striking out 13 Cubs—including Hall of Fame hitters Rogers Hornsby, Hack Wilson, and Kiki Cuyler twice each—on his way a 3–1 complete-game victory in a Series the Athletics would win in six games.

So here was Joe McCarthy, nearly 20 years later, hoping Denny Galehouse would have his Howard Ehmke moment.

It was not to be.

Galehouse gave up four runs in three innings. Kinder completed the game but also gave up four runs. Boudreau had two home runs and two runs batted in. Keltner had a home run and three RBIs. McCarthy's selection of Denny Galehouse as the playoff starting pitcher blew up in his face.

\* \* \*

A similar tale unfolded in the last game of the 1949 schedule at Yankee Stadium, Boston and New York tied for first, the pennant again going to whichever team won.

Once again, Boston was an imposing team. They led the league in scoring, home runs, and batting average. The first two hitters in McCarthy's lineup—DiMaggio and Pesky—both hit over .300, got on base over 40 percent of the time, and were among the top five in the league in runs. Batting third and fourth, Williams and Stephens were first and second in home runs, with 43 and 39, far ahead of anybody else (the four players behind them each had 24), and they tied for the league lead in runs batted in with 159—the most by any player since Jimmie Foxx had 175 for Boston in 1938. Williams again got on base in nearly 50 percent of his total plate appearances, his .343 batting average missed leading the league by less than one hit, and he scored the most runs, played the most games, and was the American League's Most Valuable Player. As the Sox took the field for the season finale, Parnell at 25–7 and Kinder at 23–6 had the two best winning percentages among American League pitchers.

McCarthy chose Kinder to start game 154 of the season. Kinder had already beaten the Yankees four times without a loss and had shut them out in his previous start a week earlier to earn his 23rd win. Since then, he had pitched in three games as a reliever, totaling four innings, meaning Kinder was pitching for the fourth time in a row on an every-other-day schedule. Not to disappoint, Kinder hooked up with the Yankees' Vic Raschi in a classic pitching duel. All Kinder gave up was a run on four hits through seven innings, but Raschi was even better. When it came

Kinder's turn to bat in the eighth inning, the Yankees led 1–0, and the Red Sox had all of two hits.

McCarthy then made two momentous decisions—first, to pinch hit for Kinder and then to replace Kinder with Parnell. While it was not unusual at the time for managers—even if they were losing—to stay with a pitcher who was pitching well in a close game in the late innings, as Kinder certainly was ("brilliant" is likely the more appropriate word), McCarthy's decision on the pinch hitter was clearly intended to start a needed rally. It was the eighth inning, after all; Kinder was not a good hitter, even for a pitcher—his batting average sitting at .130—and with one out already, the Red Sox had only five outs left to at least tie the score. That decision both worked out . . . and didn't. The pinch hitter walked but was immediately wiped out in a double play, and the Red Sox failed to score.

But bringing in the weary Parnell in relief of Kinder was a gamble, never mind that he was the ace of the staff and had won 25 games. Parnell had pitched into the fifth inning the day before, been hit hard by the Yankees, and was near exhaustion from his workload in the heated drive for the pennant. His total innings pitched on the season stood at 295, and he had made seven starts, appeared twice in relief, and thrown 59⅓ innings since the first of September. Lacking a relief ace like Joe Page over in the Yankee bullpen (or like the one he had personally developed in Johnny Murphy in the mid-1930s with the Yankees), McCarthy may have felt he had no choice but to use Parnell.

As in the final (playoff) game the previous year, this pitching decision also blew up on McCarthy. Parnell did not get an out, giving up a home run and a single before being removed for 1946 pitching ace Tex Hughson. But Hughson had been buried in McCarthy's bullpen all year, used primarily as a long reliever because of arm troubles that sidelined him and diminished his effectiveness. Hughson probably was not first out of the bullpen—hence Parnell—because McCarthy didn't have much faith in a pitcher with a 5.31 ERA who allowed more than 14 runners on base for every 9 innings of work. The Yankees plastered Hughson for three more runs. Boston scored three of their own in the ninth, which made the final score a much-closer 5–3 and raised awkward questions about what might have been had McCarthy's eighth-inning decisions been different.

\* \* \*

Was MacPhail right that McCarthy had lost his managerial edge even if his forcing McCarthy out as Yankee manager was really about consolidating his control over the ball club and its future direction?

Joe McCarthy was not only 61 years old when he assumed command in the Fenway dugout in 1948 but also had not managed since departing Yankee Stadium two years before. When the Red Sox were going badly,

McCarthy was said to smuggle whiskey into the dugout, presumably to self-medicate the sting of his team's poor performance. Although he was careful not to hound his star players, McCarthy often allowed frustration to get the better of him by making clear the New York Yankees played with greater discipline, tough-minded resolve, and dedication to winning than the Boston Red Sox. Nonetheless, despite his questionable managerial decisions in the 1948 playoff game with the Indians and the final game of the 1949 season at Yankee Stadium, the Red Sox would not even have been in position to win the pennant either year had they not overcome big deficits with McCarthy directing the action—11 games behind in sixth place in mid-June 1948 and 12 games behind in fifth place with a losing record on July 4, 1949.

The tale of those two bitter endings proves nothing about McCarthy's ability as a manager at the time. The best of managers, of whom McCarthy was certainly one, make many decisions that don't work out. It's the nature of the game, and provocative decisions by managers don't always have happy endings. Connie Mack's controversial choice of little-used veteran Howard Ehmke to start the first game of the 1929 World Series against McCarthy's Cubs mirrored McCarthy's selection to start Galehouse in the 1948 playoff game, except Mack's gamble paid off with an epic performance.

And Bucky Harris's decision as a first-year manager to use Washington ace Walter Johnson in relief for four innings, three of them extra frames, in a tie game in Game 7 of the 1924 World Series, only two days after he had pitched and lost a complete game, mirrored McCarthy's selection of Parnell to relieve Kinder in the last game of the 1949 season, except Bucky's gamble paid off when Johnson became the star and savior of the Series. Both of those worked out. McCarthy's similar decisions did not. McCarthy may not have used the best judgment, even at the time (and certainly in retrospect), but it is not as though these were ill-considered decisions.

The Red Sox failure to win their last game in both the 1948 and 1949 seasons, which either year would have put them into the World Series, marked the beginning of the end of McCarthy's managerial career. Five straight losses in a stretch where Boston lost nine out of ten games to seemingly drop out of contention by mid-June in the 1950 pennant race led to McCarthy once again being allowed to voluntarily step down as manager, except this time there would be no comeback. As it happened, from the day after McCarthy left the game for good, the Red Sox under their new manager—Steve O'Neill—had the best record in the major leagues through the rest of the 1950 season, 3½ games better than the eventual World Series–champion Yankees. Unfortunately, their having been 9½ games down in the standings at the time McCarthy retired proved too big a deficit for Boston to overcome. They finished third, four games behind the Yankees and one back of the second-place Tigers.

The Yankees, meanwhile, had won their second-straight pennant under their new manager, Casey Stengel, on their way to five in a row. If dashing Boston's hopes of winning the 1949 pennant was what gave the Yankees momentum for a new dynastic run of their own, the pivotal game for Boston's dynastic pretensions was their lost opportunity in the 1948 playoff with Cleveland. The Red Sox winning that game might have altered the course of baseball history—especially had they gone on to win the World Series, where another Boston team, the Braves, represented the National League. Perhaps the subsequent years would have been no different in how they unfolded—every season begins as a blank slate, after all—but maybe the swagger that comes from winning it all would have established an aura of invincibility that might have intimidated even the Yankees and shifted the weight of expectation and winning momentum (if there is such a thing) from New York to Boston.

After 1950, the Yankees kept on winning, and the Red Sox were on their way to spending the rest of that decade and most of the next as, at best, a marginally competitive team. By 1953, the Boston team that had been a nascent dynasty was mostly unrecognizable. Following another stellar offensive year in 1950, with 30 home runs and leading the league with 144 RBIs, Vern Stephens was bumped from shortstop, injured his knee, did not in general play well, and was finally traded away before the 1953 season. Bobby Doerr retired after the 1951 season because of a bad back. Johnny Pesky was traded to Detroit in 1952. Dom DiMaggio retired early in the 1953 season after being benched. Mel Parnell had his last productive season with a 21–8 record for fourth-place Boston in 1953. Ellis Kinder was now the best relief pitcher in the American League. And Ted Williams was flying combat missions for most of 1952 and 1953 in the Korean War, narrowly escaping death when he guided his battle-damaged aircraft back to friendly territory.

Williams was 35 years old when he returned to baseball from his second wartime service. While the Red Sox faded from contender status, a team the Yankees no longer had to worry about, Ted Williams continued as one of major-league baseball's elite players. He won back-to-back batting titles in 1957 (his .388 average coming within five hits of a second .400 season) and 1958, at the ages of 38 and 39. And, of course, Ted Williams hit a home run at Fenway Park in the final at bat of his career, maintaining his personal standard of integrity by refusing to acknowledge—even just this once—the respect, if not exactly adoration, of the Fenway faithful for his exacting discipline, intense study of "the science of hitting" (the title of a book he coauthored), and remarkable accomplishments.

\* \* \*

How closely competitive were the postwar Yankees and Red Sox? From 1946 to 1950, the Yankees and Red Sox won exactly the same number of games—473. That Boston lost one more than New York (298 to 297) is only because the Red Sox were forced to play the one-game playoff for the pennant in 1948. Not only that but Boston and New York both won 55 games against each other. Had a trifling few of their losses been wins, it could have easily been the Red Sox with three pennants (their 1946 blowout, 1948, and 1949) and the Yankees with no more than two (their 1947 blowout and 1950). And even 1950 might have gone Boston's way had they gotten off to a better start, since the Red Sox had the best record in the American League after McCarthy stepped out of the dugout.

They could have been a dominant team, perhaps should have been a dominant team—particularly after adding power-hitting shortstop Vern Stephens in 1948 and with southpaw Mel Parnell and righty Ellis Kinder emerging that year as two of the best pitchers in the league—but the Boston Red Sox from 1946 to 1950 won just one pennant. The New York Yankees, who had looked to be getting old kind of fast in 1946, wound up winning three pennants during that span after refashioning their team, particularly the pitching staff, following their disappointing performance in 1946.

Yet Boston may actually have had the better team, especially in 1948 and 1949, when considering their core regulars. Based on their cumulative wins above replacement, the Red Sox had 5 of the 10-best position players in the American League between 1946 and 1950. Williams was far and away the best player in the American League; Doerr was fourth, Stephens fifth (although the first two of those years were with the Browns), Pesky seventh, and *their* DiMaggio was tenth. The only position player on the Yankees in the AL's top 10 in cumulative WAR for those years was *the* DiMaggio, who was a very distant second to Williams in player value. Of the other Yankees, Henrich was among the league's top-10 position players for 3 years, 1947 to 1949, and 11th overall; Rizzuto was the linchpin of the Yankee infield, but not one of the league's 10-best all-around players in any postwar year until his MVP season in 1950; and Yogi Berra, who did not become their regular catcher until 1948, did not hit his stride as a great player until 1950.

While the Red Sox roster may have been graced with more of the game's best players, the margins of difference separating the two teams were both subtle and obvious.

The Yankees had far-superior depth. After McCarthy took over the Red Sox in 1948, he started his core position regulars in virtually every game and kept them in the whole game, not giving them a break. Boston position players were in at the end of 97 percent of the games they started from 1948 to 1950. Beginning with Bucky Harris, when he managed the Yankees in 1948, and certainly after Stengel assumed the reins, the Yankees not only platooned at various positions but also substituted for posi-

tion players far more often than most other teams. Between 1948 and
1950, the Yankees' starting position players played the whole game only
87 percent of the time.

And if Boston's particular strength was offense, the Yankees had a
telling advantage in pitching and defense. The Yankees had greater depth
in their starting rotation, especially beginning in 1948 when Eddie Lopat
arrived via a trade from Chicago to team with Allie Reynolds and Vic
Raschi to become one of the most notable pitching trios in baseball history. The Red Sox had a top-flight rotation when they won the pennant in
1946, but their two best pitchers that year, Tex Hughson (with a 20–11
record and a 2.75 earned run average) and Boo Ferriss (25–6, 3.25) never
again approached that level of success because of injuries. While Parnell
and Kinder were two of baseball's best pitchers between 1948 and 1950,
the remainder of the Boston staff was suspect, a significant problem even
with their imposing lineup.

Playing at Fenway Park, whose dimensions favored hitters, it is perhaps understandable that Boston's pitching was not typically one of the
best in the league. The Red Sox were certainly competent defensively,
usually among the teams with the fewest errors, but the percentage of
outs they made on balls put into play—defined statistically as "defensive
efficiency"—was mostly below the league average, which is consistent
with the team's reputation, even at the time, of not being especially good
in the field. They were certainly not up to the Yankees' standard of being
first or second in defensive efficiency every year between 1946 and 1950.

Boston's most fundamental problem, however, was being behind the
curve at a time when having a capable bullpen with a dedicated relief ace
was coming into vogue. The Yankees, on the other hand, had Joe Page,
the best relief pitcher in baseball, who was instrumental in their winning
the 1947 and 1949 pennants. By virtue of being the top pitcher in
American League Most Valuable Player voting in both 1947 and 1949,
finishing fourth and third overall, Page would likely have been the Cy
Young winner each of those years had the award existed back then.
Page's years of greatness were regrettably few, in part because he was
battling his own alcohol-fueled demons.

The lack of an ace reliever almost certainly cost the Red Sox the pennants they lost by one game. In 1948, Boston's bullpen was a mess.
McCarthy's two principal relievers—Earl Johnson and Boo Ferriss—both
had an earned run average greater than 4.50. As the Red Sox, on top of
the standings most of September, fought to hold off both the Indians and
Yankees down the stretch, McCarthy went to his bullpen only when necessary and relied on his starting pitchers to finish their victories with
complete games. Red Sox relievers won 4 and saved only 2 of Boston's 20
victories in the final month and had an unsightly ERA of 5.69. Even with
their great starting pitching, pennant-winning Cleveland, by contrast,
would not have finished the regular season in a dead heat with Boston

without the bullpen trio of Russ Christopher—who led the league with 17 saves—Eddie Klieman, and Steve Gromek. Even with the Indians' exceptional starters going the distance in 17 of the team's final 31 games and accounting for more than 80 percent of innings pitched, their relievers had a 4–2 record, 2 saves, and an excellent 2.15 ERA in 33 appearances down the stretch.

It was same story for Boston in 1949. The absence of a reliable relief ace forced McCarthy to use starting pitcher Kinder four times out of the bullpen in the last 12 days of the season, during which he also made two starts, including taking the mound for the final winner-take-all game of the season at Yankee Stadium. Going into that game, Kinder's workload in September already included 5 complete-game victories and a wearying 52 innings logged, including his relief appearances. The Yankees, meanwhile, would not have been in position to steal the pennant from the Red Sox on the final weekend of the 1949 season without Joe Page and his 13 victories and 27 saves in relief. Page saved 9 of his team's 20 victories in the final month, and 3 other games were saved by other Yankee relievers.

That Boston's bullpen was so inadequate seems surprising since McCarthy not only benefited from a strong relief corps when he managed the Yankee dynasty in the 1930s and early 1940s but also specifically cultivated Johnny Murphy to be his fireman in the bullpen. It was not until after McCarthy resigned as manager early in the 1950 season that Ellis Kinder was specifically designated by the new manager in town, Steve O'Neill, to be Boston's relief ace, a role at which he excelled into the mid-1950s.

It is hard to argue that the Red Sox did not have the superior team when considering their core players, but as to the competitive bottom line, three pennants and three World Series championships for the Yankees between 1946 and 1950 are . . . well, two pennants and three World Series championships more than Boston won. Maybe it was because Boston's pitching was not deep and—until Kinder became the relief ace in midsummer 1950—the bullpen less than effective. (True enough.) Maybe it was because the Boston offense was too one dimensional, geared to the power game. (True enough.) Maybe it was because there was little quality depth behind Boston's regular position players. (Also true enough.) Maybe it was because McCarthy had lost his edge. (Quite possibly true.)

Or maybe it was because . . . of those damn Yankees! While it is safe to say that Boston had a stronger cast of core regulars those five years than did New York—especially among position players—this advantage was not so great as to overcome the fact that the Yankees had all around better pitching, were much better defensively, had more depth on the bench, and were better managed, even though Casey Stengel was himself 58 years old when he took over in the Bronx in 1949.

# THREE

# End of the Player-Manager Era

By his own account, Bill Veeck was vexed. The Cleveland Indians' new owner—the sale of the team to Veeck was concluded in June 1946—recognized that his star shortstop, Lou Boudreau, was indispensible to the Indians' competitive success. With the possible exception of the St. Louis Browns' Vern Stephens, Boudreau was the best all-around short-stop in the game. And with Ken Keltner arguably the best third baseman in baseball, Joe Gordon still a top-notch second baseman, and Bob Feller having picked up his excellence from where he left off when he went off to war in 1942, Veeck believed the Indians had the foundation in place to be a team that could compete for the American League pennant with the Red Sox and Yankees. The problem was that the Indians' indispensible shortstop and best hitter was also their manager, and Veeck was less than happy with his manager. Unfortunately, to take away the managerial reins from Boudreau would quite likely have created an untenable situa-tion that would require trading away the best shortstop in the business and the most potent bat in Cleveland's lineup.

Veeck thought that while Boudreau was an excellent leader on the field at shortstop, as a manager he was not inclined to think strategically in the way the game demanded. After watching Cleveland end the 1946 season 18 games below .500 in sixth place, Veeck wasted no time hiring Bill McKechnie, a former National League manager whose 25 years in the dugout included leading three different teams to four World Series, to be, in effect, a "bench coach" for Boudreau. Although the Indians improved by 12 wins and finished fourth in 1947, Veeck was still not satisfied with his managerial situation. He wrote in his book, *Veeck as in Wreck*, that Boudreau managed by hunch and desperation, but he also recognized that Boudreau's popularity with Indians fans limited his options.

Veeck found that out the hard way when he spent the 1947 World Series hobnobbing with fellow owners trying to work out a deal that would send Boudreau out of town in exchange for three or four players to fill positions of weakness on the Indians. Veeck reportedly even had Al Lopez, a long-time National League catcher very well respected for his leadership skills and knowledge of the game, lined up to be his manager, if a deal could be worked for Boudreau.

The deal in the works would have been with the Browns, an exchange of the two best shortstops in the league, and would have had the added benefit of allowing Boudreau to resume his player-manager career in St. Louis. Word got around, Cleveland newspapers polled the local populous on the potential trade of the enormously popular Boudreau, the results were resoundingly against such a thing, and Veeck was inundated with letters—some of them threatening—opposed to the very thought. Veeck apologized to the team's fan base, backtracked, and made plans for the 1948 season with his star shortstop still the manager. But now, in addition to McKechnie, he bolstered Boudreau's brain trust by hiring Muddy Ruel, another former manager (of much-lesser accomplishment than McKechnie), former Indians' star pitcher Mel Harder, and former Cleveland Hall of Fame outfielder Tris Speaker as coaches.

That worked out wonderfully for Cleveland, leading to the line about sometimes the best trades are those that are never made. As a player whose excellence was already well established, Boudreau had the best year of his career with career highs in hits (199), home runs (18), runs batted in (106), batting average (.355), and on-base-plus-slugging percentage (.987). Boudreau also had the best fielding percentage among all major-league shortstops playing more than 100 games at the position. As for Stephens, he wound up being traded to the Red Sox.

While playing so well that he was nearly unanimously voted the American League's Most Valuable Player, Boudreau also managed the Indians to their first pennant and World Series championship since 1920, when Speaker was player-manager. This was the year Bob Lemon became a pitching ace in his own right, joining Bob Feller to provide the Indians with a tough twosome in the starting rotation. Rookie southpaw Gene Bearden, pitching on a bum leg from war wounds, turned out to be a pitching savior, winning 20 games—including the playoff game in Boston where Boudreau somewhat surprisingly chose to start him on only one day's rest despite his being left-handed and the game in Fenway Park. Boudreau also seamlessly integrated Larry Doby, the American League's first black player, into the starting lineup in center field. Batting mostly either second or sixth, Doby hit .301, scored 83 runs, and batted in 66 runs.

The Indians' championship season, however, was somewhat tarnished by suspicions surfacing soon thereafter that they might not have won the American League pennant without employing a high-powered gun sight used by the navy on its antiaircraft guns during World War II, courtesy of combat veteran Bob Feller, to pick off opposing catchers' signs from the center field scoreboard at Cleveland's Municipal Stadium. Having fallen 4½ games behind in early September, the Indians had the advantage of 20 of their remaining 23 games on the schedule being at home. They won 16 of those games and were 18–5 overall to finish tied with the Red Sox, forcing the one-game playoff.

If Feller's Navy-issue gun sight made a difference in the outcome of just one game, then for sure, that cheating home-field advantage deprived the Red Sox of a pennant they otherwise would have won. Three of the Indians' home wins were walk-offs, one on a two-run home run by Doby, who hit an unlikely .437 in Cleveland's final 23 home games. They jumped off to big first-inning leads three times and had 13 innings in which they scored at least three runs.

But the fact that the Indians also got outstanding pitching to shut down their opponents' offense and so completely dominated those games probably helps explain why this spy operation has not generated any of the notoriety of the similar sign-stealing enterprise that almost certainly enabled the New York Giants to likewise force a playoff for the National League pennant just three years later. The Indians outscored their opponents by more than two-to-one in their final twenty home games, limited them to one run or none in eight games, surrendered as many as four runs only five times in games that accounted for three of their four losses, won only two games that were decided by one run, both extra-inning walk-offs, and in fact had to come from behind only once in the second half of the sixteen games they won. Of their most potent batters, only Doby hit much better at home than on the road. Keltner and Gordon, who both had their best month of the season in September, hit better on the road than at Municipal Stadium, as did Boudreau. Of course, whatever the effectiveness of Cleveland's spying, there was no poignant story with a hero and victim as compelling as Bobby Thomson and Ralph Branca in 1951, which would have called attention and provoked controversy, to the legacy of Feller's naval gun sight.

Whether sullied or not, most important for Veeck was the bottom line that Cleveland set a new major-league attendance record, drawing over 2.6 million people into their cavernous stadium on the shores of Lake Erie.

\* \* \*

The 1948 Cleveland Indians were the last team to go to the World Series managed by one of its players. And Lou Boudreau, for all intents and purposes, was the last player-manager in the major leagues. Of the few that followed, all were at the end of their playing careers—now marginal big leaguers at best, regardless of how good they may have been in their prime—and none were *playing* managers, even off the bench, for very long.

The history of player-managers is somewhat episodic, with the 1930s being, arguably, the high point and the 1940s, indisputably, the last hurrah. At the dawn of the 20th century—the foundation years for the modern structure of major-league baseball, including two leagues to rival each other—many teams employed their leaders on the playing field, some quite young, as manager. When a change of leadership seemed warranted, mostly because of losing, team owners frequently turned to an active player to take over as the manager, most of whom were either stars or prominent players on the downside of their careers. They included Chicago Cubs' first baseman Frank Chance and Pittsburgh Pirates' outfielder Fred Clarke, both of whom earned Cooperstown berths based on their playing careers but whose historical identities are as "player-manager." Clarke's Pirates won four pennants between 1901 and 1909, and Chance's Cubs won four in five years from 1906 to 1910. Both managers were also among the National League's best players. Red Sox third baseman Jimmy Collins and White Sox outfielder Fielder Jones were the most prominent player-managers in the American League in the 1900s.

But standing out as managers were two in particular who did not also play for their teams—Connie Mack of the Philadelphia Athletics and the New York Giants' John McGraw. They became the archetypes of the modern major-league manager, emblematic icons—the firebrand grandmaster of strategy (McGraw) and the gentleman tactician (Mack)—whose focus on preparation and mastery of the game's nuances set the template for "baseball manager" as its own profession. They were highly visible architects of their teams' successes or failures, notwithstanding that it is ultimately the players whose performance counts most of all. Indicative of their command of the game, their mastery of ebb and flow, Mack and especially McGraw were at the forefront of innovations that became part of the manager's game-management toolkit.

The growing complexity of the game, thanks in no small part to Mack and McGraw, changed the managerial landscape. It was increasingly apparent that the most successful teams would be those that were not only the most talented and skilled in execution but also the most sophisticated in their use of strategy to win games. The skills and competitive fires of a star player like Chance or Clarke to inspire and lead his team were no longer necessarily sufficient alone to make for a good manager. Furthermore, the focus of *playing* managers was understandably divided. Whether in their prime or on the downside, they needed to devote time and energy to their playing careers.

By the 1920s, while hardly an endangered species, player-managers had become much less prevalent. The new model of a baseball manager was a "professional" who had an astute knowledge of the game and its players and who was expected to give his complete focus to the team's performance on the field. This, of course, also allowed baseball's owner-barons (the men with the money) to consolidate more of the responsibility for organizational matters into their own hands, an important consideration as major-league baseball was becoming an increasingly potent industry in its own right.

While the National League had very few player-managers with any longevity after the first decade of the 20th century, American League franchises did not give up on the paradigm. This was particularly true in the 1920s, when the Indians (with Tris Speaker), Tigers (Ty Cobb), Browns (George Sisler), and White Sox (Eddie Collins) were all managed by star players who were the face of their teams and still among the best players in baseball. Senators' second baseman Bucky Harris was the only player-manager with at least two years in the dual roles who was not a star player, but he was an acknowledged leader on the field and a popular player in Washington.

The bias against player-managers was broken by the Great Depression, making the 1930s the heyday of teams managed by core players making it to the World Series. With the economy severely depressed, teams began turning to established veteran players, often star players, when changing managers. It made more financial sense, especially for contending teams with higher player payrolls, to pay an established player something extra to manage than to hire someone else as manager who would demand a competitive wage. Five of the thirteen National League teams and three of the thirteen American League teams that went to the World Series between the stock market crash of October 1929 and 1942, the last year before major-league rosters were hard hit by the world now at war, were brought there by player-managers. In 1933 and 1934, both teams in the Fall Classic were led by playing managers. The only previous World Series where that had occurred were way back in 1903 and 1906.

The trend toward playing managers was particularly pronounced in the first half of the 1930s. Of the 23 managerial changes between 1931 and 1935, 11 went to active players who were still regulars in the starting lineup, 6 of them star players with Hall of Fame careers, including Joe Cronin twice. In mid-season 1938, the Chicago Cubs made another future Hall of Famer, their aging veteran catcher Gabby Hartnett, a playing manager. The Cubs were in third place, not far behind at the time but treading water. The move proved inspired as the Cubs came from behind to win the National League pennant. Hartnett was the last manager to lead his team on the playing field into the World Series until Boudreau 10 years later.

But even by then, it was apparent the days of the player-manager were coming to an end. The most respected managers embodied the studied approach of a wizened observer-instructor and dispassionate de-

cision-maker in the dugout—men like Joe McCarthy, whose five pennants between 1932 and 1939 were the only ones by an American League
team not won with a player-manager in charge of the action; Bill
McKechnie, whose back-to-back pennants by the Reds ended seven consecutive years in which the National League winner was managed either
by a playing manager or by a manager who had just stepped down from
the dual role; and the venerable Connie Mack, although he was now in
his 70s and thought to be growing out of touch.

After Hartnett, the only star players on their team to be elevated to
manager were Leo Durocher in 1939 and Lou Boudreau and Mel Ott,
both in 1942. Durocher may have been the Dodger shortstop, but his days
as a player-manager lasted only two years because he had no problem
deciding his playing days were over and turning his full attention to
managing once he got a look at Pee Wee Reese. The Dodgers were able to
get their hands on the hotshot prospect Reese from the Red Sox because
*their* manager, Joe Cronin, was also their shortstop and had no intention
of giving up the position, no matter how much better the kid playing on
their Louisville affiliate was, even though Cronin was well aware he was
no longer an elite player.

\* \* \*

Boudreau, Ott, and Cronin were the last three player-managers in major-
league history with any longevity in the dual roles. None of the three was
highly regarded as a manager. All three are in the Hall of Fame based on
exceptional playing careers. Ott hit 511 home runs in his career—only
Babe Ruth and Jimmie Foxx were ahead of him at the time he retired as a
player—and Cronin and Boudreau are two of the best all-around shortstops to have played the game.

By the time Cronin ended his playing career at the age of 37 after the
1944 season, he had been a player and manager at the same time for 12
years, longer than anyone else in American League history. Cronin continued on as Red Sox manager for three more years, including winning
the 1946 pennant, before stepping down to step up to be general manager
in 1948.

Mel Ott replaced Bill Terry as manager of the Giants in 1942 just as he
was beginning the final phase of a playing career that began in 1926 when
he was only 17 years old. He was now 33 but still one of the best players
in baseball. In his first year as a *playing* manager, Ott was the best offensive player in the league, according to the wins-above-replacement metric, leading the league in runs, home runs, and on-base-plus-slugging
percentage. Continuing on as both the Giants' manager and their right
fielder, Ott abjured the player part of his responsibilities in 1946. Although a knee injury was the catalyst for his staying mostly on the bench,
quality players returning from World War II gave him the opportunity to

field an outfield that did not need to include him. The Giants never had a competitive team for Ott to do much with when he was manager, and in July 1948, he was forced to step down in favor of the man who famously called him a "nice guy" — as in "nice guys finish last" — Leo Durocher, who most assuredly was not a nice guy.

As for Boudreau, the Cleveland shortstop was named manager of the team in 1942 at the ripe young age of 23 despite being the youngest player of any consequence on the roster and only 3 years and 357 games in the major leagues under his belt. He turned 24 in July. Even with his limited time in the big leagues, however, Boudreau — already the best all-around shortstop in the American League — had emerged as the team's leader in the clubhouse and on the field. And with Bob Feller volunteering for duty the day after Pearl Harbor was attacked, Boudreau was left as the undisputed star player of the Cleveland Indians, the face of the franchise.

Boudreau's ascension was, and was not, unprecedented. There were other "boy" managers before Boudreau, some quite successful, but none in the 20th century with as little major-league experience. Second baseman Bucky Harris, the poster boy of "boy" managers, already had four years in the big leagues when he was named Washington's manager at the youthful age of 27. Harris proved an instant success, as the Senators won the pennant and World Series in his first year in charge and won a second pennant the next year. Washington did not win a third pennant until 1933 when team owner Clark Griffith, remembering his success with the young Harris, made Joe Cronin, his 26-year-old shortstop, a first-time manager even though he had just five years of experience as a regular in a major-league lineup. Two years later, Cronin was player-manager in Boston.

In leading the 1948 Indians to dramatic pennant and World Series victories as their manager, while winning the MVP Award as a player, Lou Boudreau may have had the best individual season ever by a player-manager. Only one other playing manager in the 20th century in either league arguably had as great an impact on his team as a player in a single season as Lou Boudreau did in 1948 — the great Tris Speaker, now one of his coaches, who guided Cleveland to the 1920 pennant as the manager while batting .388.

Notwithstanding a huge raise Veeck bestowed upon him in the afterglow of the 1948 season, it was in fact unreasonable to expect that Boudreau the player, or Boudreau the manager, could approach such heights again. Boudreau managed the Indians for two more years, finishing third and fourth, before he was released because it was apparent his badly arthritic ankles had all but ended his great playing career. From Cleveland's perspective, Boudreau's value was primarily as a shortstop, not as a manager, so his services in the latter capacity were also no longer required. Although he was no longer owner of the team, Bill Veeck would have approved.

* * *

By the time Boudreau was released as a player by the Indians and not asked to remain as manager, the days of player-managers in the major leagues were effectively over. It was no longer sufficient for a manager to be one of the boys in the midst of the action, no matter how much leadership he showed on the field or in the clubhouse. That was a role for a team captain, perhaps, but no longer for a manager. Team owners perceived that, to be successful, they needed a manager whose responsibilities rested entirely on preparing his team, managing games, and increasingly assuming a more prominent role as team spokesman without the distraction of having to keep up his skills as a baseball player.

Old traditions die hard, however, and there continued to be a few players named managers in the 1940s and early 1950s. They were very few in number, however, all at the end of their playing careers, and none was player-manager for very long. Shortstop Marty Marion, for example—best known for his terrific defense on very successful Cardinals teams in the 1940s—still in St. Louis but now with the Browns, took himself out of the starting lineup soon after being name player-manager in June 1952 and played himself in only three games the next year before hanging up his glove. Similarly, the Cubs' Phil Cavarretta, a star player for the franchise since the mid-1930s, although still an active player, rarely put himself in the starting lineup in the two and a half years he managed at Wrigley Field. As the manager, Cavarretta found his value as a player to be greater coming off the bench as a pinch hitter.

The two most prominent player-managers since Boudreau was cast out of the job in 1950, Frank Robinson and Pete Rose, made headlines in that role for different reasons. Robinson was 39 years old and near the end of his Hall of Fame career when the Indians made him not only their manager in 1975 but also the first black man to manage a major-league team. In his two years as a player-manager, Robinson the manager limited his role as a player almost exclusively to being the designated hitter, and he played in only 85 games.

Pete Rose was closing in on Ty Cobb's career record for hits in August 1984 when the Cincinnati Reds brought him back, five and a half years after he left the Queen City for greener free-agent pastures, to manage in the town in which he staked his claim as one of baseball's immortals—and to break a record once thought unattainable. Playing regularly at first base in a platoon role as the left-handed complement to fellow aging veteran Tony Perez of the great Cincinnati teams in the mid-1970s, Rose started 110 games in 1985 and set the new hits record in September, but he was barely playing at the level of a replacement player from the minor leagues. At 45 years old, Rose never got untracked the next year and gave up his playing career to focus exclusively on managing. The bitter irony for Pete Rose was that the core of the Cincinnati team he was managing at the time he was banished from any role in the major leagues for life in August 1989 because he bet on baseball, went on to win the National League pennant and sweep the World Series the very next year, never spending even one day out of first place in their division.

# FOUR

## Enter Stengel the Grandmaster

When the Yankees fired Bucky Harris after their disappointing 1948 season, Casey Stengel was not an obvious choice to take over as manager of a franchise that had won six pennants and three World Series for Miller Huggins and eight more pennants and seven World Series for Joe McCarthy. For one thing, Stengel was 58 years old. McCarthy may have been three years older when the Red Sox asked him to assume command in 1948, but he had all those Yankee championships under his belt. Nobody had any doubts about Joe McCarthy being one of the greatest managers of all time; he was right up there on baseball's managerial Mount Olympus, along with John McGraw and Connie Mack. More to the point, however, Stengel's major-league managerial pedigree was eight losing seasons in nine years in the National League, never finishing in the top half of the standings. Rather than a reputation as a winning manager, or even a very good one, his banter and irreverence often made Stengel appear like the clownish manager of teams not to be taken seriously, so why should *he* be taken seriously?

Of course, Stengel was managing the Brooklyn Dodgers (1934–1936) and Boston Braves (1938–1943) when both were bad teams. Only once did the team he manage finish as high as fifth in the standings, and only the 1938 Braves (who, in somewhat of a short-lived identity crisis, were called the Bees at the time) at 77–75 even had a winning record. Stengel managed only eight of the 219 players named to National League All-Star teams during his years in Brooklyn and Boston. At the time of his appointment to lead the New York Yankees, Stengel had a dismal .439 winning percentage (581 wins, 742 losses) as a major-league manager.

Despite Stengel's lack of competitive success in his previous managerial experience at the big-league level, Yankee general manager George Weiss understood—or at least gambled—that Casey Stengel was a much better and more astute manager than the outcome of those seasons would suggest. Impressed by Stengel's three years as Oakland's manager in the Pacific Coast League, the minor league nearest to major-league-level quality of play, Weiss believed he could lead the Bronx Bombers back to their accustomed perch atop the American League. Still, Stengel's National League managerial career of consistently being buried in the second division made him a hard sell with the Yankees' owners, heir-to-a-family-fortune Dan Topping and construction magnate Del Webb, who were demanding to keep up the franchise legacy of dominance.

Stengel did not have much margin for error when he took over as manager, and 1949 was probably his make-or-break year with the Yankees. (It certainly would have been in the George Steinbrenner era.) Failure to win a pennant quickly not only could have meant a short tenure in the Bronx for Stengel but also likely the end of his managerial career, at least in the major leagues.

The fact that the Yankees were at the top of the American League standings from the very first day of the season until only six days and five games remained would not have helped Stengel's cause had they not won the pennant. The fact that it was *McCarthy's* Red Sox who were challenging the Yankees after having been down by nine and a half games in mid-July made matters worse. The Red Sox finally caught up in late September when they beat the Yankees in three straight games, the last in New York in the 150th game of the season, knocking Stengel's team into second place for the first time in 1949. Boston came back into Yankee Stadium for the last two games of the season with a one-game lead, needing only one win to secure the pennant. They won neither game. On Saturday, the Yankees stormed back from a 4–0 deficit to win, saving their season, and on Sunday, with the pennant up for grabs, the Yankees won again, surviving a three-run ninth-inning Red Sox rally that fell two runs short. For good measure, they went on to knock off the Dodgers in five games to return the title of World Series champions to Yankee Stadium in the Bronx.

This was the beginning of a remarkable relationship, not only between Stengel and the flagship enterprise of major-league baseball but also between Stengel and the sportswriters who covered the Yankees. All Stengel did in his first five years in Yankee pinstripes was win an unprecedented five pennants in a row and an unprecedented five straight World Series. These shall be called the "five-and-five-in-five years," and they kick-started a third wave of the Yankee dynasty that included ten pennants and seven World Series championships in the twelve years Stengel managed in pinstripes from 1949 to 1960 and extended beyond his reign to include four more pennants and two more championships until the Yankees' unimaginable collapse in 1965.

* * *

Including three and a half years in the 1960s with the newborn Mets, who were awful, as the coda to his life in baseball, Stengel won only 63 more games than he lost with a career record of 1,905–1,842 in the 3,766 games he managed. Clearly, without very good Yankee teams for 12 of the 25 years on his managerial resume, there would have been no ride to Cooperstown for Casey Stengel. With an overall managerial record of mediocrity owing primarily to his years managing bad National League teams both "before and after he was a genius," to quote Warren Spahn, who pitched for Casey in 1942 with the Braves and again in 1965 on the Mets, how much of a "genius" was Stengel as manager of the New York Yankees?

To be sure, Stengel inherited a very good team the day he assumed command at Yankee Stadium. They had won the World Series in 1947. They had entered the final weekend of the 1948 season only a game out of first place before ending up third. But the Yankees' future at the beginning of Stengel's reign was uncertain because it was obvious Joe DiMaggio was nearing the end of his iconic career.

The Yankee team Stengel led to five championships in his first five years as their manager was in transition from the DiMaggio to the Mantle eras and did not have many great players at the peak of their careers. Sure, there were six future Cooperstown residents in the Bronx during these years, but only catcher Yogi Berra and shortstop Phil Rizzuto were in their prime, and Rizzuto's Hall of Fame selection was somewhat controversial, coming only after years of intensive lobbying on his behalf. Part-time first baseman and pinch hitter–deluxe Johnny Mize was at the end of his career, his Hall of Fame merits long-since established with the Cardinals and Giants in the 1930s and 1940s, and Whitey Ford pitched only two years for the five-and-five-in-five Yankees, as a rookie in 1950 and a second-year player in 1953, sandwiching two years of military service during the Korean War.

And then there were DiMaggio and Mantle.

Joe DiMaggio was nearing the end of his career (his best years behind him) and would retire after the 1951 season, but he was still dangerous, as the Red Sox learned to their dismay in the 1949 pennant race. Hobbled by injuries in both 1949, when he played in only 76 games, and 1951, when he twice missed at least two weeks, these were not smooth sailing seasons for the Yankee Clipper.

But in 1949, DiMaggio tore the Red Sox apart, which was vital to the Yankees' winning the pennant and, arguably, Stengel's keeping his job. Even though he played in only 13 of the 22 games between the two teams, DiMaggio hit 6 home runs, drove in 14 runs, and hit .381 with an on-base-plus-slugging percentage of 1.456. Four of those home runs and nine RBIs came in three games at Fenway Park in his first 14 plate appearances of the season after he had missed the Yankees' first 65 games because of a brutally painful bone spur in his right heel. DiMaggio's was quite possibly the most dramatic return to action from an injury in baseball history, with all due respect to Kirk Gibson's pinch-hit home run to win Game 1 of the 1988 World Series, because Gibson's sidelining injury had come in just his previous game.

Mickey Mantle, called up by the Yankees in 1951, was at the beginning of his career (his best years ahead of him), giving every indication of the superstar player he would become. After struggling for most of his rookie year, Mantle emerged as the sensation he was expected to be in 1952, the first of eleven consecutive years in which his player value exceeded the five wins above replacement considered the standard for an All-Star level of performance.

Even if DiMaggio and then Mantle were the brighter and more compelling stars, Berra and Rizzuto were the cornerstone players of the 1949–1953 Yankees. Yogi Berra was still at the beginning of his career and Phil Rizzuto approaching the end of his, but they were Stengel's most valuable players on this team. Rizzuto was the AL Most Valuable Player in 1950, after finishing second in the voting the year before, with the best year of his career—125 runs, 200 hits, .324 batting average, .418 on-base percentage, and his usual stellar defense. Berra had his breakout season in 1950—scoring 116 runs, hitting 28 home runs, driving in 124, and batting .322—good for third in the MVP voting. The next year, Berra won the first of his three MVP Awards for the third wave of the Yankee dynasty, although only this one came in the five-and-five-in-five years. But Berra and Rizzuto were the only two Yankees among the league's 10-best position players from 1949 to 1953, third and fourth, based on their cumulative WAR. DiMaggio and Mantle each played in only three of Stengel's first five years. Each was among the AL's top-10 position players twice—DiMaggio in 1949 and 1950 and Mantle in 1952 and 1953.

The five-and-five-in-five Yankees did not have the overpowering lineups that characterized earlier teams in the franchise's dynastic continuum. Instead, they had a strong cadre of very capable and reliable players who blended together as a cohesive, imposing team that always found a way to win, especially when it mattered most. Foremost among them were three indispensible role players—outfielders Hank Bauer and Gene Woodling, who were often (and famously) platooned, and Gil McDougald, whose ability to play anywhere in the infield made him invaluable to Stengel from the moment he arrived in the Bronx in 1951. If the Yankees' core players in their five-and-five-in-five years were not much better relative to the rest of the league, and certainly not compared to McCarthy's regulars during DiMaggio's primetime years, they did give Stengel a solid foundation for a competitive club that was more than the sum of its parts.

Most important, Stengel inherited a trio of topflight pitchers who gave the Yankees one of the most formidable starting rotations in baseball. The hard-throwing right-hander Allie Reynolds had arrived in a trade from Cleveland on Joe DiMaggio's recommendation in time for the 1947 season and immediately became the ace on what was then a somewhat suspect staff. The left-hander Eddie Lopat also came by way of a trade, in 1948 from the White Sox. And Vic Raschi, known as the Springfield Rifle for his impressive fastball, signed by the Yankees before World War II, made it to the stadium to stay in 1947, but it was his 19 wins the next year that set up his star turn for Stengel.

The three were as tough to beat as any pitchers in baseball in the five-and-five-in-five years. They had five 20-win seasons among them, including three in a row by Raschi in 1949, 1950, and 1951. All three twice had a winning percentage better than .700, and both Lopat and Reynolds would top .700 again in 1954. They combined for a 255–117 record during the Yankees' five championship seasons, and their .685 winning percentage was 50 percentage points better than the Yankees' overall .635 record. Reynolds, in 1952, and Lopat, the following year, also led the league in earned run average.

At a time before there was a separate Cy Young Award for pitchers, Reynolds was third in the American League MVP voting in 1951 with a 17–8 record and second in 1952 when he was 20–8 and had a league-best 2.08 ERA. In neither year, however, was Reynolds the top pitcher in the MVP voting; right-hander Ned Garver finished second in 1951 on the strength of his 20–12 record for the last-place St. Louis Browns, and southpaw Bobby Shantz won the MVP Award in 1952 with a 24–7 record and 2.48 ERA for 79-win, fourth-place Philadelphia. As bankable as they were for wins on the best team in baseball, none of the Yankees' three aces—including Reynolds the two years he was so high in the MVP balloting—were among the AL's five best pitchers in any year of their run of five straight championships, based on their pitching wins above replacement.

\* \* \*

Unlike the two previous iterations of the Yankee Dynasty—the Babe Ruth years, especially after Lou Gehrig became his teammate, and the great teams of the DiMaggio era—Stengel's 1949–1953 Yankees dominated the baseball world by winning everything for five straight years without dominating the major leagues, or even just the American League, by their obvious superiority. Indeed, this Yankee team was considered even at the time as overachieving given the quality of their competition for the pennant—first, the Boston Red Sox (now managed by the Great McCarthy) in 1949 and 1950, the Detroit Tigers (for one year only in 1950), and thereafter the Cleveland Indians. The Yankees were not preseason favorites in any of Stengel's first four years in charge.

Although they won 98 games twice and 99 once, the five-and-five-in-five Yankees never once reached the 100-win plateau. The 1936–1942 Yankees, by contrast, had five 100-win seasons and just missed out on a sixth before DiMaggio was drafted for World War II. The 1926–1932 Ruth and Gehrig Yankees that won four pennants in seven years won a hundred games three times, as did Connie Mack's Philadelphia Athletics when they won three straight pennants between 1929 and 1931. Only one Yankee team in Stengel's 12 years as manager won 100 games, and that was in 1954—the year between their string of five straight championships and their next string of four pennants in a row—when their 103 victories weren't even close to enough to win the pennant because the Cleveland Indians set a new American League record for wins with 111.

While every one of McCarthy's eight pennant-winning Yankee teams left would-be competitors choking in their dust before the September home stretch, only the last of Stengel's five straight pennants was a traditional Yankee blowout of the sort McCarthy made famous. That came in 1953, when the Yankees were in first place to stay after only seven games and had an 11½-game lead by mid-June after just 60 games. Although their lead was down to five at the All-Star break, they put the pennant away with a 20–10 month of August, which extended their advantage to 8½ games going into the final month. That proved to be their final winning margin.

In 1949, by contrast, the Yankees did not win the pennant until the very last day of the season; in 1950 they finished three games up, but did not clinch until the 151st game of the season; they also did not clinch until game number 151 in 1951, although they ended up five games in front, and in 1952 it took the Yankees 152 games to secure a fourth-straight World Series appearance in a pennant race they ended up winning by two games.

McCarthy's championship Yankee teams routinely led the league in both runs scored and fewest allowed, the five-and-five-in-five Yankees, not so. While similarly well balanced between pitching and offense, they led the league in scoring only once (in 1953) and in giving up the least runs just twice (in 1952 and 1953). They had formidable competition in both those categories, however, from first the Red Sox and then the Indians, and finished second in scoring or runs allowed every year they were not first. Indicative of Stengel's five straight championship teams being better balanced than their competitors and having fewer overall weaknesses, however, they nonetheless had the best run differential in the American League every year except for 1949.

It is fair to ask whether the contemporary Indians, who bookended the Yankees' five straight championships with pennants of their own in 1948 and 1954, might have been a better team than the 1949–1953 Yankees, especially taking account of their best players at the peak of their careers. Stengel's achievement of managing the Yankees to five consecutive pennants is all the more remarkable considering the strengths of the Cleveland Indians.

* * *

Like the Yankees, the Indians had a well-balanced team. The Yankees' tough-to-beat trio of Reynolds, Raschi, and Lopat did not measure up in overall performance to Cleveland's own core of outstanding pitchers. Bob Lemon, by now the Indians' ace, had three of his six 20-win seasons in that timeframe. Early Wynn won 20 three times, and Mike Garcia did so twice. And that's not to forget Bob Feller, whose career may have been winding down but was still a formidable pitching adversary.

When Feller, Garcia, and Wynn each won 20 games in 1951, and Wynn, Garcia, and Lemon did the same the next year, the Indians became the first major-league team since the Giants in 1904 and 1905 to boast three 20-game winners in back-to-back years. Only the 1970–1971 Baltimore Orioles have done that since. And in 1955, the Indians added hard-throwing right-hander Herb Score, who as a rookie that season became the first qualifying pitcher in major-league history to strike out more batters than innings pitched.

But it wasn't just their superior pitching. The contemporary Indians also had a high-powered offense. They led the league in scoring in 1952 and were second to the Yankees the next two years, which also happened to be the years Mantle came unleashed as one of the most impressive offensive players baseball has ever seen. Cleveland led the league in home runs every year from 1950 to 1954 and were second to the Yankees in 1955. Indians center fielder Larry Doby and third baseman Al Rosen were the two best American League position players in cumulative wins above replacement in the five years the Yankees won five in a row, and second baseman Bobby Avila joined them as as one of the six best players in the league from 1951 to 1955.

Once the Red Sox faded from contender status, it was the Indians who emerged as the principal challenger to Yankee supremacy. Indeed, it was New York finishing first and Cleveland second every year in the American League between 1951 and 1955, except for 1954 when it was the other way around—the one time in Stengel's first 10 years that the Yankees did *not* win the pennant.

The Indians were a tour de force in 1954 when they upended the Yankees. Eleven straight wins in May served notice to the Yankees that six-and-six-in-six might not be a given, and eleven straight wins in September finished off Stengel's hopes for six in a row. Wynn and Lemon contributed 23 wins apiece to Cleveland's total of 111, Garcia missed out on 20 by 1, and 35-year-old Feller was 13–3 with 9 complete games in 19 starts in the last year of consequence in his great career. Art Houtteman, whose promising career with the Tigers was derailed after being drafted during the Korean War, showed signs of his former excellence with a 15–7 record in 25 starts for Cleveland in 1954.

Batting second, third, and fourth, Avila, Doby, and Rosen powered the offense. Avila led the league in batting with a .341 average. Doby, on the strength of his leading the league with 32 home runs and 126 RBIs, likely had the stronger case for MVP than Yogi Berra, who won the award, but may have been hurt in the voting by splitting 10 first-place votes with his teammate Avila. Rosen, whose league-leading 43 home runs and 145 RBIs to go along with a .336 batting average the previous year made him the MVP—he missed the Triple Crown by one percentage point in his average to Mickey Vernon's .337—had 24 homers and his fifth-straight 100-RBI season.

While the Yankees may have claimed four pennants to the Indians' one in those five years, they won only nine more games (491 to 482) and had twelve fewer losses (276 to 288), the difference between wins and losses being that New York did not have to make up three rainouts in 1953 because they had the pennant well secured since early in the season. Moreover, Cleveland's 482 wins between 1951 and 1955 were only five less than the 487 games won by the five-and-five-in-five Yankees.

\* \* \*

If the Yankee supremacy so evident in their five consecutive championships was not built on the foundation of total domination, like McCarthy's great Yankee teams in the pre–World War II half of Joe Di-Maggio's career, much of the credit belongs to the manager who presented himself as a seemingly madcap "Ole Perfessor." Casey Stengel came to the Yankees with a reputation as somewhat of a clown. After proving himself a serious manager by winning the 1949 pennant, he cultivated his wiseacre persona during his championship Yankee years (and beyond, as the face of the National League expansion "Amazin's"—the New York Mets). Stengel was a master of spin before "spin" became an art form for handling public relations, but he was also deadly serious about baseball. He was not just a funny guy managing a very good team.

Arguably already a senior citizen, at 58, when he assumed the managerial reins in the Bronx—(life expectancy for a U.S.-born male in 1949 was about 65, and when Stengel was born in 1890, it was 46, according to census data)—Casey Stengel was at the peak of his creative engagement with baseball. He was at his most brilliant and intuitive as a manager, mastering every aspect of the game. Constantly maneuvering for advantage, many of his in-game moves defied convention and begged for explanation, and although deciphering what he said (or meant) sometimes required interpretation of Stengel-speak, after-the-fact explanations the Ole Perfessor did indeed offer. Everything he did seemed to work.

Stengel was masterful at structuring his roster and in using his bench strategically to get the offensive advantage he wanted at any singular moment he believed crucial. Juggling players in and out of the lineup and pinch hitting even for starting position players, Stengel always seemed to find the right combination of players for the Yankees to come out on top in the American League. He enabled players who were not everyday core regulars, like Johnny Mize, Bobby Brown, and even Tommy Henrich in 1950, to be significant contributors to the Yankees' success.

Contrary to the blowout pennants to which Yankee fans had become accustomed in the McCarthy years, Stengel was often forced to manage under the stress of competitive pennant races down the stretch. In his 12 years at the helm, he was a perfect five-for-five in pennant races not decided until the final week of the season. The Stengel Yankees won by being relentless, resourceful, and virtually unbeatable when they had to be. They played their best baseball in the final month of tight pennant races.

Whether or not thanks to Stengel's managerial genius, the Yankees thrived when first place was on the line late in the season, meaning they were either tied for first or no more than a game ahead or a game behind in the standings at the start of play. With the American League pennant up for grabs in each of his first four years in pinstripes, Stengel managed a total of 45 games with first place directly at stake in September and won 30 of them. That's two out of three.

Their winning in 1949 was epic, inspiring books like David Halberstam's classic *Summer of '49*. The Yankees played host to the Red Sox on the final two days of the season, trailing Boston by one game, with no alternative but to win both games if they were to win the pennant. Their manager's career potentially on the line, the Yankees did exactly that. Stengel's future was assured, even if his legacy was not quite yet made. (It took the Red Sox 18 years to recover from that one.) The Yankees never led by more than three games the entire month of September, and in the waning days of the season, they were 6–3 in games with first place at stake.

The next year, the Yankees went into Detroit trailing the Tigers by half a game and were only one up on third-place Boston with 16 games remaining. Winning two of the three games, Stengel's team left the Motor City in first place, never to look back. They won nine of the fourteen games they played with first place up for grabs in September 1950, ending up with a three-game advantage over Detroit.

Going for three in a row in 1951, the Yankees were one game behind Cleveland in mid-September with only fourteen left on the schedule, when the Indians came to New York for a two-game series. Stengel started Reynolds (14–8 at the time) and Lopat (19–8). Cleveland's manager, Al Lopez—who had caught for Stengel in both Brooklyn and Boston and was in his first year as a manager—started Feller (22–7) and Lemon

(17–12). Reynolds and Lopat both pitched complete-game victories, allowing the Indians only two runs in the two games, and now it was the Yankees in first place by a game. Cleveland won only three of its last eight, while the Yankees won nine of their last twelve, which decided the pennant five games in favor of New York. Stengel managed his team to a 12–7 record with first place on the line in September.

It was more of the same in 1952. There was not a day since June that the Yankees were not on top, but the Indians stayed close. The Indians finally caught up on August 22 when Garcia (16–8 after the game) beat Reynolds (whose record dropped to 15–8) in the first of a two-game series with the Yankees visiting Cleveland, and the two teams were deadlocked. The next day, Raschi (15–3 after the game) hurled the Yankees back into first place alone with 1–0 shutout over Wynn (now 16–11). The Yankees never had to share first place again, but their final margin of victory was only two games because the Indians refused to fold and were not eliminated until they had only two left to play. Beginning with Raschi's victory in Cleveland, the Yankees won all eight of the games they played with first place at stake until time ran out on the Indians.

With Mantle coming into his own, Stengel's teams thereafter were rarely, if ever, underestimated and typically began the season as the presumed favorite to represent the American League in the World Series. Stengel finally got to enjoy a cakewalk to the pennant in 1953—his fifth in five years at the Yankees' helm—after which he had to endure a September in which New York was left in Cleveland's dust, even though the 1954 Yankees won 103 games.

But in 1955 it was back to high-stress managing for Casey Stengel. Once again, the Yankees got the better of the Indians in a pennant race that was not settled until just three games remained on the schedule. By now, the Yankees were a different team based on their core regulars. In particular, they no longer had Reynolds, Raschi, and Lopat. And now they also had to contend with the Chicago White Sox, who were the team in first place—by half a game over both the Yankees and Indians—when August turned to September. The White Sox faded, the Indians did not, and the Yankees overcame a two-game deficit to Cleveland in mid-September by winning nine of their final eleven games to dethrone the defending American League champions by three games. The Yankees were 17–6 in September, including 9–3 in games with first place on the line.

\* \* \*

What really distinguishes the 1949–1953 Yankees and explains their five-and-five-in-five success, however, is that they did not have a losing record against any of their pennant-race rivals—7 other teams with at least 90 wins, including 3 in 1950 alone—against whom they played 20 percent of their games, the equivalent of a full 154-game schedule. They won 5 of those 22-game season series and split with the second-place Tigers in 1950 and distant second-place Indians in 1953. Their record against those seven 90-win teams was 89–65. No other team in history over any five-year period could claim as high a winning percentage against rival contenders as Casey Stengel's 1949–1953 Yankees.

A major reason for their success was Stengel's assuring that his best pitchers—Allie Reynolds, Vic Raschi, and Eddie Lopat—were lined up to start against the Yankees' top-tier opponents with appropriate rest, even if it meant some discontinuity in their days between starts. From 1949 to 1952, with the pennant race still up for grabs each year, Stengel's trio started 27 of the 33 games that the Yankees faced off with contending rivals in late August and September. The Yankees won 17 of those games, with Reynolds, Raschi, and Lopat posting a 15–8 record in their 27 starts.

Stengel was judicious in the use of his other starters rounding out the rotation. Hard-throwing right-hander Tommy Byrne started 30 games and had his breakout season in 1949 with a 15–7 record—the second-best winning percentage on the team after Reynolds—but Stengel gave him only five starts against pennant-race rivals Boston and Cleveland. Unlike the Big Three, Byrne had yet to earn Stengel's trust in his competitive ability to pitch effectively against Yankee rivals for the pennant because he had limited major-league experience coming into the season.

And in 1950, Stengel made sure that rookie southpaw Whitey Ford, called up in July, could flourish at the big-league level before entrusting him with big-time games. Ford won all nine of his decisions in twelve starts, but only two of those starts and one of his victories were against a team with a winning record. When Ford returned from his two-year Selective Service commitment in 1953, he quickly became Stengel's ace and was used accordingly against the teams the Yankees needed to beat to win the pennant. In 1953, 8 of Ford's 30 starts were against the second-place Indians—he was 4–2 in those games—and 5 of his other starts, all of them victories, came against the up-and-coming, third-place, 89-win White Sox.

In large part because of Reynolds, Raschi, and Lopat, no contender suffered more at the hand of the New York Yankees than the Cleveland Indians. In the close pennant races the two teams fought, the difference in outcomes was most apparent in their records against each other. Second to the Yankees for much of the summer of 1949 in defense of their championship the year before, losing 12 of their 22 games against the Yankees, including 4 of their last 6 matchups in August and September, was not helpful to the Indians' cause. In 1950, Cleveland was within two games of New York and Detroit, tied for first in late August, before losing four straight to the Yankees effectively ended their chances. The Indians won only eight of their games against the Yankees and wound up six games behind in fourth place.

It was more of the same in 1951. This time, despite their being the team with three 20-game winners, the Indians were overwhelmed by the Yankees' 15–7 record against them. Stengel's trio of big-game starters—Reynolds (5–1 against Cleveland), Raschi (3–2), and Lopat (5–2)—won 13 of those 15 games, while losing 5. For Cleveland, Bob Feller—whose 22 wins led the league in his last outstanding season—won only two of six decisions against New York, while Bob Lemon (3–3), Early Wynn (1–4) and Mike Garcia (1–3) accounted for the remainder of their seven triumphs over the Yankees but also for 10 losses.

Cleveland fared better head-to-head thereafter. They lost the season series again in 1952, beating New York only 10 times, but held the Yankees to their worst record against any team. Not that it did them any good in 1953, when the Yankees won their first runaway pennant under Stengel, but the Indians split the season series and were once again the most difficult team for New York to beat. The two teams split their 22 games again in 1954, although this time it was Cleveland winning the pennant decisively—by eight games—or as decisively as can be, considering the runner-up Yankees also won more than a hundred games. Finally, in 1955, the Indians beat the Yankees in their season series, taking 13 of 22 games. It was the first time in the Stengel era that the Yankees lost a season series to any pennant-race rival, of whom they faced off against 11 from 1949 to 1955. But, of course, New York again came out on top of the AL standings.

New York's trio had the edge over Cleveland's three aces going head-to-head in the three years, 1951 to 1953, that both teams' top threesome were intact and the Yankees and Indians were the only teams directly competing for the American League pennant. Reynolds (7–5), Raschi (10–4), and Lopat (9–5) combined for 26 wins and 14 losses against the Indians—a .650 winning percentage, not far off their excellent collective .668 winning percentage (147–73) overall for those years. Cleveland's top three starters combined for a 180–110 (.621) record from 1951 to 1953 and threw more than a third as many innings as New York's top three but were only 23–25 against the Yankees. Lemon and Wynn both had losing records facing the Bronx Bombers at 8–9 and 6–9. Garcia alone had a winning record at 9–7. No surprise, the Yankees won all three pennants.

* * *

Perhaps the Cleveland Indians should have done better than they did with the quality of core players they had—notably Avila at second base, Rosen at third, Doby in center, and a starting rotation that featured Lemon, Wynn, and Garcia in their prime and a perhaps underused Bob Feller in his waning years. The Yankees outscored the Indians by 156 runs between 1951 and 1955 and, even though Cleveland had superior starting pitching, allowed 75 fewer runs. Over five 154-game seasons, those differences are virtually inconsequential. But they are consistent with the two teams being so close competitively that the Yankees, winners of four pennants to Cleveland's one, won only nine more games in that time.

The most crucial difference explaining New York's overwhelming advantage in trips to the World Series, however, may well be that the Yankees were 84–70 and the Indians 75–79 in the 154 games they each played against other teams with 90 wins, which included the White Sox in both 1954 and 1955. In their games against each other, the Yankees won 58, the Indians 52.

Just as blow-away pennants were a Yankee hallmark of the McCarthy years, rising to the occasion in games specifically against their principal rival for the pennant characterized the Stengel years. In his 12 years in New York, Stengel's Yankees won 10 and split 4 of the 16 season series they played against all other American League teams with 90 wins or that finished second without 90 wins in any given year. The only series they lost were to the Indians in 1955 and the pennant-winning White Sox in 1959. Their 198–154 (.563) record against top-tier competition equates to 87 wins over the standard 154-game schedule played at the time.

The rivalry between New York and Cleveland ended once the Indians became less competitive, beginning in 1956. While the Indians did finish second that year, there really was no pennant race. Cleveland was 10½ games out by mid-July and thereafter got no closer than 7 behind New York. It wasn't until 1959 that the Indians were again in the hunt, rebounding to second place.

Apparently not satisfied with his team's makeup, however, General Manager "Trader" Frank Lane—who by this point in his career often seemed to be making trades just for the sake of doing so, rather than with a grand strategy in mind—traded away Cleveland's two best position players in 1959, outfielders Rocky Colavito and Minnie Miñoso. Colavito tied Harmon Killebrew for the most home runs in the American League with 42, and his 111 runs batted in fell one short of the league leader. Miñoso's .302 average was fifth in the league, and his player value was the fifth-best among AL position players in 1959. None of the players Cleveland got in return contributed much to the Indians, who descended into decades of competitive mediocrity. Looking back 30 years later, Cleveland sportswriter Terry Pluto called it the "Curse of Rocky Colavito."

The Yankees, meanwhile, continued on with their dominance of the 1950s. Of historical note, the 1953 Yankees were the last team ever to appear in a World Series without an African American or black Latino player on the roster. They did have white, Hispanic, Cuban-born Willy Miranda as a backup infielder, however. He did not play in the World Series.

# FIVE

## Last of the Titans and Baseball's Expansion Imperative

The opening of the 1950 World Series in Philadelphia's Shibe Park—the oldest baseball stadium in the major leagues dating back to 1909—was surely a bittersweet moment for the grand old man in baseball, Connie Mack. Not only at age 87 did he finally step down at the end of the season after 50 years as the only manager the American League team in the City of Brotherly Love ever had, but it was the Philadelphia Phillies and not the Athletics who brought the city its first World Series in 19 years.

Success in Philadelphia-baseball terms had long been synonymous with Connie Mack's Athletics. The Athletics had won two of the first five pennants in American League history. That was just the beginning because Mack thereafter assembled two of the greatest teams in history. Frank "Home Run" Baker, Eddie Collins, Eddie Plank, and Chief Bender were the core of the team he managed to four pennants and three World Series victories in five years between 1910 and 1914. Lefty Grove, Mickey Cochrane, Jimmie Foxx, and Al Simmons were the heart of the team that interrupted the success of the Ruth–Gehrig Yankee dynasty, winning three consecutive pennants and two World Series between 1929 and 1931.

One third of the way into the 20th century, the Mack-owned, operated, and managed Philadelphia Athletics had won 9 pennants—second only to the New York Giants' 11 during that time. Those achievements notwithstanding, however, between 1915 and 1924 and virtually every year since 1934, the Athletics were one of the worst teams in major-league baseball.

\* \* \*

But the same-town Phillies were even worse. The Philadelphia Phillies spent most of the first half-century perfecting the art of futility. Limited financial resources, poor executive management, and having to play in Baker Bowl until they became Mack's tenants at Shibe Park in 1937 certainly did not help their cause. Although they did bring a fifth World Series in six years to Philadelphia in 1915 by winning the National League pennant, while the Athletics plunged from the top of the standings into last place, that was the only pennant the Phillies had won before 1950. The Phillies remained competitive for two years after their 1915 pennant, then gave away the best pitcher in baseball—Grover Cleveland Alexander, who had three consecutive 30-win seasons for them from 1915 to 1917—mostly for the money. For the next three decades, the National League franchise in Philadelphia was notorious for its ineptitude. They finished last 16 times and next-to-last 8 times in the 31 years from 1918 to 1948. They had only one season with a winning record in all that time.

The Philadelphia Phillies were the surprise team in major-league baseball in 1950. Their resurrection had begun during the war when the National League brokered the sale of the debt-ridden franchise to Bob Carpenter, heir to the du Pont family fortune. Being a moneyed man, Carpenter prioritized building a competitive team, including putting money into signing and developing top-notch talent. These investments began paying off in 1949, when the Phillies had their first winning season since 1932 and finished third, no longer the doormat of the National League.

But the Phillies were not assumed to be ready to compete with the powerhouse Dodgers, or even the Cardinals or Braves, for top of the heap. They got off to a strong start in 1950 and engaged in their first pennant race since the days of Alexander the Phillies Great. After going 20–8 in August, the Phillies entered the September stretch with a comfortable, though not necessarily insurmountable, lead of 6½ games with 29 left to play. The Dodgers, however, owing to rainouts earlier in the season, still had 35 games on their schedule and, with Robinson, Campanella, Newcombe, Reese, Snider, Hodges, and Furillo, a far more veteran and formidable team.

The upstart Phillies, by contrast, were called the Whiz Kids for their relative youth and inexperience. Paced by 23-year-old Robin Roberts in only his third season, 21-year-old southpaw Curt Simmons also in his third season, and Jim Konstanty in the bullpen, the Phillies had the best pitching in the league. Their core lineup of youthful gamers included two 23-year-olds, center fielder Richie Ashburn and shortstop Granny Hamner, both in their third season at the top of the batting order; right fielder Del Ennis—who was only 25 but an established big-league veteran with five years on his resume—batting clean-up; and 24-year-old third baseman Willie "Puddin' Head" Jones, in only his second full season, batting fifth.

Making a statement that the pennant race wasn't over, the Dodgers came into town in early September and won three of four, but the Phillies recovered from that setback to boost their lead to 7½ games in mid-September. It was Philadelphia's largest lead of the season, and with only 11 games left, their lead seemed commanding, if not outright secure. Time was rapidly running out on Brooklyn. But four of the Phillies' remaining games were against the Dodgers, three against the Braves, and the other four against the Giants, the team with the best record in the National League since the Fourth of July. And their last nine games of the season would all be on the road. Plus, the United States was again at war—this time in Korea—which called into duty the National Guard unit in which Curt Simmons served.

Simmons seemed on his own way to 20 wins with a 17–8 record and had a 3.40 earned run average when he was called into service. His three starts in September gave no indication that having already pitched over 40 innings more than his previous career high was diminishing his effectiveness; he allowed only 4 earned runs in 24 September innings—the last of which, sadly for Philadelphia, was on September 9. Rookie right-hander Bob Miller, who had not been a regular in the starting rotation since early August, and veteran right-hander Ken Heintzelman, who had not started a game since July, essentially took Simmons' spot in the rotation alongside Roberts (whose 20–11 record was the first of 6 straight 20-win seasons), Russ Meyer (9–11), and Bubba Church (8–6) for the final weeks of the schedule.

Miller lost two of his three starts after Simmons was called up, surrendering 9 earned runs in 17 innings, and Heintzelman won one and lost one of his two starts. Jim Konstanty, who at the end of the season became the first reliever in history to win a Most Valuable Player Award on the strength of his 16–7 record and 16 saves, was overworked and ineffective as the season drew to a close. Pitching in six of the final ten games—four times working at least two innings, and twice at least three—Konstanty lost twice, blew a save, allowed three of five inherited runners to score after he came in, and had a 6.23 ERA in thirteen innings.

The Dodgers came to Philadelphia for two games in late September, won both and sent the Phillies on the road with their lead down to five games. Philadelphia's first stop was Boston, where they won two of three to eliminate the Braves from contention. Now only the Dodgers had a chance, and the Phillies played their part by losing all four of their next games in New York at the Polo Grounds. By the time the Phillies came into Ebbets Field to close out the season, it was the Dodgers who were the team with momentum, having won 12 of their last 15 games.

Being up by two games, all Philadelphia needed was one win to escape Brooklyn with the pennant. In the first game, Miller failed to make it out of the fifth; Konstanty, pitching in relief, was ineffective; the Dodgers won, and the two teams went into the final game of the season one game apart. Should Philadelphia lose, the National League pennant would be decided in a best-of-three playoff.

Game 154 was a classic in 10 innings, both team's aces—Robin Roberts and Don Newcombe—going the distance, Richie Ashburn cutting down the would-be walk-off winning run at the plate trying to score from second on a single up the middle in the bottom of the ninth, and ending with first baseman Dick Sisler hitting a three-run home run off Newk in the tenth to send the Phillies to their first World Series since 1915. And thus did the Phillies avert what would have been, at the time, the most epic collapse in history—losing a 7½-game lead with only 11 left on the schedule. They would leave it to a later Phillies team, in 1964, to have that distinction. The Phillies went on to lose the Series in four straight to the Yankees, thus ending their season by losing nine of the last ten games they played.

Notwithstanding two future Hall of Famers on their roster—Roberts and Ashburn—and their pennant, the 1950 Philadelphia Phillies were a tease. They were not in the same competitive class as the Dodgers and the up-and-coming Giants (who would add Willie Mays in 1951), and Philadelphia did not factor into any pennant race again until 1964. If the Whiz Kids were going to win, 1950 was going to have to be their year. Even with Roberts the best pitcher in baseball the first half of the 1950s— leading the league in wins four straight years, in complete games five straight years, and in innings pitched five straight years—and with Ashburn one of the best outfielders in the game the entire decade, the Phillies dropped to fifth place with a losing record in 1951 and spent most of the rest of the decade mired in mediocrity.

Until 1949, the Athletics drew more fans to their ballpark than the Phillies in all but six years, and three of those years were Alexander's 30-win seasons. Even when both teams were perennial bottom dwellers, it was Connie Mack's team that more Philadelphians came out to see. Despite the fact that the 1948 Athletics were actually competing for the American League pennant until the end of August and looked to be on the upswing, the next year it was the Phillies that outdrew Mack's teams.

The two Philadelphia clubs finished the 1949 season with the same record and the same deficit behind the pennant winners in their league, although the Phillies were third in their standings compared to the Athletics coming in fifth. And in 1950, when the Whiz Kids captured the fancy of Philadelphians, the Athletics celebrated Mack's 50 years at the helm by being the worst team in baseball. In 1950, 1.5 million people spun the turnstiles at Shibe Park, but nearly 80 percent of them—1.2 million—came to see the Whiz Kids. The Phillies were now the favored team in the City of Brotherly Love, a fact not lost on the Mack-family ownership of the Philadelphia Athletics. This was the beginning of the end for the Athletics in Philadelphia.

* * *

When Connie Mack retired to become essentially *president emeritus* of the Philadelphia Athletics, he along with Clark Griffith and Branch Rickey were the last of baseball's titans who built and nurtured the structure of the modern game. He did as much as any manager in the first part of the 20th century to develop the profession of manager as its own discipline. Mack was tied with Joe McCarthy for the second-most pennants won by a manager in major-league history until then with nine—one behind John McGraw, another of baseball's early 20th-century modernizers. In his primetime years as a manager, which admittedly was a long prime (he was well into his 60s when he managed the 1929–1931 Athletics to three straight pennants), Mack was a master at teaching the art of baseball, and his players were well schooled in how to play the game. Mack arguably developed and managed more great players than any manager in history, including McGraw.

But Connie Mack was also owner of the franchise, with the financial responsibilities that ownership entails. In the first part of the 20th century, it was not uncommon for managers to be part-owners of the teams they managed. McGraw was with the Giants. Griffith was with the Washington Senators. Wilbert Robinson was with the Brooklyn Dodgers, who were nicknamed the Robins for most of his years in the dugout. Mack became the controlling owner of the Philadelphia Athletics in 1912 when he secured the shares to 50 percent of the franchise.

Because, as an owner, Mr. Mack had to be concerned as much about the bottom line as competitive success, his career arc as owner-manager was defined by building a great team that dominated baseball between 1910 and 1914, which he disbanded, ostensibly to save his franchise from insolvency, followed by a decade of awful teams until he had sufficient financial resources to build up another great team, which he again disbanded, ostensibly to save the franchise from insolvency as the Great Depression tightened its grip on America. The second time, however, Mack did not invest in trying to rebuild a competitive team.

The first time Mack disbanded his championship team for economic reasons, after the 1914 season, occurred when the United States was in the midst of a bad recession and the existing major leagues were being challenged by the upstart Federal League enticing veteran star players with higher salaries than they were making in the established order. Even though his team won its fourth pennant in five years, attendance at Shibe Park was down by 39 percent in 1914. Four teams in the American League drew more fans to their games than the defending World Series–champion Athletics. But attendance across the major leagues was down two million fans from 1913 because of tougher economic times. (There is no record of Federal League attendance during its two years in operation. The upstart league shared only two cities with the AL and

NL—Chicago and St. Louis—and quite likely drew some fans from Cubs, White Sox, Browns, and Cardinals games.) While the Federal League challenge caused many teams in the two established major leagues to substantially boost the salaries of their star players, Mack refused to do so for financial reasons—either because he couldn't or simply wouldn't.

Mack began to rebuild as soon as he was financially able, however, and by 1929, he was again managing baseball's most formidable team . . . which he began taking apart in 1933. But the second time, Mack did not wait out his financial woes, eventually to rebuild. Whether chastened by the universal economic hardships of the Great Depression or lacking the stamina to *want* to invest the time and energy required for rebuilding (he was already 68 years old when the Athletics won the 1931 pennant), the financial bottom line was more important to Connie Mack—*owner* of the Philadelphia Athletics—than the winning bottom line. Even after World War II brought an end to the Depression and baseball attendance surged once the war ended, Mack stayed a minimalist in his approach to spending on his team.

Operating with limited financial resources, the Athletics descended ever lower into the depths of the American League. Mack spent little on scouting and incubating a minor-league system to groom players for Philadelphia. Unwilling to pay high salaries, Mack was more than willing to sell or trade promising young players to other clubs if the price was right and replace them with players who would command less money. From 1933 until he finally retired in 1950, Mack managed only three winning teams—all between 1947 and 1949. The Athletics finished last 10 times and next-to-last twice. Mack's Great Depression breakdown of his team was the start of nearly 40 years that the Athletics would spend in the wilderness, including a horrendous 13-year sojourn in Kansas City, before finally putting together a championship team in Oakland in the 1970s.

But if the financial constraints were real, Connie Mack's position as both owner *and* manager of the Philadelphia Athletics was also inherently contradictory. In the 1930s and 1940s, he subordinated his instinct to win as a manager to his impulse as an owner to maximize whatever profits there were to be had from owning a major-league baseball team. Mack's economic calculus apparently was, "I can make more money finishing last than first" because "with a last place ball club, you don't have to raise anybody's salary," as he was quoted in David Kaiser's book, *Epic Season*, on the 1948 pennant race. Mack may have been trying to justify his skinflint approach to ownership when he asserted in his 1950 autobiography, *Connie Mack: My 66 Years in the Big Leagues*, that baseball fans, in Philadelphia at least, were in any case more inclined to watch a team "fight to become champions" than to support a consistently winning team, evidence to the contrary in New York. He apparently believed the best circumstance to boost attendance was to have a competitive team fighting to return to the top—neither mired in the bottom muck (hopeless) nor unchallenged at the top (boring).

Assuming this sentiment reflected his true thinking, the idea that building a winning team that competed for pennants would boost revenues by increasing fan interest and attendance was not relevant to Connie Mack. What appeared to be relevant for Mr. Mack, *owner*, was the law of diminishing returns. Even with the end of the Depression and then World War II, Mack apparently calculated that the increase in attendance revenues from building a consistently competitive team could not keep pace with the expenditures necessary for achieving success. Or, more specifically, Mack assessed that the cost in player salaries of fielding a winning team, let alone investing in his minor-league farm system to build a foundation for winning, was prohibitive to making a profit, especially in a two-team city that was not New York or Chicago.

* * *

Just as for half a century there were no changes in major-league baseball's all-white demographic, the game's geography had not changed either. From 1903 to 1952, the same 16 big-league teams played in the same 10 U.S. cities. Four cities had one team from each league—Boston, Chicago, Philadelphia, and St. Louis—and a fifth, New York City, had three big-league teams, one in the Bronx, another in Manhattan, and the third in Brooklyn, which until 1898 had been its own city. The five cities that the two leagues shared were also the five largest cities in the United States, according to U.S. census data, at the time the major league's geography was cemented—seemingly in perpetuity—in 1903, the year the American League put the team that would become the Yankees in New York. But the national demographics were changing and the population shifting.

By 1930, however, while New York with 6.9 million people, Chicago with 3.4 million, and Philadelphia with nearly 2 million were still the three largest cities—and would remain so through 1950—St. Louis had dropped from fourth-largest city in 1910 to seventh and Boston from fifth to ninth. The ability of St. Louis, where the Cardinals and Browns had shared Sportsman's Park since 1920, and Boston to support two big-league teams was increasingly open to question.

It was not as though there were not big-city alternatives for a financially struggling franchise in any major-league city to move. The fourth- and fifth-largest cities by population in the 1930 census were Detroit—whose 1.6 million citizens could presumably support a second team in addition to the Tigers, certainly if both were competitive—and Los Angeles. Baseball's manifest destiny had not yet extended to the West Coast, however, for the practical reason that commercial air travel was still in its infancy and the distance was too great for train travel—the mode of transportation big-league teams relied on. But Baltimore, the 8th-largest

U.S. city, Minneapolis and St. Paul, whose combined population would have made it 10th largest, and even number 12 Milwaukee were all within Eastern Seaboard–reach by rail.

While the very successful Cardinals in the early 1930s considered moving to Detroit because of disappointment that their winning ways had not resulted in surging attendance, major-league owners bought into premise that their franchises needed to be geographically stable to remain viable, even if two teams in some cities no longer made sense and the population base in other cities could support a big-league team. Furthermore, in the broader context of "organized" baseball, there was no enthusiasm for disrupting minor-league teams that held sway in those cities, particularly those that had transactional arrangements for major-league-ready players or were becoming affiliates of major-league franchises as Branch Rickey's concept of the farm system took hold. And baseball had the antitrust exemption granted by the Supreme Court decision in 1922 that finally addressed issues raised by the now-defunct Federal League to fall back on. The exemption allowed the collective body of teams in their respective leagues to prevent, in the name of franchise stability, owners of financially struggling teams from moving to greener pastures.

At least until the economic impact of the Great Depression, it was still possible for the return on investment of putting together a competitive team to turn around a financially troubled franchise, even with market competition from another franchise in the same city. Philadelphia, St. Louis, and Boston all had years where both teams had good attendance. Until the Depression, there was little reason to think these cities could not support two competitive major-league teams. But with World War II over and the Depression in the past, this possibility became increasingly untenable, even with the dramatic surge in attendance that accompanied the end of the war.

Notwithstanding the advantages of the antitrust exemption, baseball was forced to grow up from the parochial industry it had been and modernize its business strategies. And it was apparent that some cities weren't big enough for two teams. The situation was most dire in St. Louis and Boston, where one of the two teams in each city was consistently at the bottom of the standings and unable to compete with the other for a fair share of ballpark attendance.

* * *

In St. Louis, that team was the American League Browns. The Cardinals dominated the baseball scene in the Gateway City after they began to regularly win National League pennants in 1926. The only year the Browns drew more fans to Sportsman's Park than the Cardinals was 1944, when both St. Louis teams won their league's pennants, probably only because the Browns not only competed for the pennant for the first time in more than two decades but also won a close race that went down to the final day. It was the only pennant ever won by the Browns, and it quite likely was possible only because the rosters of the best American League teams—including the Yankees and Red Sox—were more decimated by the wartime service of star players.

The Browns quickly faded from contention to their more traditional place buried in the second division when many of baseball's best players returned to the baseball wars in 1946. The Cardinals remained one of the best teams in baseball and one of the most popular. In 1950, more than one million fans watched the Cardinals play at Sportsman's Park. The Browns' attendance was less than 250,000—by far the fewest fans to see any of the 16 major-league teams play ball in 1950.

Bill Veeck did not believe the Browns could survive in St. Louis when he bought the team in 1951. The Gateway City belonged to the Cardinals, who had a history of winning ways, not to mention Stan Musial. The Browns had a history of losing and lacked the financial resources to offer their fans—what few they had in St. Louis—a more promising future. The fact that Veeck presided over a substantial boost in Browns' attendance in 1952 to over half a million for the first time in six years did not make their position in St. Louis any more tenable.

Veeck first looked into moving the Browns to Milwaukee, where he had gotten his start as a baseball owner in 1941 with the Milwaukee Brewers in the minor-league American Association. The Brewers, however, were now an affiliate of the Boston Braves, who consequently held organized baseball's "territorial" rights to Milwaukee, causing Veeck to turn his attention east to Baltimore. Now the sixth-largest city in the United States with a population just under one million, according to the 1950 census, Baltimore had a rich tradition of baseball dating back to the 19th century, and the city had built a modern ballpark suitable for a major-league team.

When beer baron August Anheuser Busch bought the Cardinals in February 1953, Veeck knew the Browns were finished in St. Louis because he did not have the resources to compete with the Busch family fortune. As big-league teams convened for the rites of spring training, Veeck lobbied his fellow American League owners to approve moving his team from St. Louis to Baltimore for the 1953 season. Contrary to expectations, since he had lined up the support of Baltimore city officials, he was denied. The owners voted overwhelmingly against him. It was in fact a vote against *him*—Bill Veeck, a controversial gadfly in the cliquish world of major-league franchise owners.

No doubt affected by the news about the Browns wanting to skip town just before the season started, their attendance plummeted to less than 300,000 in 1953. American League owners finally approved their move to Baltimore but only after Veeck sold the franchise to a consortium of buyers in the city. Renamed in honor of the city's great 1890s major-league team and outstanding minor-league teams that followed, the Orioles may have drawn more than one million fans in their first year in Baltimore in 1954, but they were still the same old Browns with their seventh-place finish, a whopping 57 games out of first place. The Orioles did not escape the bottom half of the standings until 1960.

* * *

While Veeck was kept from moving to Baltimore in 1953, the Boston Braves were *not* denied their petition that same spring for approval by the National League to move to Milwaukee. Having used public money to build a new stadium, city officials used Veeck's interest in Milwaukee as leverage with the Braves to either give up their territorial rights or move there themselves.

Like the Browns in St. Louis, the Braves had a history of mostly losing seasons buried deep in the standings since the demise of their late 1890s dynasty, which went by the name Beaneaters. They stunned the baseball world with their stirring 1914 championship season, when they surged from last place in late July to win the pennant by 10½ games and then swept Mack's heavily favored Athletics in the World Series but faded quickly from contention after that. From 1917 until 1947, the Braves never finished better than fourth and were always struggling to make financial ends meet. During most of those dark years, however, the Red Sox were just as bad, their penance for having sold out their fans by selling Babe Ruth to the Yankees for the then-exorbitant price of $100,000 in December 1919. Neither Boston team was overwhelmingly favored by the fans.

That changed when Tom Yawkey bought the financially fraught Red Sox in 1933. Notwithstanding this was the middle of the Depression, Yawkey immediately began to pour money into the team. He could afford to because Yawkey was a man of considerable wealth derived from his family's timber and mining interests. He spent half a million dollars in cash, along with surrendering a few bit players, to bring Lefty Grove, Joe Cronin, and Jimmie Foxx to Fenway in the 1930s.

By World War II, the Red Sox were clearly in competitive mode with Ted Williams, Bobby Doerr, Dom DiMaggio, and Johnny Pesky in the lineup. The Red Sox had still not challenged the powerhouse Yankees in a real pennant race, but they had the star attractions. Without players like those, the Braves could not compete with the Red Sox for Bostonian affections; only a third of the fans who paid to see major-league baseball in Boston in the first decade of the Yawkey reign did so at Braves Field. Boston was a Red Sox town.

In 1946, like every major-league franchise, the Braves benefited greatly from Americans' desires to put the Great Depression and World War II behind them. But the Braves were also on the upswing. After having been in a precarious financial position for decades, the downtrodden franchise was purchased in 1943 by a trio of heavy-construction magnates led by Lou Perini who immediately began investing in the club's future.

Most significantly, the new owners ramped up their scouting and rebuilt a farm system that had atrophied even before the war to only three affiliates, all in the lower minor leagues. They scouted and signed Alvin Dark, who became one of baseball's premier shortstops. By 1946, the Braves had 12 minor-league affiliates and their first Triple-A team. In 1947, they secured the American Association team in Milwaukee to be their Triple-A affiliate. At the major-league level, the Braves recruited Billy Southworth, who had led the Cardinals to three straight pennants from 1942 to 1944, to be their manager when his contract with St. Louis expired after the 1945 season; acquired first baseman Earl Torgeson from the Pacific Coast League; purchased (with some minor players thrown in) accomplished major leaguers third baseman Bob Elliott, second baseman Eddie Stanky, and outfielder Jeff Heath from the Pirates, Dodgers, and Browns; and they had Warren Spahn and Johnny Sain back from the war to headline their pitching staff.

The Braves finally had a team that could compete with the Red Sox for Boston fan allegiance. Both teams, finishing third in their leagues, broke one million at the gate in 1947. Coming off their pennant the previous year, the Red Sox drew 1.4 million to Fenway Park, and the rapidly improving Braves saw 1.2 million enter Braves Field. Bostonians nearly had the privilege of watching both its teams play in the World Series the next year when the Braves won their first pennant in 34 years and the Red Sox finished the schedule tied with Cleveland for first, only to lose the one-game playoff at Fenway to determine who would face off against the Braves. The Braves' attendance of nearly 1.5 million was only about 104,000 less than went to Fenway Park.

But the Braves' success both competitively and in attendance was short lived. In part undermined by player animosity toward Southworth's increasingly abrasive and seemingly arbitrary managerial style, the Braves could not capitalize on their 1948 success and plummeted to fourth place and a losing record in 1949. The Red Sox remained one of baseball's powerhouse teams. In 1951, the Braves' attendance was back to below half a million, while 1.3 million Bostonians went to Fenway Park.

Even with a grand strategy and the financial means to improve the team through scouting and player development, including shortstop Johnny Logan and third baseman Eddie Mathews already in the pipeline, it was apparent to Perini that Boston—the 10th-largest city with a population of about 800,000—was not a big enough market to support two teams. Bostonians were making clear their preference was the American League team. When the Braves sank to seventh place in 1952 and their attendance to 281,278—by far the fewest fans of any major-league team, including the hapless Browns in St. Louis—Perini determined that Milwaukee was the place to be. His team having operated at a loss of nearly $1.3 million since 1950, Perini estimated that staying in Boston would be a losing proposition to the tune of $1 million in red ink every year. "This is no sudden thing," he said. "I've known for two years it was inevitable. Boston simply is not a two-club city."

The Braves' move to Milwaukee proved an instant eye-opening success. In each of their first six years, the Milwaukee Braves led the major leagues in attendance. In the first five of those years, no other team came close. In 1954, they became the first National League team in history to break the two-million barrier in attendance, a string they ran to four years in a row, as the Braves attracted fans regionally from across the Upper Midwest. They were not challenged by any team in attendance until 1958, when the Dodgers were new to Los Angeles and came within 126,000 fans of the Braves in Milwaukee.

And perhaps most important, the historically hapless Boston Braves quickly became one of the National League's most formidable teams in Milwaukee. After finishing second, third, and second in their first three years in their new home city, the Braves came within a game of the 1956 pennant, displaced the Dodgers as the class of the National League by winning decisive back-to-back pennants in 1957 and 1958, won a stirring World Series against the Yankees in 1957, and then tied the Dodgers for first place at the end of the 1959 season schedule before losing the pennant in a playoff.

\* \* \*

The Braves' move to Milwaukee in 1953 was the first time in 50 years that a franchise was allowed to relocate and the first time since 1902—when, ironically, an original American League team called the Brewers left Milwaukee for St. Louis to become the Browns—that a new city was added to the major-league map. The impoverishment of second-rate teams in two-team cities could no longer be justified. To keep franchises in place that clearly did not have the financial resources to compete, simply because it had been that way since the turn of the century in a very different America, risked ultimately undermining the viability of the game itself.

It especially made no sense to do so when there were other populous markets not only capable of supporting a major-league franchise but willing to invest public funds to attract big-league teams, as both Baltimore and Milwaukee did in building modern baseball stadiums. Within a year of the Braves' move, the Browns were in Baltimore as the Orioles. And two years later, the Athletics abandoned Philadelphia for Kansas City, expanding the geographic reach of the major leagues for the first time beyond the Mississippi River.

But it was not as though Philadelphia could not support two major-league teams. Still the third-largest city in the country with a population over two million in 1950, Philadelphia was home to 400,000 more citizens than St. Louis and Boston combined. The City of Brotherly Love was certainly a large enough market for both the Athletics and the Phillies, at least if both franchises demonstrated a commitment to invest in their teams. Even if the Whiz Kids failed to deliver more on the promise of 1950, the Phillies kept hold of their star players—Robin Roberts, Richie Ashburn, Del Ennis, Granny Hamner, Willie Jones, Curt Simmons, and Jim Konstanty—into the middle of the decade. But the Athletics both would not and could not keep their best players.

Aside from Mack's self-defeating belief that the good citizens of Philadelphia would not support a winning team, his options to invest in rebuilding his team were in fact quite limited. Like Washington's Clark Griffith, but unlike most of the other owners—including the Phillies' rich new owner, Bob Carpenter—Mack had no profitable business or independent wealth outside of baseball. Moreover, even as the investment of capital was becoming increasingly important to baseball operations in postwar America, neither Mack nor Griffith was inclined to bring on investors whose stake in the franchise might diminish their control and still less to sell to buyers who had more financial resources to devote to building a competitive team. For Mack and Griffith both, their teams were family-owned enterprises that they wished to hand down to their progenitors, notwithstanding that this paradigm of ownership was no longer viable. And to make matters worse, the Mack-family ownership was dysfunctional, with Connie's heir-apparent sons fighting over control of the franchise, especially after he retired in 1950 from day-to-day operations.

By the end of the 1954 season, Mack-family ownership of the storied franchise was no longer tenable. They were deep in debt and the franchise close to insolvent. Their attendance had gone down from 627,000 in 1952, when the Athletics surprisingly finished fourth with a winning record, to barely over 300,000 coming to see a last-place, 103-loss team play at Shibe Park. The Athletics' draw had not been that low since the mid-1930s during the Great Depression. And the Phillies had more fans come to see them play in the same ballpark every year since 1949, including a more than two-to-one advantage in attendance in both 1953 and 1954.

The Macks had to sell. Although there was a late bid by a group of Philadelphia businessmen who promised not to move the franchise, American League owners approved the sale of the Philadelphia Athletics to Chicago businessman Arnold Johnson, who was clear in his intention to move the franchise to Kansas City—a city of less than 500,000, only 20th in population size among U.S. cities. The deal was strong-armed by Yankee owners Del Webb and Dan Topping, who had an extensive business relationship with Johnson and used their influence to persuade their fellow league owners that there was no future for a profitable American League franchise in Philadelphia.

Now only New York and Chicago, the two largest cities in the United States, had two major-league teams. That lasted only until 1958, when both the New York Giants and Brooklyn Dodgers moved to California, leaving New York City with only one team until the New York Mets were born in 1962 as part of an expansion scenario that major-league owners, content with the structure of organized baseball that had existed since 1901, were resistant to happening. Their hand was forced by Branch Rickey, in the final act of his career (and his life).

* * *

Once Connie Mack had retired, and after Washington Senators' owner Clark Griffith died in 1955, Branch Rickey stood standing as the last of the titans from early in the 20th century who helped to shape modern major-league baseball. Rickey found himself in retirement after the 1955 season when Pirates' owner John Galbreath refused to extend his contract as general manager, although he was retained as a high-priced consultant. Ever the visionary, however, Mr. Rickey—the architect of the farm-system concept of affiliated minor-league teams at every level to develop and control players that all big-league franchises eventually adopted just to stay competitive, not to mention the man who dared to buck tradition by signing and promoting Jackie Robinson and then Campanella and Newcombe—had one last grand ambition that ultimately changed the structure of major-league baseball.

His was quixotic quest that was doomed to failure because the powers that be in the game were opposed and could still count on the antitrust exemption that had been granted by the Supreme Court more than 30 years before. While Rickey's last crusade did not achieve fruition on its own merits, it led directly to the expansion era that began in 1961 and ultimately to the realignment of each league into two divisions less than 10 years later.

The genesis of Rickey's last stand was a belief nurtured soon after the war ended that major-league baseball's scope needed to expand to stay relevant given the dramatic changes that seemed inevitable in the postwar era. The United States was now at mid-century with a vibrant postwar economy and a surging population. While the U.S. population in 1953 was double what it was in 1903, the major leagues still had the same two leagues with the same 16 teams, all in the eastern half of the country, that there were back then. The West was increasingly populous and important to the country's economy.

If the franchise moves of the Braves, Browns, and Athletics in the first half of the 1950s proved anything beyond assuring their financial survival, it was the wisdom of the major leagues' expanding their geographic map. The fact that the Dodgers and Giants left New York and were so well received in Los Angeles and San Francisco reinforced the point. Besides the big boost in attendance for each team that moved, including the Dodgers and Giants on the West Coast, the attractiveness of regional markets became apparent.

Rickey took advantage of a perception in the late 1950s that baseball was in a state of unhealthy malaise. Even with great players like Willie Mays and Mickey Mantle, Stan Musial and Ted Williams, Hank Aaron and Al Kaline, Warren Spahn and Whitey Ford, Ernie Banks and Luis Aparicio—and that's just naming a few—the game was seen as somehow stale in a dynamic country. The game seemed slow to adapt, if at all, to changing times. Action on the field was often said to be plodding, homogenized, bereft of the unexpected. Stadiums built 40 years before seemed tired and obsolete, no longer the throbbing heartbeat of a neighborhood accessible to the masses by public transportation, now located in unattractive areas hard to get to by car. There were more recreational options for Americans' leisure time, including plopping down in front of the television. The televising of major-league games was thought to depress attendance at the ballpark. All of which seemed to explain the dip in attendance in the 1950s that some believed was a warning sign that the national pastime was imperiled. Americans seemed less interested in baseball.

There was merit to all those perceptions, with the possible exception of attendance. Given the explosive growth of major-league attendance once the country was no longer at war, a decline was likely inevitable. Baseball represented a return to normalcy, and Americans celebrated by shattering major-league attendance record in 1946 when more than 18 million showed up at major-league ballparks. New records were set in each of the next two years with attendance peaking at 21 million in 1948. Attendance was still over 20 million in 1949 but declined each of the next four years to about 14.4 million in 1953.

But from 1950 to 1953, the United States was back at war—this time on the Korean Peninsula—a war that seemed unusually brutal, in harsh conditions, perhaps a harbinger of an ultimate atomic conflict with the Soviet Union, and required the conscription of 1.5 million men, interrupting their lives. After the Korean War was over, without a clear American victory, attendance at big-league ballparks bumped up again in 1954 to about 16 million, reached 17 million in 1957, topped 19 million in 1959, and was up to nearly 20 million in 1960. Moreover, even if not as high as the first postwar years, major-league attendance as a percentage of the U.S. population in any year of the 1950s was greater than in any year before World War II.

Regardless of what conclusions were drawn about Americans' long-standing love affair with baseball, however, the major leagues entered a midlife crisis of existential angst. The powers that be with few exceptions were stuck in adherence to hidebound tradition. Branch Rickey's belief had turned to conviction that the game needed to be saved from itself. He was convinced baseball needed a growth spurt beyond two leagues and sixteen teams to keep pace with the growing population, economy, and infrastructure of the United States. The full-court press to put a new National League team in New York City, led by influential and well-connected New York attorney Bill Shea, and parallel scrutiny by Congress of baseball's antitrust exemptions gave Rickey the leverage he needed to move on his proposal that what baseball most needed for the long-term health of the game was a third major league.

It would be called the Continental League. It was founded in August 1959, Branch Rickey was named president, and Bill Shea predicted the new league would take the field in 1961. There were to be eight teams in populous North American cities—including Toronto, Canada—but New York was the only city the new league would share with any existing major-league team. Because of the city's size, importance, and influential media, having a franchise in New York was crucial for the new league to be successful. Rickey did not advocate that the new league be a rival to the two existing major leagues or try to pilfer their players, as both the fledgling American League at the turn of the century and the ill-fated Federal League in 1914 and 1915 had done. He estimated it would take four or five years before Continental League teams would be capable of playing at the existing level of major-league baseball.

With Rickey unwilling for his upstart league to raid players because he believed in the sanctity of the reserve clause, the Continental League was doomed to be a failed enterprise without major-league buy-in. Needing access to players in the existing minor leagues to make a go of it, Rickey tried to persuade major-league owners that all of baseball would benefit if they were supportive of the Continental League. Facing congressional legislation that threatened to strip major-league baseball of all or most of its antitrust exemption, Commissioner Ford Frick in 1960 proposed that instead of a new league, the owners would support "expansion" with each league adding two teams—including a new National League team in New York City. Rickey, arguing—correctly, as it turned out—that four new teams would start at a gross competitive disadvantage to the established franchises that would take years to overcome, insisted the solution was a separate league where all eight teams started out on an equal footing.

In the end, Rickey was outmaneuvered. Having been lobbied hard by major-league owners, Congress was leaning toward legislation that would declare all the major sports—including baseball—to be largely exempt from antitrust regulations. Nonetheless, knowing they had skirted a disaster and that Congress was watching how events unfolded, the owners understood they had little alternative but to commit to expansion.

The American League picked off Minneapolis, one of the Continental League cities, when Calvin Griffith wanted his Senators to leave Washington. Having inherited the franchise when uncle Clark Griffith passed away, Calvin presided over the franchise with the worst annual attendance of any major-league franchise since the Braves, Browns, and Athletics left their original cities. The National League picked off New York, when Bill Shea was promised a team, although Shea in the end merely lent his name to the new stadium in Queens rather than being an owner of the Mets.

Promises to include two of the other proposed Continental League franchise cities in expansion now, and the remaining four in the not-too-distant future, pulled the rug out from under Rickey's vision of the Continental League. It turned out, however, that Houston was the only other Continental League city to get a team in the first wave of expansion, joining New York as the two new NL teams in 1962. The two AL expansion franchises, which began play a year earlier, were in Los Angeles to offset the NL's getting a team in New York and in Washington to replace Griffith's now Minnesota Twins. The next wave of expansion, in 1969, did not include any of the other proposed Continental League cities.

\* \* \*

Connie Mack, who died in 1956, was voted into the Hall of Fame in 1937. Clark Griffith, who died in 1955, was voted into the Hall of Fame in 1946. Branch Rickey died in 1965. He was elected to the Hall of Fame two years later by the Veterans Committee. For all he did that bucked tradition to shape the modern game—develop the model for player development and minor-league affiliates, end the segregation of major-league baseball, advocate the need for expanding the major-league map to catch up to how much the country had grown—Branch Rickey deserved to have been immortalized in Cooperstown during his lifetime.

# SIX

## Brooklyn's Answer to New York

When Branch Rickey took over the baseball operations of the Brooklyn Dodgers in 1943, he understood that they were a team soon in need of a more youthful makeover. The previous two years had been all about the Dodgers and Cardinals—a team Rickey had rebuilt to championship caliber before his final five-year contract in St. Louis expired after the 1942 season. They had engaged in back-to-back pennant races for the ages. First, the Dodgers held off the Cardinals in 1941 on the strength of a 40–18 record over the last two months. Then St. Louis surged from a 10-game deficit in early August to overtake Brooklyn and win the 1942 pennant by going 44–9 the rest of the way, which they followed up by stunning the Yankees in five games to win the World Series. The St. Louis and Brooklyn battle for supremacy seemed to promise tight National League pennant races that would extend to at least the mid-1940s, but in 1943, America's intensifying involvement in World War II intervened.

In the first year of massive call-ups and voluntary enlistments of major-league players, the Dodgers were significantly undermined by three of their most indispensable players—shortstop Pee Wee Reese, center fielder Pete Reiser, and relief ace Hugh Casey—going off to war. The 1943 Dodgers finished third, far out of the pennant chase. Losing a key starting pitcher, Kirby Higbe, and second baseman Billy Herman the next year further crippled the club, which ended the 1944 season in seventh place. The Dodgers improved to finish third in 1945. Outfielder Dixie Walker and pitcher Curt Davis were the only key players from the 1941 and 1942 Dodgers who stayed in Brooklyn for the duration of the war years.

Although they did lose two-thirds of their starting outfield in 1943 when Enos "Country" Slaughter and Terry Moore donned military fatigues, the Cardinals were less hobbled by wartime call-ups of their core

71

players. St. Louis retained enough of their core players to completely dominate the National League in both 1943 and 1944. Stan Musial being called up in 1945, however, was too much for the Cardinals to bear and very likely cost them a fourth-consecutive pennant. They lost to the Chicago Cubs by three games.

That the Cardinals benefited from the Dodgers being hurt much more by wartime player losses is correct but only to a point. Even though the Cardinals were able to keep more of their core players during the war years than most other teams, most notably the Dodgers, they still had holes to fill as a result of ballplayers becoming soldiers, sailors, and airmen, particularly on their pitching staff.

But even conceding that the Dodgers lost a greater number of important players to the war than the Cardinals, Rickey—moving from St. Louis to Brooklyn—realized better than most that the two teams were likely on different trajectories even had the Second World War not intervened. Specifically, the 1942 Cardinals were a young team getting better, while the 1942 Dodgers were older and possibly on a plateau. Five of Brooklyn's regular position players and two of their three pitchers with 20 or more starts that year were 30 years or older, compared to only one core regular that age on the St. Louis roster—30-year-old Terry Moore. Back then, unlike today when professional baseball players are so much better conditioned and benefit from the marvels of modern medicine and surgery (not to mention major-league baseball's end-of-the-20th-century fling with performance-enhancing drugs) to keep them going longer, being 30 years old was to be on the slippery slope toward the end of one's baseball career.

The same as with Boston and New York over in the American League, once the war was over and the major-leaguers-turned-soldiers returned to being players, Brooklyn and St. Louis were poised to resume their fierce prewar rivalry for the National League pennant. That promise was more than fulfilled with the two teams ending the 154-game 1946 schedule tied at the top, necessitating the major league's first-ever playoff—three games to determine a pennant winner, which the Cardinals won in two.

While the Cardinals returned with much the same team they had in 1942, Rickey already had the Dodgers in transition. Of the seven players 30 years or older as regulars on the 1942 Dodgers, only right fielder Dixie Walker—who was not called into service during the war—was still a regular on the 1946 Dodgers. The six other regulars from 1942 were either no longer on the team or no longer effective players. Two pitchers back from the war who were instrumental to the Dodgers' success in 1946, Higbe and Casey, were now over 30. The future seemed to be in the hands of Reese and Reiser, both only 27 after three years away, and 29-year-old second baseman Eddie Stanky, who Rickey had obtained from the Cubs during the 1944 season.

But Rickey had something else in mind that not only laid the foundation for a would-be dynasty but also shook up an entrenched and sacrosanct convention of the major-league baseball establishment. Even as the Dodgers were fighting the Cardinals for the National League pennant in 1946, the seed of Branch Rickey's rebellion against the major league's unwritten, but nonetheless universally understood, segregationist, white-players-only policy was germinating in Montreal in the person of Jackie Robinson.

\* \* \*

Running parallel to the New York City, Bronx-based Yankees, in the New York City borough of Brooklyn, the Dodgers were every bit as dominant in ruling the National League during the 1950s. They were a dynasty of their own. The Yankees met the Dodgers in six of the ten World Series between 1947 and 1956, perfectly coinciding with the major-league career of Jackie Robinson.

While the focus was on Robinson, Rickey had signed two other black players with indisputable major-league ability to play for Class B Nashua, Roy Campanella and Don Newcombe, with a longer timetable for their promotion to Ebbets Field in mind. Excelling for the Montreal Royals, Robinson proved he could play on the biggest stage and earned his spot on the major-league club in 1947, but the success and progression of Campanella and Newcombe in the minor leagues was just as important for the long run—for the Dodgers, for baseball, even for America.

Rickey's careful paving of all three of their paths in the minor leagues paid enormous dividends. Robinson was the major league's Rookie of the Year in 1947, helping the Dodgers to a pennant while playing out of position at first base because Stanky was set at second. Campanella immediately established himself as the best catcher in the National League when he was called up from the Dodgers' Triple-A team in St. Paul in July 1948. Newcombe made a case for himself as one of the best pitchers in baseball when he was crucial to the Dodgers' success in winning another pennant in 1949 and was voted the National League's Rookie of the Year. Brooklyn's winning accomplishments during these years with three black players as cornerstones to their success validated not only the courage and wisdom (in terms of being in it to win) of Branch Rickey's decision to break the major-league color barrier but also assured there was no going back on integration.

Brooklyn's 1947 pennant was the generational pivot point for the Dodgers that Rickey was instrumental in masterminding. From a team whose featured stars included right fielder Dixie Walker, second baseman Eddie Stanky, and hard-drinking, friend of Ernest Hemingway, ace reliever Hugh Casey, the only core regulars on the 1947 Dodgers who would be central to the 1949 to 1956 eight-year run of the team that would be immortalized by New York baseball writer Roger Kahn as the Boys of Summer were Robinson, Reese, and Carl Furillo. Walker, a club-house ringleader in the Dodgers' southern contingent of players threatening in spring training not to play with a black teammate, was traded after the 1947 season despite being a Brooklyn fan favorite—the "people's choice." Stanky was also traded, so that Robinson could play second base, his most natural position. The alcohol-fueled Casey self-destructed and was let go the next year. Reese, who despite being from Kentucky was not part of the incipient rebellion against Robinson, was the only veteran dating back to the prewar Dodgers to continue on as one of the Boys of Summer. Furillo had been a rookie in 1946.

Winning five pennants in eight years and twice losing out by the closest of margins, the 1949–1956 Dodgers were clearly the National League's most dominant team with historically great players in the prime of their careers. They were arguably a better team than their direct American League contemporaries over in the Bronx—the New York Yan-kees—at least when taking into account advanced metrics on player performance. In fact, every year except for 1954—when Brooklyn finished five games deep in second place and their Bronx rival also finished second, even further behind, but with 103 victories—it was the Dodgers who had the higher team WAR. The Boys of Summer failed to match the Yankees' five consecutive pennants from 1949 to 1953 only by virtue of losing their last game of the season, famously each time, in both 1950 and 1951.

No major-league team in the 20th century had the longevity of suc-cess—eight years—with the same core group of players as the Brooklyn Dodgers from 1949 to 1956. Not even any of the various great Yankee teams. With Gil Hodges at first, Robinson at second through 1952 and then alternating between third and left field, Reese at shortstop, Duke Snider in center, Furillo in right, Campanella catching and staff ace New-combe (except for two years of military service during the Korean War) playing all eight of those years, starting pitcher Carl Erskine and relief ace Clem Labine as regulars on the pitching staff for six of the eight years, pitcher Preacher Roe and third baseman Billy Cox as regulars for five, and Jim Gilliam alternating between second and the outfield playing in four of those years, Brooklyn won five pennants and finished second three times.

In four of their five pennants, the Boys of Summer Dodgers had the best record in the major leagues, better even than the Yankee teams they faced in the 1949, 1952, 1953, and 1955 World Series. And two of their bridesmaid years went down to the last game of the season. In 1950, the Dodgers lost to the Philadelphia Phillies in the regular-season finale in frustrating fashion. After having the potential game-winning run that would have forced a three-game playoff gunned down at the plate in the last of the ninth, Newcombe surrendered a three-run home run to Dick

Sisler that gave the game and the pennant to Philadelphia in the tenth. If that was frustrating, the very next year was heartbreaking, Brooklyn famously losing to their New York City National League rivals on Manhattan Island after blowing the 13½-game lead they held on August 11 on the dramatic Bobby Thomson "The Giants win the pennant! The Giants win the pennant!" home run in the third and deciding 1951 playoff game.

The 1951 pennant race was almost the exact inverse for the Dodgers of the 1950 race. On September 19, 1950, third-place Brooklyn trailed Philadelphia by a seemingly insurmountable 9 games with only 13 days, but 17 games, remaining. They won 13 of their next 16 games, however, while the Phillies were losing 9 of 12, setting up a showdown in their regularly scheduled meeting on the last day of the season at Ebbets Field. Brooklyn was one game down with first place on the line. Only center fielder Richie Ashburn's throw and Sisler's home run, along with Robin Roberts's great pitching, prevented the 1950 Phillies from an implosion as great as the Phillies implosion in the last weeks of 1964.

The only pennant race that the 1949–1956 Dodgers failed to compete in all the way until the end of the schedule was in 1954, when they finished five games back of the Giants, who benefited from Willie Mays having his breakout season. Even then, however, Brooklyn trailed by only a game and a half with four weeks remaining before falling out of contention relatively quickly with eight losses in their next ten games.

The first and last of the five pennants the Dodgers won were just like the 1950 and 1951 pennant races they lost. Tight affairs, fought to the end. The Dodgers battled the Cardinals all summer in 1949, never leading by more than two games nor trailing by more than two and a half after July, before securing the pennant with an extra-inning victory on the last day of the season. And in 1956, Brooklyn won a three-team dogfight by one game over the Milwaukee Braves—who would win the next two National League pennants—and the upstart (for one year only) Cincinnati Reds. The 1956 Dodgers spent all summer in second or third place and did not reach the top of the standings until mid-September.

Brooklyn's middle three pennants, by contrast, were comfortably in hand as the season entered the September stretch. The Dodgers began the final month of the 1952 season with a nine-game lead and were never threatened even as the Giants whittled that down to four and a half by the time the schedule expired. In the summer heat of 1953, the Dodgers' blazing hot 48–14 record in July and August opened up an 8-game lead entering September on their way to a 13-game margin of victory and a franchise record of 105 wins that stands to this day. Despite their season-long dominance, "next year" still did not come for Brooklyn in 1953; the Yankees, having already beaten the Dodgers in the 1941, 1947, and 1949 World Series, did so again. And in 1955, the Dodgers started the season with 10 straight wins, won 22 of their first 24 games to give them a 9½-game lead by May 10, secured the pennant by a 13½-game margin, and most importantly, this was "next year" as they beat the New York Yankees in the only World Series the Dodgers were to win while resident in Brooklyn.

\* \* \*

No other National League team in history, including the 1990s Atlanta Braves, had as strong a core group of players with regard to player legacies as the 1949–1956 Dodgers. Arguably, not even any of the dynastic teams in Yankees history—whether in the Ruth and Gehrig era, the DiMaggio and Mantle eras, or the Derek Jeter–Mariano Rivera era—had a roster of star players as impressive as the 1950s Brooklyn Dodgers. Of the eight position players who were regulars in the starting lineup of the 1949–1956 Dodgers for at least four years, four are in the Hall of Fame for having outstanding playing careers, and five were not only the most productive National Leaguers at their positions during those years but also among the NL's ten-best position players between 1949 and 1956, based on their wins above replacement.

For the five years between 1949 and 1953, nobody in baseball was as outstanding on the field of play as Jackie Robinson. His 42.3 wins above replacement for those five years was the best in the game, although Stan Musial was a close second with a 41.4 WAR. The best player in the American League in that time was Cleveland's Larry Doby, with 28.3 wins above replacement. Ted Williams was in the Korean War in 1952 and 1953, but based on his 20.2 wins above replacement in the three years before he was called into service, it is unlikely he would have matched either Musial or Robinson had he played all five years.

Robinson's average annual player value exceeded the eight wins above replacement that denotes an MVP-quality season, an award he in fact won in 1949. Playing in every game and leading the league with a .342 batting average in 1949, Robinson was at his most productive against the Cardinals, which was an especially good thing for Brooklyn since St. Louis was not eliminated from contention until the final day of the season; his .378 batting average off Cardinals' pitching was his best against any team, as were his 24 runs batted in.

Consistency was a Jackie Robinson hallmark during these years. He hit over .300 in at least four months of each year, including the final month of every season. Robinson had another outstanding season in 1953, batting .329, but he was shifted from second to third base and the outfield to accommodate having lost some of his speed and defensive agility as a result of turning 34 in January. Alternating between third base and left field thereafter, Robinson played just three more years before retiring after the 1956 season.

The 1953 season was the last in which Robinson played at an elite level. It was also center fielder Duke Snider's breakout year as an elite player, as it also was for Mickey Mantle over at Yankee Stadium. After having hit 50 home runs the two previous years combined, Snider's 42 in 1953 were the first of five consecutive 40-home-run seasons. Before Snider, only Babe Ruth for seven straight years from 1926 to 1932 and Ralph Kiner for five from 1947 to 1951 had breached the 40-home-run barrier with such consistency year to year. Snider's power was not exclusive to dimensions of Ebbets Field, which was relatively favorable to home runs; 44 percent of the 207 home runs he hit from 1953 to 1956 were in other teams' ballparks. With Snider batting third, Robinson fourth, and Campanella, having the best season of his career, usually batting fifth in the Brooklyn lineup, the Dodgers scored a staggering 955 runs in 1953—the most by a National League team in 23 years—on their way to 105 wins, a blowout pennant, and, of course, the requisite World Series defeat at the hands of the Yankees.

As outstanding as Snider's year was in 1953—the best of his career based on the WAR metric for player value—it was his teammate Roy Campanella who took home the National League's MVP Award on the strength of his own 41 home runs and his league-leading 142 runs batted in. (Snider was third in the voting.) Campanella was also the NL's Most Valuable Player in 1951, when he hit a career-high .325 with 33 homers and 108 RBIs, and for a third time in 1955, with 32 home runs, 107 RBIs, and a .318 average. Although his big-league career was relatively short at only 10 years, off to a late start at age 26 because of major-league baseball's institutional discrimination against black players and tragically cut short by a crippling car accident, Campanella was the best catcher in National League history (with all due respect to Gabby Hartnett) until Johnny Bench in the 1970s.

Pee Wee Reese, Robinson's double-play partner at shortstop, was the stabilizing center of gravity for the Boys of Summer. Although he turned 31 in late July of 1949, the six years from 1949 to 1954 were the best stretch of his Hall of Fame career, with Reese averaging 5.4 wins above replacement—an All-Star-level quality of play. There was some sentiment that he should have been named player-manager when Charlie Dressen stepped down as Dodger manager after the 1953 season, even though player-managers by this time were largely a relic of the past. Reese is not known to have lobbied for the position, and the job went to Walt Alston. Reese was the fifth-best position player in the National League between 1949 and 1956, based on the WAR metric, and was the best shortstop in the league, if not in all of major-league baseball, until eclipsed by Chicago Cubs rookie Ernie Banks in 1955. Reese turned 37 in the middle of that season.

The Boys of Summer legacies of Robinson, Snider, Campanella, and Reese earned each of them an eternal home in Cooperstown. There are still many advocates for first baseman Gil Hodges being there as well. By far the best first baseman of his era, Hodges was as consistent a run-producer as there was in the game. Although he never led the league in RBIs, Hodges drove in 100 runs for 7 consecutive years between 1949 and 1955, the only player in that era to do so, and he was a deft defensive first baseman. Hodges's quiet leadership has made him, in historical telling, the moral center of Brooklyn's baseball universe in the 1950s.

Carl Furillo was a reliable presence for the Dodgers in right field and the batting order throughout these years. His .344 batting average was the best in the majors in Brooklyn's offensively outstanding 1953 season. Known as the Reading Rifle for his home in Pennsylvania and the strength of his throwing arm, Furillo's reputation for gunning down base runners—he had 24 outfield assists in 1951 alone, including starting 6 double plays—made caution the watchword for runners trying to take an extra base on balls hit his way.

Brooklyn's only positions of weakness during the Boys of Summer years were at third base and left field. Billy Cox was the Dodgers' mostly regular third baseman from 1949 to 1952, more for his defensive prowess than his very modest abilities at bat. His deficiencies at the plate put him on the sidelines when Jim Gilliam, a much better hitter, made the club in 1953 and forced the move of Robinson and his body of age-declining skills to third. Cox nonetheless started 86 games at third that year so that Robinson could play left field—a position of vulnerability made so by the Dodgers' decision over the winter to trade veteran power-hitting Andy Pafko to Milwaukee for cash and a marginal big-league outfielder, Roy Hartsfield, who was assigned to Montreal and never got a call up to Brooklyn.

The Dodgers had seemed to solve their perennial left-field problem, a position they had struggled to fill since the end of World War II, when they obtained Pafko from the Cubs at the trade deadline in June 1951. Made at a time when they were already leading the Giants by six games, the move seemed to fortify the Dodgers' pennant chances. Brooklyn's ignominious failure to protect their 13½-game lead of August 11 certainly cannot be pinned on Pafko, who hit 8 of his 30 home runs in September and 2 more in the first 2 games of the playoff for the pennant with the Giants, and he drove in 32 runs in 30 games down the stretch. Pafko followed that up with 19 home runs in 1952. What could be wrong with an outfield of Furillo, Snider, and Pafko going forward?

Nothing, except that Brooklyn's baseball executives had other plans. Because the Dodgers had numerous strengths and Pafko was very well paid, perhaps *too* well paid, trading the 32-year-old outfielder might have been in part a move to save salary with little perceived risk of damaging the club's prospects. But it might also have been they had other plans for left field—specifically Sandy Amorós. A Cuban-born black Hispanic, Amorós had hit .337 for the Dodgers' Triple-A team in St. Paul in 1952 to earn a promotion to Brooklyn in August. Notwithstanding his impressive showing in spring training, Amorós was sent back to Triple-A for the 1953 season, this time to Montreal.

With Robinson, Campanella, and rookie Jim Gilliam all slated to start the season at Ebbets Field, and it being only six years since Jackie Robinson integrated organized (white) baseball, Brooklyn executives (who no longer included Branch Rickey) apparently concluded the time was still not right for so many black players to be starting on a major-league team, according to Roger Kahn. Leading the International League in batting, Amorós had another outstanding year in Triple-A. Not having Amorós in Brooklyn, however, did not hurt the 1953 Dodgers, who romped to the pennant with Robinson often in left and Cox starting at third more often than thought likely in the spring.

With their impressive corps of position players, the Dodgers were an offensive juggernaut. Beginning in 1949, when their 879 runs were the most by a National League team since 1930, Brooklyn led the league in scoring six times in eight years, and they were second in runs the two other years (1954 and 1956). Snider, Hodges, and Campanella were the power behind Brooklyn leading the major leagues in home runs seven years in a row from 1949 to 1955.

\* \* \*

But as dominant as they were offensively, the Boys of Summer had their flaws—more so than the contemporaneous Yankees—which typically surfaced in the World Series. Their biggest weakness was a persistent lack of depth on their pitching staff. Brooklyn's pitching was merely good, not in a class by itself like their hitting. In only five of the eight years was Brooklyn one of the National League's top-three teams in fewest runs allowed. The only year their pitching led the league in earned run average was 1955, when the Dodgers outscored their game opponents by nearly 200 runs (as did the Yankees, by the way).

Dodger pitchers had the disadvantage of half their games being in Ebbets Field, a ballpark that favored hitters. More runs were scored in Ebbets Field than in any other National League ballpark in five of the eight years from 1949 to 1956. While National League pitchers collectively gave up *more* runs on the road than they did at their home parks during those eight years, it was the other way around for Brooklyn's pitchers at Ebbets Field. They also gave up nearly a third more home runs at Ebbets than was the league average for other teams' pitchers in their home ballpark. Nonetheless, home *is* home, and Dodger pitchers in four of the eight years had a better earned run average at Ebbets Field and, in all but one year—1954, when they did not win the pennant—held the opposing team to a lower batting average at home than in away games.

Led by Don Newcombe and Preacher Roe, Brooklyn's pitching was at its best in the first three of their eight Boys of Summer years, although they came away with only the 1949 pennant. They each notched 56 wins between 1949 and 1951. One of the game's premier power pitchers and averaging over 260 innings in his first-three big-league seasons before being drafted in 1952, Newcombe was durable and an intimidating presence. Roe won nearly three-quarters of his decisions with a 56–20 record those three years, including 22–3 in 1951. Arm problems limited him to only 25 starts and 8 complete games in 1952, but Roe was still almost unbeatable at 11–2.

Otherwise, however, the Dodger staff was in some disarray with numerous pitchers worked into the rotation behind Newcombe and Roe. The most notable among them was Ralph Branca, whose claim to fame was surrendering Thomson's home run, which ironically would not have cleared the fence in Ebbets Field. Branca never lived up to the promise of his 21–12 season as a 21-year-old in 1947 and was inconsistent at best when he had the third-most starts among Brooklyn pitchers from 1949 to 1951. Whether shell-shocked by the Thomson home run or unable to recover from a back injury in spring training the next year, Branca was never the same and was let go by Brooklyn less than two years later.

Newcombe's return to baseball in 1954 helped to stabilize the Dodger rotation. Although Newcombe struggled to regain his touch his first year back with a 9–8 record in only 25 starts, he and Carl Erskine were the foundation of the Brooklyn rotation for the remainder of the Boys of Summer years. They were not as formidable a pair as Newk had been with Roe. Erskine had a terrific year in 1953 with a 20–6 record, leading the league in winning percentage, but did not again approach that level of success.

Don Newcombe is the only core pitcher for the Boys of Summer who received serious Hall of Fame consideration. Although twice revisited for consideration by the Veterans Committee after his initial eligibility to be voted in by the baseball writers expired, the two years Newcombe lost in 1952 and 1953 when he was drafted during the Korean War probably doomed his Cooperstown prospects. Newcombe made 102 starts for Brooklyn in his first three years in the majors and had a 56–28 record at the time he went into the service. He was 26 years old and at the peak of his career. After pitching poorly his first year back from the service, Newcombe went 20–5 in 1955 and 27–7 in 1956 to lead the pitching staff in both pennant-winning years. Only two National League pitchers have since matched Newcombe's 27 wins in 1956. Newcombe not only won the very first major-league Cy Young Award for his pitching brilliance in 1956, when every one of his 27 wins was needed in a pennant the Dodgers won by a single game, but he was also the National League's MVP.

Other core starting pitchers for Brooklyn during these years included Billy Loes from 1952 to 1955, the veteran Russ Meyer in 1953 and 1954, the up-and-coming Johnny Podres in 1954 and 1955 before he was drafted into the military, and Roger Craig in 1956. The Dodgers benefited enormously in 1956 when Sal Maglie was acquired from Cleveland early in the season, which helped compensate for the loss of Podres to Uncle Sam. Despised in Brooklyn when he pitched for the Giants, it is doubtful the Dodgers would have won the 1956 pennant without Maglie's 13–5 record in 26 starts, given that only two games separated the top-three teams.

A major failing of the Dodgers was their difficulty replacing Hugh Casey, released after the 1948 season, in the bullpen. The Dodgers had no real relief ace until Joe Black burst onto the scene with 54 relief appearances and 15 saves in 1952. Black's tenure as Brooklyn's ace reliever—and his career in the major leagues—turned out to be short-lived. The Dodgers finally resolved their bullpen issues when Clem Labine emerged to become their relief ace in 1955, a role he held until the team left Brooklyn for the sunnier climes of Los Angeles.

\* \* \*

While the Yankees had Casey Stengel holding court for the entire time, the Dodgers had three managers during their Boys of Summer years. The "boys" would have been justified to feel whiplashed between extremes in managerial style. They went from the brilliant intensity of the egocentric Leo Durocher to "Kindly Old" Burt Shotton, KOBS for short (an appellation given him by *New York Post* writer Dick Young that gives a sense of his personality), twice in that order—Leo in spring training 1947 to KOBS for the season and about half of 1948 with each—to the brilliant intensity of another egocentric, Charlie Dressen, to the stolid Uncle Smoky Alston. "Brilliant," of course, is what both Durocher and Dressen thought of themselves.

As a player, Burt Shotton was a contemporary of Casey Stengel's before World War I although Shotton's career was centered in the American League and Stengel's in the National. He was in retirement after a long career as a player, manager, and coach when Rickey called him in an emergency to take over the Dodgers just as the 1947 season was getting under way. Shotton had played for Branch Rickey, who was his manager on both the St. Louis Browns and the Cardinals, and the two men had great respect for each other. The emergency was that Durocher, who had been the Dodger manager since 1939 and who quelled the spring-training rebellion led by star outfielder Dixie Walker against Jackie Robinson by warning they could either play with Jackie or not play for Brooklyn at all, was suspended for the season by the commissioner because of his association with unsavory characters.

Shotton was three years older than Stengel would be when he took over the Yankees, and, like Stengel, his prior major-league managerial experience was managing bad National League teams—in his case, the Philadelphia Phillies from 1928 to 1933—with only one winning season and a .403 winning percentage to show for his efforts. Shotton, however, was supposed to be merely a place holder for the duration of Durocher's suspension, and despite having just led Brooklyn to the World Series, he stepped aside when Durocher was reinstated for the 1948 season. Durocher being Durocher, however, and the fact that the Dodgers were playing poorly, motivated Rickey to persuade Horace Stoneham, owner of the rival New York Giants, that Leo was just the guy who could reverse his team's decade of lost causes. Once he had engineered Durocher's taking over the Giants, Rickey once again asked Shotton to manage in Brooklyn.

While 1948 was by now a lost cause, Shotton—with the core of the Boys of Summer now fully intact—led the Dodgers to the 1949 pennant. The fact that the next year Shotton rallied the Dodgers from a 9-game deficit to the Phillies with only 17 games remaining and the Dodgers were still in play on the final day of the season was not enough for him to keep his job, assuming that, at age 65, he still wanted to. Shotton's departure, however, was a virtually foreordained consequence of Walter O'Malley's forcing out Branch Rickey after the 1950 season in a battle for ownership control of the Dodgers. Burt Shotton was Mr. Rickey's man, and everything having to do with Branch Rickey, except the great team he assembled, was not looked upon fondly by Mr. O'Malley.

Shotton's replacement was Charlie Dressen, who had been Durocher's alter ego as his most influential coach until he left Brooklyn to become a coach for the Yankees in the year Durocher was suspended from baseball. Widely considered one of baseball's best and brightest minds, the feisty Dressen was the perfect managerial antidote to those—including many New York baseball writers—who thought the elderly, wizened Shotton was too laid back and perhaps behind the times. Thomson's home run may have ruined the rookie manager's coming-out party in 1951, but Dressen recovered to manage the Dodgers to pennants each of the next two years, after which he overstepped O'Malley's redline by demanding a multiyear contract to return to the Ebbets Field dugout.

Replacing Dressen, the much more remote Walt Alston was not quickly embraced by the Dodgers' veteran players. While he had his detractors, Dressen had the closest bond with the Boys of Summer of any of their managers between 1947 and 1956. Dressen was much more beloved as a manager by Robinson, Campanella, and Newcombe than Durocher or Shotton before him or Alston after him, perhaps because his less rigorous and disciplined approach to managing games was more in the style his black stars were accustomed to in the more free-wheeling Negro Leagues.

Alston's biggest challenge when he assumed the reins was earning the loyalty of his team. Although he had managed Brooklyn Triple-A affiliates for six years and had helped groom many Dodger players for the major leagues, Alston was not the obvious choice to take over in the

Brooklyn dugout. (Many thought Pee Wee Reese the obvious choice, but the shortstop wasn't interested.) Once on the job, notwithstanding a Triple-A resume of winning success, many of the Dodger veterans—most famously Jackie Robinson—thought Alston's managerial abilities were not up to major-league standards. Alston was perceived in particular as insufficiently attentive to game situations and was further perceived as too laid back. There was more of an emotional distance between players and manager than there had been under Dressen and even a certain lack of respect for Alston, especially by Robinson, although it must be remembered Jackie had his own axe to grind.

Handling Jackie Robinson's highly competitive ego and relentless desire to be a cornerstone of the team when his skills were clearly diminishing was a sensitive issue for Alston. They clashed about both playing time and managerial style, with Robinson thinking Alston was not sufficiently intense and aggressive as a manager. The sands of time beginning to wind down his career just as Alston took over the team in 1954, Robinson never really got along with the last manager he would play for, but being the man he was—chosen by Branch Rickey for the purpose he was—Jackie Robinson understood that ultimately this was a matter of fair competition, based on merit, not race or dimming star power. Robinson realized that his skills were eroding, that he no longer was the great player he had been, and that Walt Alston as manager had the responsibility to field the best team he could on any given day, even if it often meant the name "Jackie Robinson" was not to be in the starting lineup.

After Dressen had just led the Dodgers to back-to-back pennants— and it would have been three in a row if not for Thomson's home run— short of winning the World Series, Alston really could only go downhill. He did not have a triumphant debut managing the best team in the National League, as *his* Dodgers won 13 fewer games and finished 5 games back of Durocher's hated Giants. However, while the concept of "expected wins" based on runs scored versus runs allowed had yet to enter the imagination of baseball statisticians, Alston by that standard had a very successful year as manager given that his team should have won only 81 games instead of the 92 they actually won. For whatever reason, O'Malley brought him back on another one-year contract in 1955—the second of 23 he would sign with the Dodgers—and Alston made the most of his second chance. His team got off to a tremendous start with 10 straight wins on their way to a runaway pennant (by 13½ games) and Brooklyn's first and only World Series championship. Walt Alston's future was secure, at least for the moment.

The Dodgers won another pennant the next year, surviving a three-team race that was not decided until the final game of the season. By this time, however, the Boys of Summer were aging. Robinson and Reese were 37, Campanella and Furillo were 34, Hodges was 32, Newcombe was 30, and Snider was a year shy of 30. Not only were the 1957 Dodgers effectively out of the running by mid-August—although they did finish third—but attendance was lagging badly, Ebbets Field was too small and becoming a dump, and O'Malley's efforts to secure land and infrastructure support from the city for a new ballpark had been stymied. Meanwhile, Los Angeles beckoned, and the following year, the Dodgers and Giants brought major-league baseball to the West Coast. Neither team did well in 1958, but both were part of another three-team race for the National League pennant in 1959. The Dodgers won, but the team was no longer . . . the Boys of Summer.

# SEVEN

## Durocher the Spymaster

Leo Durocher, who famously said "nice guys finish last"—also the title of his autobiography—might also plausibly have rhetorically asked, "Who said cheaters never prosper?" It is not known that he ever did say so in specific reference to a grand strategy that had a decisive bearing on the greatest comeback pennant victory in history, but—ever the gamesman—if Leo didn't, he certainly should have, just to mess with our heads.

This speaks, of course, of the revelation about half a century after the fact by Joshua Prager in first a *Wall Street Journal* article and then his book, *The Echoing Green*, that Durocher installed a coach, Herman Franks, in the manager's office of the Giants' clubhouse beyond center field in the Polo Grounds to look through a telescope at opposing catchers' signals, relay them through an electrical-buzzer system to the Giants' bullpen in deep right field, from where they would be flashed to the Giants hitters in their turn at bat. The implication of this revelation is that Bobby Thomson would not have tagged Ralph Branca for arguably the most famous decisive home run in baseball history if not for spying from the center-field clubhouse, that indeed the 1951 New York Giants would not have come back from their 13½-game deficit of August 11 to finish the 154-game schedule in a flatfooted tie with Brooklyn, giving Thomson his date with history.

It was not, however, as though technology-aided spying on opposing teams' signs did not have a long history in major-league baseball. Stealing and deciphering signs from the dugouts and by players on the field of play has always been an accepted part of gamesmanship in major-league baseball. Teams and players self-police the practice, however, because being too obvious is to invite meaningful retribution against either the offending party or, more often, a proxy victim—usually the batter who might have to evade a deliberate bean ball. Using spyglasses and tele-

85

scopes to pick off signs and relay them to the batter, however, has always been considered out of bounds precisely because they are used outside the field of play, such as by hiding in scoreboards or doing so from the bleacher seats. Unlike players and coaches studiously stealing signs on the field or from the dugout, which both teams can do, home or away, technology-aided spying outside the playing-field perimeter is almost always by the home team, which has the advantage of controlling the environment that the visiting team does not.

Just three years earlier, in 1948, it was the world-champion Cleveland Indians who may have benefited from illicit scoreboard sign-stealing. While they had to overcome a four-and-a-half-game deficit in early September and had the advantage of almost all their remaining games being at home, the Indians were in the race all year. There was not the dramatic background context to Thomson's home run, and so this episode is more a forgotten footnote in history than Prager's revelation, which threatens the integrity not only of the Giants' pennant drive but also of the home run itself.

* * *

The spying began on July 20 against the Cincinnati Reds. The Giants began the day in second place, seven and a half games back of the Dodgers, having lost six of the eleven games they had played thus far in their current home stand. But it was not as though the Giants were having difficulty scoring runs. They had scored 69 runs in those 11 games, more than 6 per game, and knocked out 22 home runs. Their team batting average stood at .259, up from .250 in early June, and they were second in the league to the Dodgers in scoring. The Giants' problem was their pitching. Only the last-place Pittsburgh Pirates had given up more runs to this point in the season, and the Giants had given up 61 runs in the first 11 games of this home stand, almost as many as they had scored.

Nonetheless, when recently acquired but seldom-used reserve infielder Hank Schenz told Durocher about how he used to hide in the Wrigley Field scoreboard and spy on the catcher's signs when he was with the Cubs, and, oh by the way, he still had the high-powered telescope that facilitated that signals-intercept operation, Leo Durocher was intrigued. And even though pitching was letting down the Giants more than their hitting in this 5-and-6 home stand, Durocher was also motivated. A Polo Grounds electrician (a Brooklyn fan, it turns out) was put on the job to install the wiring and buzzer between the clubhouse and the Giants' bullpen, and the technology-aided sign-stealing began.

With Franks using Schenz's high-powered telescope in the manager's office of the center-field clubhouse for the first time, the Giants erupted for three runs in their half of the first against Ewell Blackwell, still one of the toughest pitchers in the league to hit, on their way to an 11–5 blowout victory. After having limited the Giants to only four earned runs in 18 innings in two starts and a relief appearance against them so far in the season, Blackwell this game failed to survive the first inning. The Whip, as he was nicknamed, also became the losing pitcher in the second game of a doubleheader the next day when he came on to pitch the last of the ninth in a tie game and gave up the game-winning run on a walk, an error, and a single in the Reds' 9–8 loss at the Polo Grounds.

Surely this was cheating. If this illicit spying on opposing catchers' signals allowed the New York Giants to steal even just one victory during the regular season, it had a decisive impact on the 1951 pennant race because just one win less and the Giants' dramatic surge toward the National League pennant would have come up one game short. There would have been no Miracle of Coogan's Bluff, and Bobby Thomson's name would likely be lost to history. But it does beg the question: just how much of an advantage was the advantage of having a spy in the center-field clubhouse?

\* \* \*

Contrary to what might have been expected, having magnified spying eyes out beyond center field did not result in the Giants' scoring appreciably more runs at the Polo Grounds than elsewhere. In the 28 home games they played from July 20 until the end of their 154-game schedule, the Giants not only averaged nearly one run less per game than before what might be called "operation sign catcher" went into effect, but their runs per game was only marginally better at the Polo Grounds than in 38 remaining games they played on the road. And after August 11, when the Giants hit their low point in games behind and faced having to win at an unprecedented pace, their scoring ratio of five runs per game *on the road* was far better than the 4.5 they averaged at home. Despite their outstanding 49–17 record to close out the season from July 20, which does not include the three-game playoff they forced with the Dodgers, the Giants' total runs were only fourth best in the National League and matched by the Pirates, who won 19 fewer games on their way to a seventh-place finish.

And, however valuable the spying may have been, it rarely allowed the Giants to jump on the opposing pitcher for big leads in their first innings at the Polo Grounds, forcing the visiting team to play from deep in the hole from the very beginning of the game. After mauling Blackwell for three runs in the bottom of the first on the first day of "operation sign catcher," the Giants scored that many runs in the first inning of only 2 of their 27 remaining scheduled games at home. Three of the National League's seven other teams had 4 games at home after July 20 in which they scored at least three runs in the first inning.

Nor were the Giants able to take advantage with "big innings" of at least three runs. Every National League team but one—the Philadelphia Phillies, who finished sixth in the league in scoring—had more big innings after July 20 at their home parks than the Giants' total of 13 in 28 games at the Polo Grounds. Moreover, the Giants' distribution of three-run innings at home was not weighted toward the late innings, when big innings might facilitate a comeback or provide breathing room in a close game.

The Giants' unique and unknown home-field advantage also did not result in their winning many games by blowout margins of five or more runs. Only 10 of their 22 blowout victories that year were at the Polo Grounds, and just 3 of those came after Durocher set up his spy operation to benefit his hitters, which included the very first day Franks took up his position with the telescope in Durocher's office. In fact, the Giants won twice as many games by five runs or more on the road—six—as at home from July 20 until time ran out on the season.

One might expect that foreknowledge of what pitch is coming would have been especially valuable in games in which the Giants were forced to make up a deficit if they were to win. Of the Giants' 23 wins at home from July 20 to the end of the schedule, 10 were in games in which they trailed at some point after the first inning, but while stealing signs by illicit spying may have made the difference in at least some of their home victories, the Giants' come-from-behind record at home was not unusual in league context. The Dodgers, even as they saw their lead steadily erode, also won 10 games at home coming from behind in games, and the last-place Chicago Cubs had 12 come-from-behind victories at home.

Whether knowing what pitches were coming was the deciding factor in any of the Giants' five walk-off wins at the Polo Grounds after July 20, which became six when Thomson hit his game-ending pennant-winning home run in the third game of the playoffs, four other NL teams matched their total. The Dodgers had five walk-off wins at Ebbets Field in the same timeframe, the Reds had five in their home at Crosley Field, the Phillies five at Shibe Park, and the Cubs six last-at-bat victories in Wrigley Field. Durocher's team was less successful coming from behind on the road, where they trailed after the first inning in only 7 of their 26 wins, but the fact that they won 19 away games without having to play from behind indicates they were effective in scoring first and protecting their lead—one of the many marks of a winner.

\* \* \*

Beginning with Blackwell's start against them on July 20, the Giants won a remarkable 23 of their 28 remaining games scheduled at the Polo Grounds. But they would not—indeed, could not—have won the 1951 pennant had they not also played exceptionally well in other teams' ballparks, where they did not have the advantage of spying on what pitches the opposing catcher was calling. The Giants actually had 10 more games to play on the road than they did at their own ballpark. And play exceptionally well they did, with a 26–12 record away from home to finish their schedule.

Perhaps the better metric is their home-versus-road record after the Giants hit their nadir on August 11. They had just come off a 17-game road trip in which they won 9 and lost 8. That included losing three straight in Brooklyn on August 8 and 9, which ended with the Dodgers' celebrating their sweep by serenading the Giants with "Roll out the Barrel" from the neighboring clubhouse in Ebbets Field. Fortuitously, after being shut out by the Phillies at home on August 11 to fall 13½ games behind the Dodgers, the Giants had more games left at home with 23 than the 21 they had scheduled on the road. Of the 16 straight wins they reeled off beginning on August 12 to get back into the pennant race, all but 3 were at the Polo Grounds.

But the vagaries of scheduling were that, even though the Giants began their dramatic surge with the advantage of 20 of their next 23 games being at home, they ended with the disadvantage of 18 of their final 21 games being on the road. On September 5 when the Giants started a 14-game road trip still trailing the Dodgers by 6 games, they had only 3 home games remaining. If the Giants were going to win this thing, it would have to be on the road.

Going 10-and-4 on the trip, they whittled Brooklyn's lead down to 4½ games at the beginning of their final 3-game home stand against the Boston Braves. Scoring precisely four runs each game, the Giants swept the Braves at the Polo Grounds, but that still left them two and a half back, with two games remaining in Philadelphia and their last two in Boston. They won all four, while the Dodgers lost four of their final seven, also all on the road, to end the scheduled season tied for first, necessitating that fateful three-game playoff to decide the National League pennant. While their 20–3 record at the Polo Grounds after August 11 was the foundation for the Miracle of Coogan's Bluff, winning 14 of 18 games on the road in September was indispensable to the New York Giants' catching the Brooklyn Dodgers.

Although it is not obvious that their unique home-field advantage had much effect on their run production in the aggregate, it seems quite likely it made a very big difference in their most crucial home stand of the season—14 games from August 21 through September 3, including 2 against the Dodger team they were chasing down. Since it began with them trailing Brooklyn by eight games—a significant margin so late in the season—and because this was their last extended home stand of the year, the Giants needed to exploit every edge they had from playing at home, even an illicit one such as their center-field clubhouse telescope.

After September 3, the Giants had only three games remaining at the Polo Grounds and not until the next-to-last weekend of the season.

Perhaps suspiciously, the Giants won 11 of those 14 games, scoring 77 runs in an offensive outburst. Late-inning rallies to overcome a deficit were decisive in four of those victories, starting with the first game of the home stand when a six-run eighth erased a four-run Cincinnati lead. Two were walk-off victories where the Giants trailed going into their last at bat—a two-run ninth to snatch a 5–4 win from the Cardinals on August 24, and a two-run twelfth inning on August 27 to stymie the Cubs, who scored to break an extra-innings tie in the top half of the inning. The Giants were also unusually prolific in their power game, hitting 25 home runs, many of them at timely moments, during that 14-game home stand. They had nine multi-home-run games and four in which they blasted at least three home runs.

And nothing all season, until Thomson's epic home run, was quite like the Giants' delicious dismantling of the hunted and, by now, increasingly haunted Brooklyn Dodgers, by 8–1 and 11–2, on September 1 and 2. They hit seven out of the park in the two games, which scored 14 of their 19 runs off Brooklyn pitching. After Don Mueller, a modest power threat at best, tagged Dodger pitchers for three round-trippers in the September 1 game, Prager relates that Brooklyn coach Cookie Lavagetto told manager Charlie Dressen: "You notice when we come here, we never fool anybody? We throw a guy a change of pace, he seems to know what's coming?" The next day, Mueller hit two more.

\* \* \*

Prager recounts in *The Echoing Green* how Durocher canvassed his clubhouse to ratify his grand scheme to steal opposing catchers' signs for the benefit of his hitters. Although some players indicated they preferred to trust in their own visual acuity, intuition, and skill, their manager's case was compelling enough—delivered perhaps in inimitable Durocher style, making the point in a way his team would understand they couldn't really refuse—that the system went into effect the following day, apparently to the detriment of one Mr. Ewell Blackwell, who, of course, may have just had a bad day.

None of the core regulars on the 1951 Giants—all of whom, except catcher Wes Westrum, started every game after August 12—has ever admitted that his offensive exploits, especially those that turned games, had anything to do with Herman Franks squinting through a telescope, pushing a buzzer to the bullpen, and someone in the bullpen conveying the sign to the batter. Thomson, Mueller, first baseman Whitey Lockman, second baseman Eddie Stanky, and Westrum—although only with home runs—were all players whose at-home performance from July 20 until the end of the season suggests they *might* have benefited at crucial moments from knowing what pitches were being served up.

The player most associated with having benefited from this spying was Bobby Thomson, whose walk-off, come-from-behind, three-run home run off Ralph Branca is now generally assumed to be because he knew what was coming.

The right-handed-batting Thomson was leading the Giants in home runs and was second on the team to Monte Irvin in runs batted in as of July 20, but mostly he had struggled at the plate. With the arrival of rookie Willie Mays, Thomson was displaced from his starting center-field job in late May, by mid-June he was being platooned in the outfield with Don Mueller, a left-handed batter, and by the end of the month, his batting average was down to .220. Thomson's stock had fallen to the point where Durocher tried to deal him to the Cubs for outfielder Andy Pafko before the June 15 trade deadline. The Cubs dealt Pafko to Brooklyn instead.

In his platoon role, and doubtless unhappy about it, Thomson had started only 9 of the Giants' first 16 games in July, when two things happened—third baseman Hank Thompson suffered what amounted to a season-ending injury on July 18, and Durocher decided he really liked the idea of spying on catchers' signals, which began on July 20. The first certainly presented an opportunity for Thomson. After being shopped around by the Giants, he was now their new third baseman. The second *may have* facilitated Thomson's dramatic turnaround at the plate; he finished the year with 32 homers, which would be his career best, and a .293 batting average, the second highest of his career.

Thomson never said that his surge to the finish was a consequence of knowing what pitches were coming in home games. Indeed, Durocher's decision to use Thomson in a platoon role may have been the first step in rehabilitating his season. Thomson was already on the upswing, hitting .333 since the beginning of July, which had brought his average up to .237 when he started at third base in place of the injured Thompson for the first time on July 20, the telescope also in place and Herman Franks in the clubhouse for home games for the first time. He went 3-for-5 that day to raise his average another seven points. From then until the end of the season, including the playoff with Brooklyn, Thomson hit .356 at the Polo Grounds—114 percentage points better than his home-field batting average in the Giants' first 48 home games.

But Thomson was even more productive on the road, where he could not benefit from illicit spying on catchers' signals. In 39 road games after July 20, including the first game of the three-game playoff played at Ebbets Field, Thomson hit .357—126 points better than he had in 39 road games before—with 13 home runs and 34 RBIs. Those power numbers were much better than the 3 home runs and 18 runs batted in he had at the telescoped and wired-up Polo Grounds, and one of those home runs and three RBIs were on that immortalized swing of the bat against Branca.

Whitey Lockman and Eddie Stanky also hit substantially better at home after the spy operation went into effect. Unlike Thomson, neither did nearly as well away from home. Stanky's batting average was 76 points higher at the Polo Grounds than in away games, in which he batted below .200, suggesting he might have liked the unique home-field advantage set up by Durocher.

Although he is one of only two players in Prager's account—Irvin was the other—who supposedly did not want to know what pitch was coming, even from a runner on second base picking off signs, the data is compelling that Lockman may have benefited as much as anyone from the Polo Grounds spy operation. His hitting performance at the Polo Grounds was much better at home than before July 20 and much better than in other teams' ballparks, particularly his ratio of home runs and RBIs. All six of the home runs Lockman hit from then until the end of the season were at home, and his 21 RBIs in 9 fewer games at the Polo Grounds were 5 more than on the road. Lockman had key hits in three of the four late-inning rallies that turned seeming defeat into victories in that crucial August 21 to September 3 home stand.

Catcher Wes Westrum's offensive productivity dropped off sharply after July 20, both home and away. In the Giants' remaining home games, however, Westrum had some crucial clutch hits for a guy who hit only .131 in games at the Polo Grounds from then until the end of the season. On August 15, his two-run home run off Branca broke up a 1–1 game in the eighth. Against Cincinnati on August 21, Westrum's three-run home run in a six-run eighth erased a 4–1 deficit. And on August 26 against Chicago, Westrum ended a tie game with a walk-off home run that gave the Giants their 13th-consecutive win in what would become a 16-game winning streak.

And then there's right fielder Don Mueller. He did not hit as well for batting average at home after July 20—65 points less than before—and had a higher average in away games, but Mueller sure did channel his inner Babe Ruth when it came to hitting home runs at the Polo Grounds after spying eyes were in position to help.

Bobby Thomson may have hit the home run that killed off the Dodgers, but it was Don Mueller who most deserved to be called the Dodgers' killer. Seven of the sixteen home runs Mueller hit in 1951 were off Brooklyn pitching, six of them at the Polo Grounds—all six of which were after Durocher's spying operation went into effect, including five in the two games the Giants crushed the Dodgers at home on September 1 and 2. His five home runs in consecutive games tied the major-league record then held by Cap Anson (set in 1884), Ty Cobb (1925), Tony Lazzeri (1936), and Ralph Kiner (1947). All four are in the Hall of Fame.

No one is mistaking Don Mueller for a Hall of Fame slugger—certainly not Babe Ruth, who never hit as many as five home runs in consecutive games. Mueller had hit only 18 home runs in his entire career coming into that two-game series with Brooklyn, and he would hit only 42 more over the next six years to retire with the not-very-imposing total of 65 for his entire career. As for the real Babe, Ruth did hit five home runs in two days in 1927 and six in two days in 1930, but both times that was over three games because of doubleheaders.

The data does not indicate that the three other regulars in the Giants' lineup either wanted to or were able to exploit Durocher's spy operation to any great advantage. Alvin Dark's batting average in home games was 101 points lower than before, and he hit 97 points better on the road than at home. Monte Irvin's hitting carried the team at least as much as Thomson's, but his batting statistics at the Polo Grounds once the spy system went in effect, while not as good as before, were not indicative of any trend one way or the other. When Durocher was canvassing his clubhouse to get his team's buy-in, Irvin, according to Prager, had the temerity to tell his manager that he didn't need any extra help to be a dangerous hitter. During the Giants' miracle comeback drive, Irvin proved his point by making a practice of going into other teams' homes and tearing the place apart. He hit .340 with 9 home runs and 44 RBIs in 39 road games after July 20, including the first playoff game, which was in Brooklyn.

As for rookie Willie Mays, although he did not play as well on the road as at home during that time, there is nothing in his comparative before-and-after home-field statistics to indicate he exploited the Polo Grounds advantage. His most recent biographer, James S. Hirsh, wrote that Mays was circumspect on the issue.

\* \* \*

In a neutral context, one can plausibly argue the data suggests that the Giants' spying on catchers' signals from beyond center field provided only marginal advantage. Their scoring average on the road was almost the same as at home and much better after August 11; they did not pounce on the opposing pitcher for many runs in the very first inning of home games to grab a big early lead; they won twice as many games by blowout margins away from home and had the second-fewest big innings where they scored three or more runs in their home ballpark among National League teams; they did not have an unusual number of comeback rallies at home compared to other teams in the league; and, let's not forget that the Giants had more games on the road after July 20, where failure to play as well as they did would have doomed their quest, whatever advantage they exploited at home.

The Giants, however, did hit very well in their most crucial home stand of the season from August 21 to September 3, including late-inning rallies to come from behind to win four games. Had that home stand gone badly, the Giants' hopes of going for the pennant would have ended.

But the context is not neutral. The Giants had to fight back from a large deficit to force the three-game playoff with the Dodgers. While the overall impact of having a center-field spy might have been marginal, a marginal advantage is not the same as irrelevant. It seems likely—if not probable—that at least several of the Giants' home victories were facilitated by knowing what pitches were coming. Win just one fewer game than they did in their remaining 66 games after Herman Franks made himself at home in Durocher's clubhouse office with a telescopic view of the catcher's fingers and Brooklyn would have been the National League champion without a playoff.

Of the 23 games the Giants won at home from July 20 to the end of the scheduled 154-game season, 10 were by one run. They lost only one home game by a single run. While it cannot be proven that any of those one-run victories were because of their spy advantage, it is worth considering that the Giants scored at least three runs in an inning in four of those games and—more significantly—came from behind after the first inning in seven of their ten one-run victories.

Of note in those come-from-behind victories were Lockman's eighth-inning double off Ewell Blackwell—the very first victim of the Polo Grounds spy operation back on July 20—to break a 3–3 tie against Cincinnati on August 22, Lockman's and Thomson's (following Irvin) hitting consecutive singles to start a game-ending two-run rally that overcame a 4–3 deficit in the ninth on August 24 against St. Louis, and Lockman's single that helped key a two-run game-winning rally in the 12th against Chicago on August 27 after the Cubs had taken the lead in the top half of the inning. Those were all during the Giants' crucial 14-game home stand at the end of August. And in their last scheduled home game of the season on September 24 against the Braves, Thomson's single started a game-tying rally in the sixth, and Mueller's single in the ninth began the game-winning rally, with Stanky's walk-off single driving him home.

It seems all but certain, therefore, that the New York Giants' miraculous comeback to win the 1951 pennant would not have happened without the elaborate spy system set up in the Polo Grounds. But it also would not have happened without a dramatic improvement in the team's pitching that coincided with "operation sign catcher."

What truly distinguished the Giants' exceptional record to close out the season was by far the stingiest pitching in the league. Riding on Larry Jansen, Sal Maglie, and Jim Hearn as their front-three starters, the Giants, who had given up the second-*most* runs in the league as of July 20, surrendered by far the fewest the rest of the season. Providing Giants' batters with a unique home-field advantage was one thing—and likely *the* crucial variable to their success—but airtight pitching, unaided by spying of any sort, that helped the Giants to outscore their opponents by nearly two runs per game in the 66 games remaining was surely just as vital.

\* \* \*

Leo Durocher managed a total of 24 seasons in two acts (1939 to 1955 and 1966 to 1973) but won only three pennants, all in his first act. The case for his Hall of Fame plaque rests on the Giants' stunning come-from-behind pennant in 1951—that they lost the World Series to the Yankees in six games is beside the point—and shocking the ostensibly much-superior Cleveland Indians in a four-game sweep of the 1954 World Series. Since much of Durocher's legacy comes from his team's dramatic finish in 1951, does deploying sidekick coach Herman Franks in the center-field clubhouse with a high-powered telescope and an elaborate signals system in the Polo Grounds tarnish his reputation as a Hall of Fame manager? Call him a scoundrel, a rogue, devious, unethical, lacking in integrity, whatever, but the New York Giants would not have won the 1951 National League pennant by cheating alone.

Durocher set the stage for the first of the Giants' two last great performances before they left for San Francisco—the second was their 1954 championship—by remaking the team he took over in July 1948. Under his predecessor, Mel Ott—the "nice guy" who Durocher was referring to when he made his Bartlett's quotation—the Giants had relied on the power game to score runs; their 221 home runs the previous year set a new major-league record. Leo demanded a more multidimensional offense.

Gone by 1950 were sluggers Johnny Mize, Sid Gordon, Willard Marshall, and Walker Cooper, who had combined for 235 of the Giants' 385 home runs in 1947 and 1948. Durocher's Giants still had sluggers—notably Bobby Thomson, who was there when Durocher arrived; Monte Irvin and Hank Thompson, who debuted in July 1949 to integrate the team; and catcher Wes Westrum, with Mays coming aboard in 1951—but now also had better speed and hitters more skilled at getting on base at the top of the order in Eddie Stanky and Al Dark, both of whom were acquired from the Braves in 1950.

The Giants' defense got much better under Durocher. After having been middle of the NL pack in turning batted balls in play into outs when he took charge, the Giants led the league in defensive efficiency in each of Durocher's first-three full seasons as manager. Better all-around defense helped the Giants' pitching, whose earned run average improved from four consecutive years as the second worst in the league before his arrival to third in 1949, second in 1950, and finally the league's best ERA when they won the 1951 pennant.

Durocher had no tolerance for players who did not play with intensity and the fierce urgency of now to win every game. It was this urgency that allowed the Giants' relentless pursuit of the Dodgers in 1951 to be successful, even when the season seemed a lost cause in mid-August. Having been on the wrong side of a similar late-season surge by the Cardinals in 1942 that eviscerated the nine-and-a-half-game lead his Dodgers enjoyed halfway through August, Durocher knew that pennant-race miracles can happen. Durocher also had no tolerance for players who weren't prepared to play, which was why, when he returned from his one-year suspension to retake the Dodger reins in 1948, he was at loggerheads with Jackie Robinson, who played with exactly the intensity and urgency Durocher demanded but reported to spring training overweight, out of shape, and not baseball-ready. And Durocher had no tolerance for players not thinking on the ball field, such as failing to take the extra base, being out of position, throwing to the wrong base, or missing the cut-off man.

If not for the Korean War, which claimed Mays for the U.S. Army in 1952 and 1953, the Giants might have made a play to compete with the Dodgers for the National League title every year, at least through 1954. Foreshadowing their remarkable stretch run in 1951, the Giants' 41–21 record in the last two months of the 1950 season was the best in the league after July and four games better than the Dodgers in Brooklyn's furious failed bid to overtake Philadelphia's Whiz Kid Phillies. And after shocking the baseball world with their relentless pursuit of the Dodgers in 1951 that culminated in Bobby Thomson's and radio broadcaster Russ Hodges's moment in history, the Giants finished second in 1952, only four and a half back, without Mays in the lineup, begging the question of whether they could have overtaken Brooklyn had they had the Say Hey Kid. Without Mays, the Giants did not compete in 1953, but when he returned from the service, they won it all in 1954. Say Hey Kid or no, the Giants imploded in 1955, costing Durocher his job.

The Giants, however, were unlikely to have been so successful without Durocher as their manager because even with future Hall of Fame players Monte Irvin—whose best years were in the Negro Leagues—and Willie Mays, and despite the compelling narratives of 1951 and 1954, the Giants were not a great team. Their bitter rivals in Brooklyn, on the other hand, had a memorably great team built around Robinson, Campanella, Snider, Reese, Hodges, Furillo, and Newcombe. Although very difficult to play for and prone to antagonizing many of his players, Durocher was an astute judge of talent and skilled at nurturing and getting the best performance from the players he believed were most important to his team's success.

For sure, Leo Durocher seized any advantage he could to win games, and he was not averse to underhanded tactics if he thought he could get away with them, which he admitted on the very first page of his life in baseball, *Nice Guys Finish Last*. In this case, his secret was safe for about half a century, even though there were unsubstantiated rumors soon after and along the way, according to Prager. However much help having a center-field spy was to Giants' hitters, they still had to win at a furious pace to overcome Brooklyn's seemingly insurmountable midsummer lead—and to do so with more games on the road than at home. As manager, Leo Durocher was the driver who engineered the greatest comeback in pennant-race history. Still, why didn't anyone think to ask: where's Herman Franks, if he's not in the dugout or on the coaching lines?

There's no cheating in baseball. Just ask Leo. He'll tell you himself.

*A version of Chapter 7, "Durocher the Spymaster," appeared in the Fall 2012 issue of* The Baseball Research Journal, *Volume 41, Number 2, and is used with the permission of The Society for American Baseball Research.*

# EIGHT

## Charlie Dressen's Worst Day at the Office

Leo Durocher's opposite in the dugout when Bobby Thomson assured himself of baseball immortality was Charlie Dressen. They were not, however, opposite in personality—well, maybe on the social circuit, where Leo flaunted his flamboyance and celebrity connections—but not as managers. They were both egocentric, intense, and thought of themselves as God's gift to baseball strategy. Baseball historian Peter Golenbock gets to the essence of Charlie Dressen when he writes in his oral history of the Brooklyn Dodgers, *Bums*, that Dressen took all the credit for the wins and heaped all the blame on his players for the losses. It is possible that Dressen was the greatest manager who never was. This was because Dressen's relentless and strident self-promotion—he would tell you himself what a baseball genius he was—got in the way of his career ambition to greatness.

Dressen's three years as manager of the Brooklyn Dodgers were the apex of his career. After leading the Dodgers to a second-straight pennant in 1953, by 13 games, Dressen demanded a multiyear contract to return to the Ebbets Field dugout. Given their 105 wins were the most any Brooklyn team had ever won, and that the Dodgers had not won back-to-back pennants since 1899 and 1900, way back when they were known as the Superbas, Dressen undoubtedly thought he had leverage with Walter O'Malley. Knowing he had Walt Alston waiting in the wings, however, O'Malley said no to Dressen, who stuck by his conviction that he deserved more than a one-year contract and thereby forfeited an opportunity to build on his legacy in Brooklyn. Baseball historian Bill James writes that, in so doing, Charlie Dressen wound up forfeiting a place in the Baseball Hall of Fame because of the Dodgers' subsequent success.

If he felt the Dodgers were unfair in refusing to give him a multiyear contract after he managed them to two straight World Series, Dressen probably should have thanked his lucky stars that he was given any contract at all after he failed to win the 1951 pennant that he had well in hand in mid-August. While the outcome of the 1951 pennant race certainly pivoted on the Giants' 37–7 record to complete the regular-season schedule after trailing by 13½ games on August 11, Dressen was accountable as manager for Brooklyn's historic collapse. After winning the first game of a doubleheader on August 11 that put the Dodgers up by those infamous 13½ games, Dressen managed his team to no better than a 26–23 record to finish the schedule, which became 27–25 after losing the three-game playoff to decide the pennant on Ralph Branca's ill-fated pitch. Dressen failed in the manager's responsibility to keep a good team with a commanding lead going strong even once it appears that a pennant is certain.

Same as the Giants, the Dodgers spent most of the month of September on the road. After losing a close 2–1 contest at home to the Giants on September 9, only 3 of the Dodgers' remaining 19 games on the schedule were at Ebbets Field, and they lost 2 of those 3 to the defending NL-champion Phillies, who were mired in fifth place with a losing record. Of their 16 games on the road, the Dodgers won only 8. Overall, the Dodgers went 9–10 to complete the 1951 schedule, but their lead had shriveled from six games on September 11, when rookie right-hander Clem Labine shut out the Reds in the first game of a nine-game road trip, to none at all after their 154th game.

Labine could have been the pitching savior for Brooklyn in 1951, if Dressen had only let him. When Labine took the mound for his first major-league start on August 28, with the Dodgers having lost 8½ games in 17 days off their once imposing 13½-game lead, Dressen's starting rotation was overtaxed and without a reliable fifth starter, for when a fifth starter would be needed, behind Don Newcombe, Preacher Roe, Ralph Branca, and Carl Erskine. Thrust into the heat of a pennant race, Labine pitched complete-game victories in each of his first four big-league starts between August 28 and September 16, allowing only four earned runs in 36 innings—an ERA of precisely 1.00.

Labine could perhaps be excused for finally having a bad outing in his fifth start, against the Phillies at home on September 21. After loading the bases in the first inning with only one out for Willie "Puddin' Head" Jones, Labine provoked his manager's ire by surrendering a grand-slam home run pitching from a wind-up instead of from the stretch as Dressen had directed. Labine figured that, with the bases loaded, the base runners weren't going anywhere and that he would get more on the pitch going with a full wind-up.

Charlie Dressen, being Charlie Dressen, chose to neither forget (a useful attribute for a manager) nor forgive (which in this case may have cost his team the pennant) Labine's decision to ignore his counsel. Labine was not used by his manager in any meaningful role in the remaining nine games on the schedule. Notwithstanding that the Dodgers' lead went from four to three to two to one to none over their next five games, and despite his exceptional first four starts at the big-league level, Labine did not start another game. He did not even pitch again until the fifth inning of the final game of the scheduled season, just after a triple had given the Phillies a 7–5 lead in a win-or-see-you-next-spring game for the Dodgers.

\* \* \*

The September reality for Brooklyn was that, as Durocher's Giants were relentlessly closing the gap, Dressen's core starting pitchers were all overworked and struggling for effectiveness. His ace, Don Newcombe, finished the season 20–9 and pitched doggedly and effectively in his last three September appearances, but he began the month badly. Four of his first five starts in September were Dodger losses, during which he pitched into the seventh inning only once—a two-hit shutout against the Giants on September 8—and had an ERA of 5.00.

Preacher Roe wound up with an exceptional 22–3 record but lost his next-to-last start, giving up four runs in eight innings as Brooklyn's lead dropped to a mere half-game with three remaining, and then gave up four runs in less than two innings on only two days of rest in the Dodgers' last game on the schedule. Fortunately for both Roe and Dressen, Brooklyn eventually won in 14 innings to force their ill-fated playoff with the Giants, thanks in large part to an extraordinary extended-relief effort by Newcombe.

After pitching mostly in relief, Carl Erskine worked his way into the starting rotation in mid-July and won seven of his eight decisions as a starter from then until mid-September on his way to a 16–12 record for the season, 8–6 as a starter. But he faltered badly in the final week, losing his last two starts while giving up 11 runs, 8 earned, in 10⅓ innings. And Ralph Branca, even before his infamous date with history, lost five of the six games he started in September, including his last four. Branca failed to last six innings in four of his September starts, in which his earned run average was an unsightly 11.35, and he had a 6.27 ERA for the month as a whole.

Labine, meanwhile, watched while Newcombe (three starts, two wins), Roe (three starts with one win, one loss, and a no-decision), Erskine (two starts, two losses), and Branca (one start, a loss) were roughed up for a 5.71 earned run average in Brooklyn's final nine games on the 1951 season schedule. But after Branca lost the first playoff game against the Giants, with Thomson tagging him for a two-run home run that proved the difference, Dressen had virtually no choice but to get over his anger at Labine and start him in the second must-win-or-the-season-ends playoff game. And indicative of his first four starts, the young right-hander shut down the Giants at the Polo Grounds, 10–0, raising the question of whether a playoff with the Giants for the pennant would have even been necessary, and the Dodgers about to meet the Yankees in the World Series, had Dressen not relegated Labine to a sit-and-don't-pitch role in the final week of the season.

Dressen was now faced with the decision of who to start on only two days of rest in the third and final game—Preacher Roe, who worked only one and two-thirds innings in his start on the final day of the season, or Don Newcombe, who ended the season pitching significant innings three times (including two complete-game starts) in five days in high-stakes, winning-is-the-only-option games for Brooklyn to force the playoff for the pennant.

With Roe likely already experiencing the sore arm that would plague him throughout 1952, Dressen chose Newcombe to pitch the biggest game of the season. This was the same Newcombe whose effectiveness in big games Dressen would deride in the future as a "terrible flaw." Despite his manager's uncharitable assessment of his big-game performance, the Dodgers would not even have been in this position, competing in a "winner goes to the World Series" game, were it not for Newcombe's extraordinary effort in each of the last two days of the scheduled season. First, on just two days of rest after his complete-game victory against the Braves, Newcombe shut out the Phillies on the next-to-last day of the season to keep the Dodgers' hopes alive. And then, the very next day—when Brooklyn absolutely had to win—he came into a tie game in the eighth inning and pitched 5⅔ shutout innings, allowing just one hit, before leaving in the 13th inning after surrendering back-to-back walks with two outs. The Dodgers won that game in the 14th to send the season into overtime, and here he was on the mound again—three days later—trying to pitch his team into yet another tête-à-tête with the Yankees.

Fatigued and pitching on guile and guts alone, Newcombe held the Giants to only one run through eight innings. A three-run eighth had given the Dodgers a 4–1 lead that Newcombe took to the mound in the ninth. He had faced 28 batters. This was after having faced 26 batters in his 5⅔ innings just three days before, when he may have given up only one hit but also walked six. Newcombe had now faced 87 batters in 22⅔ innings in three games over five days. And going back to his complete game against the Braves, it was 123 batters in 31⅔ innings over four games in eight days—two complete-game victories, his extended relief on the last day of the season, and eight innings so far against the Giants. Don Newcombe, in a word, was gassed, and thus began Charlie Dressen's most nightmarish inning in baseball.

* * *

There are various versions of manager Charlie Dressen telling his team—the Cincinnati Reds (whom he managed in the mid-1930s) by one account, the Dodgers by others—to keep it close, he'd think of something. No doubt, as that fateful ninth inning unfolded, Dressen thought through the possibilities and made key decisions based on his best calculation of what moves would have the best chance of securing the remaining three outs and returning the National League pennant to Brooklyn. In addition to taking account of the objective game situation, Dressen, like all managers, was influenced by roster limitations and gut instinct. Never underestimate the importance of a manager's instincts, especially if the manager is someone like Charlie Dressen—or his counterpart for the day, Leo Durocher—who prides himself on his ability to parse a situation and "think of something" perhaps a bit different from what most managers would ordinarily do in that situation. Dressen made four critical decisions leading up to Bobby Thomson's home run that contributed to "The Giants win the pennant! The Giants win the pennant!"

The nightmare began when Alvin Dark led off the Giants' ninth with a single. (Dark hit only .229 at home after the Giants' sent coach Herman Franks into their center-field clubhouse to steal opposing catchers' signs, compared to .330 before, suggesting that spying eyes were of no particular benefit to him.) With the left-handed-hitting Don Mueller now at bat, Dressen told first baseman Gil Hodges to hold Dark close at first rather than play off the bag and cut down the hole between first and second. Scribes in the press box wondered about this. After all, Brooklyn had a three-run lead, needed only three more outs, and Dark's run by itself was irrelevant. What was Charlie thinking?

While it is *possible* Dressen was inattentive to the circumstance, it seems more likely that because he was so focused on getting the final three outs, he may have feared that allowing that first run to score—especially with nobody out—would lead to an unraveling, a cascade of runs that would erase Brooklyn's lead, and therefore decided to play it as though it was earlier in the game. Either way, Mueller's single into right field got by Hodges, who dove to his right and just missed snagging the ball, a play many felt he could have made for at least one out had he been playing closer to normal depth.

As Monte Irvin—arguably the Giants' most dangerous hitter—came to bat, Dressen went to the mound, where he was reassured by Newcombe that he could get the final outs. On this visit to the mound, however, according to Roger Kahn—one of the baseball writers closest to Dressen, who would later write *The Boys of Summer*—Dressen's managerial instinct was less to replace Newcombe than to bring in the injured Roy Campanella to replace Rube Walker behind the plate, both because of Campy's superior skills in calling a game but especially because of his ability to motivate and focus Newcombe. Campanella had not started any of the three playoff games because a leg injury made it virtually impossible for him to run.

Dressen went against his instinct and did not make that move. A key consideration for Dressen was the huge foul area around home plate at the Polo Grounds that Campanella could not possibly cover with a bum leg. But another consideration, according to Kahn, was his concern about being second-guessed should that happen and the hitter take advantage of his new lease on the at bat to get another damaging hit. The decision not to replace Walker with Campanella may have been correct on its merits but suggests, if Kahn's account is correct, that Dressen allowed his ego to interfere with his decision making in the most important game he had managed so far in his career.

Irvin fouled out, ironically into that vast expanse of foul territory that concerned Dressen, but in a play for the first baseman, not the catcher. Whitey Lockman's double to left-center scored Dark and put the tying runs in scoring position with only one out and Bobby Thomson coming to bat. This time, Newcombe told his manager he was exhausted, and in a decision criticized and derided to this very day, Dressen called on Ralph Branca to get the final two outs and save the game.

But who else was there for Dressen to call?

\* \* \*

The underlying reality, which Dressen surely knew, was that the Dodgers no longer had a bullpen worthy of the name.

Most fans of more recent vintage remember Clyde King as one in a long line of George Steinbrenner's Yankee managers—in 1982, both after (with five intermediates) and before Billy Martin—but in 1951, he was the Dodgers' relief ace. King headlined a bullpen whose 27 wins, 15 saves, and 3.79 earned run average through August contributed directly to just over half of Brooklyn's 82 wins going into September. After winning both games of a doubleheader, pitching 3 innings of shutout relief in the first game and another inning in the second, King had a 14–5 record, with 5 saves and a 3.36 ERA. But having pitched 23⅔ innings in 11 games in 26 days since July 27 took a toll on his arm, and King was never the same again—as in never. He appeared in only 10 games the rest of the season, with a 10.67 ERA, and in 58 games the next two years with an ugly earned run average of 5.16 before his big-league pitching career came to an end.

Without King pitching effectively, Dressen was forced to rely increasingly on his starting pitchers to go the distance in Brooklyn's valiant effort to hold off Durocher's charging New York Giants. Except for the season finale against the Phillies, every Brooklyn victory in September required a complete game from the starting pitcher. Brooklyn relievers, meanwhile, had a collective 5.03 earned run average since the beginning of September. And so, Charlie Dressen really had no reliable relief pitcher to replace Newcombe as Thomson approached the plate.

There was Bud Podbielan, who pitched in seven games and had the most relief innings for Brooklyn in the final month. He was the winning pitcher in the 14-inning season finale against the Phillies that set up the playoff, but Podbielan had pitched in only 54 big-league games in parts of three seasons, rarely in the high-stakes situation he was thrust into in that game against Philadelphia. Following Branca, King, Erskine, Labine, and Newcombe in relief of the day's short-lived starter, Preacher Roe, Podbielan was in fact just about the last pitcher Dressen had available to use in that game. It seems highly unlikely, given his relative inexperience, that Dressen even considered Podbielan in a game of this magnitude, with the very pennant at stake—just two more outs needed.

There was Johnny Schmitz, who had not pitched in eight days. Schmitz, however, had given up four runs in four innings in his previous appearance and was a southpaw against whom the right-handed-slugging Thomson was batting .385 in his career with 10 hits, including a pair of doubles and a home run. In 1951, Thomson had a double in two at bats off Schmitz. So Schmitz also was not really an option for Dressen in this situation.

King and right-hander Phil Haugstad were both woeful in September, King giving up 12 earned runs in 9 innings, including two in one inning in the final game against Philadelphia, and Haugstad surrendering nine earned runs in seven innings—including a home run to Thomson in the Giants' 11–2 blowout of the Dodgers on September 2. Haugstad had pitched in only 27 major-league games and would pitch in only 9 more.

Dressen had once had the right-hander Erv Palica in his bullpen. Despite having proven himself with a 13–8 record in a swing-starting pitcher-reliever role under Dressen-predecessor Burt Shotton in 1950, Palica was banished to Dressen's doghouse for being "gutless," apparently for not trusting enough in his fastball. In any event, the uniform Palica was now wearing was that of the U.S. Army, having been drafted in mid-September to serve during the Korean War.

With Labine having just pitched a complete game the day before, Dressen was left with only with three possible options among his corps of starting pitchers. One was Roe, but he was apparently not considered, whether because of arm trouble, the inability to get outs in his last start, or a combination of both. Instead, Dressen had both Ralph Branca and Carl Erskine getting ready for this moment.

Bobby Thomson was batting .333 against both pitchers in 1951. He was 3-for-9 against Erskine and 4-for-12 against Branca. And he had tagged both Brooklyn pitchers for two home runs, his pair off Erskine coming in May and his pair off Branca both hit since the beginning of September, including a two-run shot that was the difference in the opening game of the playoff. Branca had faced the Giants three times since the beginning of September, with Thomson torching him for three hits in six at bats, two of which went the distance. Erskine had not pitched against the Giants since August 8 at Ebbets Field, when he gave up only one run in seven innings of relief to earn the 12th of his 16 victories on the year. He got Thomson out all three times they faced each other that afternoon—which were the last three times the two had stood 60 feet 6 inches apart.

The popular account of why Branca and not Erskine is that Dressen's decision was made after "Oisk" bounced a pitch warming up in the bullpen. The subtext of how this decision is portrayed is along the lines of Dressen losing his grip, not thinking clearly in the heat of the moment. What was he thinking, letting Branca pitch to Bobby Thomson, who had been treating Branca like a batting-practice pitcher in the last three games they faced each other—including the game-winning shot just two days before?

What was he thinking? We of course can only speculate, but what Dressen certainly must have known was that Erskine had been having control and location problems of late. In his last three appearances of the season (two starts and one in relief), Erskine had given up eight walks—only one intentional—in 12⅓ innings. And he had averaged 4 walks per 9 innings in 38⅓ September innings, compared to 3.6 per 9 in 151⅓ innings through August. Upon hearing of Erskine's bounced pitch while warming up to enter the game, Dressen may have been reminded of the young right-hander's lack of control in his recent appearances and concluded this was too much of a risk with two runners in scoring position, the pennant on the line.

\* \* \*

Even if bringing in Branca was a reasonable decision given the alternatives, especially if he was indeed concerned about Erskine's recent inability to pitch consistently within the strike zone, Charlie Dressen still had one immediate decision to make: whether to pitch to Bobby Thomson with the tying runs in scoring position, one out and first base open . . . or . . . intentionally walk the veteran Thomson to load the bases and take his chances with the rookie Willie Mays waiting on deck. And batting behind Mays was another rookie, Ray Noble, who had entered the game as a defensive replacement in the top half of the inning after Durocher had pinch hit for his starting catcher, Wes Westrum.

Bobby Thomson was on a roll with a hot hand. With two hits already in this game, Thomson had extended his hitting streak to 15 games, and he had now hit safely in 22 of his last 23 games. Most of those were on the road, by the way, where Thomson would not have benefited from knowing what pitches were coming courtesy of Durocher's Polo Grounds spy operation. Thomson was hitting .457 with 37 hits in 81 at bats in those 23 games, including 6 home runs.

Willie Mays, by contrast, was a 20-year-old rookie with tremendous promise who was in a batting funk. Not only did he have just one hit in ten at bats so far in this three-game playoff against the Dodgers. Not only did he have just 3 hits in his last 32 at bats (.094). Not only had he struck out in 10 of his last 32 plate appearances. Not only did he have just seven extra-base hits since the end of August, only one a home run. But Ralph Branca totally owned Willie Mays. Mays had come up to bat 19 times against Branca, and Branca had gotten him out 17 times. Finally, although perhaps unbeknownst to the Dodgers, the kid was scared to death waiting in the on-deck circle, thinking the Giants' season might come down to him.

In his manager's mind, parsing the situation, thinking through the possible outcomes of his various options, Dressen could have decided that rather than risk Branca pitching to Thomson—especially given that game-winning two-run home run just two days before—it would be better to intentionally walk Thomson to load them up *even if* Mays were to drive in a run while making an out—an important caveat—which would make it two outs with Noble up next. What are the odds, Dressen might have asked himself, that a backup catcher, and a rookie besides, could win this thing for the Giants? Ray Noble had only 141 at bats in his career with a .234 batting average and was hitting only .207 against right-handers. He had never faced the right-handed Branca.

Although deliberately putting the potential winning run on base, as an intentional walk to Thomson would have done, was certainly not an optimum move—and few managers, especially in Dressen's time, would think to do so—discretion in this case might have been the better part of valor because Thomson was hot, Mays was not, and Giants' manager Durocher had no viable pinch-hitting options to bat for Noble. He had used both Bill Rigney and Hank Thompson, his best players on the bench, to pinch hit in the eighth inning and then been forced to put Clint Hartung into the game as a pinch runner for Mueller, who broke his ankle sliding into third base on Lockman's double.

Walking the lock-in veteran to pitch to the struggling rookie and then, if necessary, another rookie after that would have been a move worthy of a manager who prided himself on his baseball genius, on his ability to outthink the guy in the other dugout (or, in this case, the third-base coach's box, where Durocher now stood). It would have been risky, to be sure. But Charlie Dressen went with the more conventional wisdom of not putting the possible winning run on base, especially not in the bottom of the ninth. He allowed Ralph Branca to pitch to Bobby Thomson. And we all know how that turned out for him.

# NINE

## The Age of Enlightenment
## about Relief Pitching

Lost in the drama of the Thomson home run was the fact that the lack of a strong bullpen, or really any reliable relief pitching at all, is what cost the Dodgers the pennant. Had this been 11 years later, when the 1962 Dodgers again lost a three-game playoff to the Giants to decide the National League pennant, they would have brought in Ron Perranoski to pitch in such a crucial situation. In more recent years, even if Clayton Kershaw was pitching, it likely would be Kenley Jansen, who strikes out half the batters he faces, coming into the game in the ninth inning to protect the lead and secure the victory.

By the 1950s, exemplary relief pitching to backstop starting pitchers was increasingly recognized as a crucial element to winning success. Both the Dodgers, when winning pennants in 1941 and 1947 and forcing a playoff with the Cardinals for the 1946 pennant, and the Yankees in their 1947 and 1949 championship seasons had a singular relief ace who was as indispensible as any other pitcher on their staff—Hugh Casey in Brooklyn and Joe Page in the Bronx. Nonetheless, the proposition that a lockdown "closer" to win and save games in relief was not just nice to have, but essential, was still not gospel. The time-honored assumption that strong starting pitching was a necessary foundation for championship teams and a bias that starting pitchers were expected to go the distance (at least in their victories) still prevailed.

\* \* \*

It may not be on his plaque in the Hall of Fame, but Page's manager in his breakout year of 1947, Bucky Harris, is often associated with introducing the "relief ace" to major-league baseball. That would be Fred "Firpo"

Marberry, widely regarded as the trailblazer for relief pitching. Harris's Washington Senators would not have won the close 1924 pennant race and might not have won again in 1925 without Marberry as their relief ace. His 20 wins and 30 saves accounted for more than a quarter (26 percent) of Washington's 188 victories in their back-to-back pennant-winning seasons. How Harris used Marberry had only one, somewhat inexact, precedent—15 years earlier, when Giants' manager John McGraw made Otis "Doc" Crandall the first major-league pitcher to be primarily a "relief ace."

Since the beginning of baseball time, pitchers were groomed and expected to be starting pitchers. No thought was given to the concept of relief pitching being its own discipline until McGraw with Crandall. Even as the percentage of complete games had gradually declined from nearly 90 percent at the beginning of the 20th century to about two-thirds by 1908, relief pitching was thought of in terms primarily of finishing up for a starting pitcher so badly scored upon or physically exhausted or hurting that he was mercifully removed from the game. Relief pitchers were rarely in the game at the end of victories, and then mostly after the starting pitcher had been routed and their team had made a big comeback. McGraw's genius was in realizing that victories don't necessarily have to come from complete games. Sometimes bringing in a fresh arm to complete a game is the best way to secure a victory.

Other managers, more quickly in the National League than the American League, soon followed McGraw's lead, mostly because it made sense. By 1908, in large part because of McGraw's influence, 10 percent of victories in the National League were games completed by relief pitchers, who would have to wait for more than half a century to be officially awarded the "save" they so deserved (although their "saves" were counted retroactively according to a 1969 definition that credited a save for any victory completed by a relief pitcher regardless of the size lead that pitcher was asked to protect, some of which were quite large). As the value of using a reliever to save a victory or to go for the win in close games gained currency among major-league managers, the overwhelming majority of wins were still complete games.

Moreover, all managers at the time, including McGraw, went to their strength—their best starting pitchers—for most of the occasions they brought in a reliever to affect the outcome of a game. The first great relief pitcher in the game's history was also one of the best starting pitchers in history—the Chicago Cubs' Three-Finger Brown. While throwing at least 21 complete games of his own every year from 1908 to 1911, Brown also led the National League in saves all four years. Between his starting and relief roles, Brown was directly involved in fully one-third of the Cubs' total victories those four years, which included two pennants and twice finishing second. When he came in to relieve, it was almost always with the game in the balance.

By using Doc Crandall primarily as a reliever from 1909 to 1913, McGraw either imagined or anticipated a future of designated relief pitchers. Crandall's role, however, was more as a dedicated "finisher" of games than a forerunner to the concept of "closer"—a pitcher dedicated to wrapping up a close game in the final inning or two—and Crandall still started in more than a third of the games he pitched for McGraw. At a time when pitching was all about having the ability, stamina, and durability to pitch the entire game—and no self-respecting pitcher, or manager, expected anything less—the concept of carrying a pitcher on the staff exclusively as a reliever was so radical that even McGraw did not take his Crandall initiative to that logical extension. It would not be until the early 1920s that McGraw did so, with Claude Jonnard, who filled the role of Giants relief ace for three years before resuming his long career as a starting pitcher in the minor leagues.

Although the percentage of complete games dropped below 60 percent by the mid-1910s, the overwhelming majority of victories were finished by the starting pitcher. And because managers made fewer than 1.5 pitching changes in the games their starting pitcher failed to go the distance, mostly in losing causes, there simply was not a significant requirement to have a stable of relievers in an established bullpen. "Saves" leaders were typically starting pitchers called upon between their own starts to preserve victories in the late innings or "multi-role" pitchers who started fewer games than their team's best pitchers and appeared more often in relief.

Of the 34 pitchers between 1913 and 1924 who led their league in saves (there were multiple saves leaders in several years), 20 also made at least 20 starts, and another made 19. Not until the 1920s was the pitcher with the most saves typically a "genuine" relief pitcher. It was no longer unusual, however, for promising rookie pitchers to begin their careers working primarily out of the bullpen. If they were any good they moved into the starting rotation or became multi-role pitchers, both starting and relieving. If they were not, their major-league careers were short-lived.

Bucky Harris changed all that with Marberry. Marberry's 6 wins and record-setting 15 saves in 1924 were instrumental to the Senators' beating out the Yankees by 2 games to win the pennant in Harris's first year as a manager. Having pitched in only 11 big-league games the previous year, Marberry's relief role was not at the time unusual. As effective as he was, and throwing as hard as he did, the 25-year-old Marberry would ordinarily have earned a starting role based on his performance in 1924. Instead, Harris kept him in the bullpen, using Marberry almost exclusively in relief in all five of the years he managed in the first of his three tours in Washington. Marberry appeared in 273 games for Washington from 1924 to 1928, only 40 of them starts. In his 233 relief appearances, Marberry's 39 wins and 64 saves accounted for nearly 25 percent of his team's 429 victories. His 22 saves in 1926 stood as the record until Joe Page saved 27 for the 1949 Yankees.

No other pitcher had ever before pitched as many games almost exclusively in relief for as long as Firpo Marberry during those five years. He pitched at least 36 games in relief every year. Before him, only five pitchers had ever had back-to-back seasons appearing 30 times out of the bullpen. Much in the manner of late 20th-century closers, not only did Marberry throw hard—very hard—but also he displayed a fearsome, stalking, intimidating presence on the mound. More importantly, however, having a pitcher as effective as Marberry in his bullpen allowed Harris to better pace the mid-30s veteran pitchers on his staff—Walter Johnson, George Mogridge, and Stan Coveleski—whose effectiveness was indispensible to the Senators' success.

Being a "relief ace" was still a long way from being the road to career success for a pitcher, but Marberry's success in the role did not go unnoticed. While managers remained resistant to the idea of using talented young pitchers like Marberry in relief roles for very long before making them starters, they increasingly *did* see value in extending the careers of proven, reliable veteran pitchers by making them primarily relievers—which still did not necessarily mean "relief ace" to win or save close games.

Until the mid-1930s, by which time complete games were down to about 45 percent, managers continued to rely on some of their top starting pitchers to close out victories rather than use their designated relief pitchers for such an important task. Lefty Grove was the Three-Finger Brown of his generation. In the midst of 7 consecutive 20-win seasons from 1927 to 1933 as the premier starting pitcher in all of baseball, Grove pitched 94 times in relief with a 22–12 record and 38 saves. He led the major leagues in both wins (28) and saves (9) in 1930. Consistent with the prevailing dismissive attitude of using talented pitchers in the prime of their careers in the role of relief ace, Marberry was moved into the starting rotation in 1929 when legendary Washington pitching ace Walter Johnson, who so benefited from Marberry's presence, replaced Bucky Harris as manager of the Senators.

After Harris with Marberry, it wasn't until the Yankees' Joe McCarthy in 1935 that another manager specifically developed a young pitcher—in his case, Johnny Murphy—to be his designated relief ace and kept him in that role for many years. McCarthy was blunt in telling Murphy that he was unlikely to stick as a starting pitcher but he would be of considerable value to the Yankees as a reliever. Unlike other managers of his day, McCarthy rarely used his top four starters out of the bullpen in the years his Yankees dominated baseball. Instead, he routinely carried three pitchers he used almost exclusively in relief, with Murphy designated as both his "fireman," coming into games in the late innings with runners on base to douse the flames of an opposition rally—and, indeed, one of Murphy's nicknames was Fireman—and his "closer" (to use today's terminology), coming in specifically to save games without a pitcher necessarily being in trouble.

McCarthy used Murphy judiciously, efficiently, and when it mattered most. Murphy figured directly in the outcome of the game in nearly 70 percent of his total relief appearances from 1936 to 1943, when the Yankees won seven pennants in eight years. The Yankees led the league in saves five times, and Murphy had the most saves of any pitcher four times. Notwithstanding the demonstration of his value to the Yankees' success, and though the percentage of games saved was inexorably increasing, few teams followed McCarthy's Johnny Murphy model of grooming and nurturing a specialist to win and to save games in the late innings. Complete-game victories were still the gold standard for self-respecting, top-flight starting pitchers, and nearly all managers gave them their due.

At the time World War II began to significantly impact the major leagues in 1943, the percentage of complete games had been relatively stable at between 45 and just less than 50 percent since the late 1920s, as had about two-thirds of all victories being finished by the starting pitcher. The number of wins involving relief pitchers either getting the victory or the save—in some cases a reliever got the save for another reliever getting the win—hovered around 40 percent.

There was no longer any doubt about the necessity of having a viable bullpen, but its relative importance in the grand strategy of the game was still open to question. There were no formulas or set patterns for using bullpens more strategically, and most teams' relief corps lacked stability and cohesiveness from one season to the next. The pen was still primarily a way station for aging veterans, up-and-coming pitchers aspiring to be starters, or marginal pitchers trying to hang on. The idea of relief pitching as a unique discipline to be developed and nurtured was still either disdained or beyond consideration. McCarthy's Yankees were the only team with a bullpen plan.

The crucial importance of having a singular relief ace was on display by the Yankees' Joe Page and the Dodgers' Hugh Casey in 1947. Both relievers were instrumental to their teams' pennant triumphs. After being less than successful in three years trying to work himself into the starting rotation under McCarthy, the hard-throwing Page, now working for Harris, won 14 and saved 17 while striking out nearly 8 batters every 9 innings as the Yankees lapped the AL field. His manager had a ritual toast after many Yankee victories, according to Hall of Fame broadcaster Red Barber in his book on the 1947 season, *When All Hell Broke Loose*: "Here's to Joe Page." In Brooklyn, meanwhile, Casey had a 10–4 record in relief and 18 saves, the most ever by a National League pitcher, as his team also had the pennant all but cinched by September.

Although other highlights endure in the popular account—Jackie Robinson's daring on the base paths, Al Gionfriddo's robbery of Joe Di-Maggio, Bobby Browns 3-for-3 as a pinch hitter, and Cookie Lavagetto's bottom-of-the-ninth two-out hit that not only broke up Bill Bevens's no-hitter but also turned him into the losing pitcher—the 1947 World Series ultimately came down to Page versus Casey. Casey pitched in six of the seven games, was directly involved in all three of the Dodgers' victories with two late-inning wins and a save, and allowed the Yankees only one run in his 10⅓ innings of work. Page pitched in four games, but they included four innings to close out game 1 with a save and five scoreless innings for the win to close out game 7. He faced the minimum batters possible in his stellar game 7 performance, allowing only one batter to reach base—on a ninth-inning single—who was erased in a double play that ended the Series, the Yankees triumphant . . . again.

The age of enlightenment about relief pitching was at hand.

\* \* \*

Leo Durocher was at the forefront of managers implementing more nuanced and sophisticated strategies for handling their pitching staffs. While he was relatively conventional about letting his starting pitchers complete games as long as they had the stuff and the stamina, Durocher made more pitching changes in games his starters failed to finish than most other managers of his time. He was also willing to pinch hit for a pitcher in the late innings of a close game where other managers might leave him in the game if the pitcher, including a reliever, was throwing well.

Durocher went through four stages in how he employed his pitching staff during his first career as a major-league manager from 1939 to 1955, each of which was determined to a great extent by the quality of his starting pitching. In his eight and a half years managing in Brooklyn, the only time Durocher did *not* have good pitching was during the war years from 1943 to 1945. The quality of his pitching staff when he managed with the Giants, however, was more variable.

Before wartime baseball took its toll, there was nothing unusual about how Durocher used his pitching staff. The percentage of complete games by Brooklyn's starters was consistent with the league average. When the Dodgers narrowly won the 1941 pennant and when they narrowly lost the next year, Whit Wyatt and Kirby Higbe were both workhorses who Durocher was willing to trust deep into games. In games that his starting pitchers did not finish, Durocher made about the same number of pitching changes—1.7 on average during the four years—as the league average. But at a time when few teams used any one quality pitcher almost exclusively in relief, Hugh Casey had become Durocher's go-to reliever.

Durocher had also used Casey primarily in relief in 1940, but that was because he was not effective as a starter. When Durocher moved Casey to the bullpen in July 1941, the Dodgers were in a dogfight for the pennant with the Cardinals, and the move was strategic. Casey had a 9–4 record at the time, but in 7 of his 13 starts had either failed to last 5 innings or had given up at least 5 runs. Once he assumed the role of relief ace, Casey made only 5 starts the rest of the way—all in doubleheaders when Durocher needed an extra pitcher. Durocher used him 11 times in the September stretch, which started with the Dodgers and Cardinals in a first-place tie, all in relief to finish games, and Casey excelled with a 4–2 record, 3 saves, and gave up just 3 runs in 21⅓ innings. The Dodgers would not have outlasted the Cardinals to win their first pennant since 1920 without Hugh Casey in the bullpen.

Perhaps the genesis for what became Brooklyn's perennial postseason existential angst, Casey was much less successful in the World Series. Called upon to hold the Yankees at bay in a scoreless tie in the eighth inning of Game 3 at Ebbets Field, Casey gave up four consecutive singles and wound up the losing pitcher. The next day, having entered the game in the sixth inning, Casey was protecting a 4–3 lead that would have tied the Series and had the Yankees down to their last strike—which he got, except that strike three got past catcher Mickey Owens, Tommy Henrich reached first base, and Casey proceeded to unravel, surrendering a single, a walk, and a pair of doubles that resulted in the Yankees winning the game on their way to another Fall Classic triumph for the Boys in the Bronx.

Despite his World Series meltdown, Casey was indisputably the relief ace Durocher thereafter relied on in games the Dodgers had a chance to win if he felt his starter could not go the distance. In 48 relief appearances in 1942, Casey finished 29 games for the Dodgers, figuring directly in the outcome of 20 of them with a 6–1 record and 13 saves. Then it was off to war for Hugh Casey.

Thus began the second stage in the evolution of Durocher's bullpen management. Durocher became quicker to remove his pitchers, both starters and relievers, when they got into trouble. Brooklyn starters completed only a third of their games between 1943 and 1946, substantially below the league average of about 43 percent complete games.

The 1946 season was a watershed year for how Durocher used his bullpen. Even though the war had ended and most wartime veterans were back in the game, Brooklyn's starting pitchers from 1941 and 1942 were for the most part gone, with only Higbe remaining. Unusual for any team finishing the schedule in first place—tied, actually, with St. Louis, forcing a playoff that the Cardinals won—Brooklyn had the second-*fewest* complete games in the league. Only the Giants completed fewer starts, but that wasn't surprising because they finished last and gave up the second-most runs in the league. That the Dodgers were next to last in complete games *was* surprising since the 3.04 earned run average by their starting pitchers was second best in the league, behind the Cardinals, and substantially better than the league-average starters' ERA. Durocher went to his bullpen a record 223 times in the 105 games his starters failed to complete in 1946, meaning he made an average of 2.1 pitching changes per game after removing his starting pitcher.

Casey was back in 1946, after three years in the service, and he was superb with an 11–4 record and 1.81 ERA in 45 games coming out of the bullpen. Although Casey was in at the end of twice as many games than any other Dodger pitcher, he had only 5 of the major-league-leading 28 saves by Brooklyn relievers. Perhaps as a carryover from managing less-practiced pitchers during the war years, Durocher used virtually all of his pitchers in relief with the game on the line, his decision on whom to call depending on the game situation. The next year, Casey was the Dodgers' undisputed bullpen ace but not for Durocher, who was suspended for the entire 1947 season.

* * *

The third stage of Durocher's progression in managing his bullpen came in his first three full seasons as Giants manager, 1949 through the miracle year of 1951. Durocher once again had solid starters he allowed to go for complete games if they were pitching effectively. Giants pitchers completed 43 percent of their starts, well above the league average of 38 percent. Larry Jansen, the Giants' ace when Durocher arrived, and Sal Maglie, who he moved into the starting rotation to stay in July 1950, were two of the National League's best pitchers.

In seeming contradiction to the Giants' having more complete games than any other National League team except the Braves—who had Spahn and Sain—Durocher continued his practice from Brooklyn of making substantially more pitching changes in games his starters did not finish than most of his contemporaries, including managers with bad pitching staffs whose starters survived many fewer starts. From the time he took over at the Polo Grounds halfway through the 1948 season until 1952, the Giants used more relievers in non-complete games than any other team in the league. Also similar to how he managed his bullpen with the 1946 Dodgers, Durocher did not rely on any one reliever to win or save close games. Even though he usually had two pitchers he used almost exclusively in relief, Durocher often called on one of his starters to get crucial last outs in games. Maglie saved four games in five relief appearances for the Giants in 1951, to go along with his 37 starts and 22 complete games.

The fourth stage of how Durocher handled his pitching staff began in 1952 and lasted until he was fired from the Polo Grounds dugout as soon as the 1955 season ended. The first two of those years, the Giants' starting pitchers were in the bottom half of the league in earned run average and complete games. Jansen hurt his back in 1952 and never recovered his former effectiveness, and Maglie, while still pitching effectively, was no longer able to go the distance as often now that he was on the high side of his mid-30s. Durocher continued to use an average of two relievers in games his starters failed to complete, more than most of his fellow managers.

But now he also had a dedicated relief ace in the person of Hoyt Wilhelm. Because Wilhelm was an *artiste* of the knuckler, Durocher was able to use him with unprecedented frequency. As a 29-year-old rookie in 1952, Wilhelm's 71 relief appearances were the second-most ever by a major-league pitcher, just two years after the Phillies' Jim Konstanty pitched 74 games in relief, and he led the league in relief appearances again in 1953 with 68. No pitcher, not even Konstanty, had pitched so many games in consecutive seasons. Wilhelm not only pitched in nearly half the Giants' games, earning 26 saves, but 34 percent of his appearances were on back-to-back days and another 30 percent on just one day of rest. And Wilhelm in 1952 and 1953 averaged over two innings per game.

The arrival of the durable Johnny Antonelli in a trade from Milwaukee, the coming of age of second-year pitcher Ruben Gomez, and the return to form of Maglie gave the Giants one of the league's most formidable corps of starting pitchers in 1954, a major factor in their winning the pennant. Durocher still called in relievers more frequently than any other manager except for the sixth-place Cardinals' Eddie Stanky, who had to cope with one of the worst pitching staffs in the league. And now Durocher had the hard-throwing Marv Grissom, already 36, whose career had been mostly in the minor leagues, to complement the soft-tossing Wilhelm in his pen. This only slightly reduced Wilhelm's workload, even though Grissom became the pitcher Durocher was most apt to call on to save games.

With Wilhelm and Grissom, Durocher was one of the first managers to recognize that, just as the teams with the best pitching staffs had at least two first-rate starting pitchers, so too should a manager be able to rely upon more than one first-rate reliever. He had two, and he used them in a combined total of 227 games for the Giants in 1954 and 1955 before his time ran out in New York.

That both were so effective gave Durocher tremendous flexibility. Wilhelm was used more frequently on short rest—over half his appearances were on one day of rest or the very next day—and primarily between the sixth and eighth innings. Consistent with the knuckler's pattern of use the two previous years, Durocher called on Wilhelm as often when the Giants were losing by one or two runs as when the game was tied or they led by a run, and he averaged about two innings of work per outing. Grissom was used primarily between the seventh and ninth innings, by far most often when the Giants had the lead, and so got the preponderance of save opportunities. Grissom was in at the end of 68 games with 25 saves in 1954 and 1955, Wilhelm in 44 games with 7 saves, all coming in 1954.

* * *

Making as many pitching changes as he did with clubs that were generally winning teams and often in the pennant chase, Durocher was the most strategic and systematic manager among his contemporaries in structuring his relief corps to anticipate contingencies. The concept of bringing in a reliever in the middle of an inning to squelch rallies in closely contested games was by now universal, with due regard for managers' judgments on whether his current pitcher—especially an ace starting pitcher—had enough left to pitch his way out of a jam. Durocher, however, was quicker to replace a pitcher in trouble and less likely than other managers to give him the chance to work out of his predicament, unless he was a *trusted* starting pitcher with good stuff still pitching effectively in the game.

Durocher was also an early master of making pitching changes to match up to specific batters, depending on the game situation. He emphasized having a southpaw in his bullpen for the situations where he might need to get a tough left-handed batter out. This is of course the mission of so many southpaws in major-league bullpens today, who are employed solely to pitch to, and get out, the one tough left-handed batter at a crucial moment late in the game. Unlike today's managers, who have the benefit of much-larger pitching staffs than in Durocher's day when teams typically carried no more than eight or nine pitchers on their roster, rarely did Durocher have a left-hander he could use almost exclusively in relief. Most of the lefties he relied on for situational relief were also starting pitchers, including the veteran Larry French in 1942, Vic Lombardi in 1945 and 1946, and Monte Kennedy and Dave Koslo with the Giants from 1949 to 1951.

The only southpaw the Giants had in 1954 who pitched almost exclusively in relief was Windy McCall, causing Durocher to sometimes use left-hander Don Liddle as a reliever for situational purposes. Durocher turned to Liddle out of the pen 9 times in 1954—he also started 19 games—and each time the first batter he was called in to face was left-handed. Five times Durocher brought him in with runners on base, twice with the bases loaded. Liddle was the reliever Durocher brought in to pitch to just one left-handed batter in Game 1 of the World Series. With two on and nobody out in the eighth inning of a tie game, pitching in relief of starter Sal Maglie, it was Liddle who threw the pitch that Vic Wertz hit that made Willie Mays an icon.

The Polo Grounds still in an uproar over Willie's surreal catch and spin-around throw, Cleveland manager Al Lopez opted to pinch hit for switch-hitting right fielder Dave Philley, who did not hit left-handers well, with the right-handed-batting Hank Majeski, who did. Durocher did not hesitate in removing Liddle for his hard-throwing right-handed relief ace, Marv Grissom. As Liddle is said to have said upon leaving the mound, his work done for the day—he got his man. Grissom got out of the inning and became the winning pitcher with two additional innings in relief when Dusty Rhodes hit a three-run pinch-hit walk-off home run off Cleveland ace Bob Lemon in the 10th.

A similar situation played out, twice, in Liddle's Series-winning start in Game 4, three days later. With two out and two on in the seventh inning and the Giants holding a 7–3 lead, Durocher removed Liddle from the game after he gave up a hit that brought the tying run to the plate in the person of right-handed lead-off batter Al Smith. Durocher called in right-hander Hoyt Wilhelm to get him out, which he did. The next inning, with one out, two on, and the dangerous left-handed-slugger Wertz coming up and representing the tying run, Durocher brought in southpaw Johnny Antonelli to relieve Wilhelm. No great play was needed by Mays this time, as Antonelli struck out Wertz and the next batter and then pitched a scoreless ninth to wrap up the Giants' improbable Series victory.

\* \* \*

Durocher's opposite in the 1954 World Series, Al Lopez—a former catcher, and a good one—was arguably the only American League manager who thought creatively about his bullpen even though, in both Cleveland, from 1951 to 1956, and Chicago, from 1957 to 1965, his teams always had excellent starting pitching. At the beginning of his managerial career, Lopez was more traditional in his approach to relief pitching, like most American League managers in the early 1950s, often using his starters as relievers late in close games. Early Wynn, Bob Lemon, and Mike Garcia—three of the best starting pitchers in baseball at the time—accounted for 20 of the Indians' 37 saves in Lopez's first two years in Cleveland. While starting 203 games in 1951 and 1952, those three also pitched 53 games in relief. The only starting pitcher Lopez spared from relief duties was the aging Bob Feller, who relieved only once while making 62 starts.

Lopez backed away from using his core starting pitchers so often as relievers in 1953, and dependable bullpens soon became a hallmark of Lopez's consistently competitive teams. Like Durocher, he embraced the concept of having two reliable dedicated relievers, rather than just one, whom he could use in the late innings of close games. In 1954, when Cleveland set the AL record for victories with 111, Lopez split the role of relief ace between three pitchers used almost exclusively in the bullpen—hard-throwing rookie right-hander Ray Narleski; veteran southpaw Hal Newhouser, the former ace of the Tigers now at the end of his career; and rookie left-hander Don Mossi. He called on Narleski and Newhouser most often in the seventh inning or later with the game tied or the Indians ahead by no more than two runs. Narleski and Mossi remained Lopez's go-to relievers in his remaining years at the helm in Cleveland, with Narleski, same as in 1954, getting the lion's share of saves.

Lopez followed the same pattern of having two dedicated relievers to win or save games in the late innings when he moved to Chicago. They were veteran right-hander Gerry Staley—formerly a starting pitcher with the Cardinals who Lopez moved into an exclusively relief role—and Turk Lown, who had been relief ace for the cross-town Cubs in 1956 and 1957, also a right-handed pitcher. Indicative of Lopez's willingness to use them virtually interchangeably with the game on the line, Lown had 15 saves to lead the league, and Staley had 14 when the White Sox won the 1959 pennant. Both Lown and Staley, however, were already well into their 30s when first introduced to Lopez, so by the early 1960s, Al Lopez was looking for a new pair of ace relievers.

The arrivals of Eddie Fisher from San Francisco in 1962 and Hoyt Wilhelm from Baltimore in 1963, both knuckleball pitchers, gave Lopez the foundation for possibly the best one–two reliever combination major-league baseball had yet to see. After two years where he used Wilhelm as his principal "savior"—(the term "closer" was not popularized until 25 years later)—in 1965, Lopez began using them interchangeably to close out games. Often alternating days on call, Fisher saved 24 that season, and Wilhelm had 20 saves.

\* \* \*

The new age of enlightenment about relief pitching was in its formative stages in the 1950s, as managers were mastering the art of how to use their bullpens for effect. The trend was the same for both leagues, but their paths were not quite in sync.

Continuing a trend that began before the war, National League managers made more pitching changes in games their starters did *not* complete than their American League counterparts every year in the 1950s, even though the two leagues seesawed in which had the higher percentage of complete-game starts in any given year. Consistent with giving *fewer* innings to their relievers, AL managers were more likely as a group to leave a starter who was pitching well in the game for the duration, certainly if their team had the lead but even in a losing cause; a higher proportion of complete games were *losses* in the American League in all but one year of the decade, and fewer games were won in the AL by a relief pitcher every year.

While NL managers went to their bullpen more often, they typically used individual relievers for fewer outs, which probably contributed to more attention paid on the makeup of their relief corps. Perhaps most significantly, National League teams were more likely than in the American League to have the same pitcher in the nearly exclusive role of "relief ace" for multiple years. Every NL team during the decade had at least one pitcher who was the team's relief ace for at least four consecutive years. There was much less continuity of ace relievers on AL teams from one year to the next. Boston with Ellis Kinder, Cleveland with Narleski and Mossi, and Chicago with Fritz Dorish in the first half of the decade and Staley and Lown when Lopez was manager were the only teams in the league who boasted the same top reliever for at least four successive years.

Not surprisingly, therefore, most of the heralded relievers in the 1950s were National Leaguers. Besides Wilhelm and Grissom on the Giants, the Phillies' Jim Konstanty became the first relief pitcher to win a Most Valuable Player Award when he "saved" the Whiz Kids' way to the 1950 pennant; Clem Labine was Mr. Reliable in the Dodgers' bullpen from 1953 to 1959; and by the end of the decade, Roy Face of the Pirates had put himself in the argument with Marberry and Murphy as the best relief pitcher in the history of the game over at least five successive years. The only American League relief ace of such prominence was Kinder from midsummer 1950 to 1955.

Face was arguably the prototype of the modern relief ace. Page, Casey, and even Konstanty in 1950 were all workhorses out of the pen in their best years, their managers sometimes calling on them in the early innings and relying on them in some cases to pitch more than a third of the game. Face exited the bullpen only in the late innings, most often with the game on the line and usually for less than two innings at a time. When he won 18 of 19 decisions in relief in 1959, Face entered the game most often in the eighth inning or later and never before the seventh. He pitched an inning or fewer in 27 of the 57 games he appeared.

\* \* \*

Whatever general philosophical differences on structuring their bullpens and employing relievers there may have been between the two leagues was largely erased by the end of the decade. With complete games having fallen below 30 percent to stay, AL teams became fully invested in their bullpens in the 1960s, including nurturing young pitchers with good stuff to be their ace reliever over many successive years—a concept they had not fully embraced, as the NL did, in the 1950s. In 1966, the Baltimore Orioles, with quite possibly the best bullpen any team had yet assembled—including Stu Miller, Eddie Fisher, Eddie Watt, Moe Drabowski, and Dick Hall—won a blowout pennant by 9 games despite throwing only 23 complete games. Their bullpen accounted for more than a third of Baltimore's innings and won or saved all but 20 of the Orioles' 97 wins.

Testifying to relief pitching coming of age in the American League, most of the top relievers in baseball in the 1960s were on AL teams, foremost among them Wilhelm and Fisher in Chicago, John Wyatt in Kansas City, and Dick Radatz in Boston. They were all of fixtures in their teams' bullpens over multiple years, saving the day for their teammates. Radatz became the prototype of the big (six and a half feet), intimidating, flame-throwing fireman. Pitching 207 games in relief for the Red Sox between 1962 and 1964, Radatz struck out 487 batters in 414 innings—an average of 10.6 per 9 innings—and his 40 wins and 78 saves accounted for more than half of Boston's victories.

For most of the decade, the American League had appreciably fewer complete games and more saves than the National League—a disparity perhaps best explained by the NL having arguably the greatest generation of starting pitchers in history. National League managers recognized and honored the fact that pitchers like Sandy Koufax, Juan Marichal, Don Drysdale, Bob Gibson, Tom Seaver, Ferguson Jenkins, Gaylord Perry, Jim Maloney, and Jim Bunning all had the ability and the drive to finish what they started. There were many fewer starting pitchers of such magnitude in the American League in the 1960s, making AL managers more inclined to trust their ace relievers to close out victories. This trend would reverse in the 1970s, when it was the AL that had more top-quality starting pitchers and the designated-hitter rule went into effect, precluding the need to remove a pitcher for any reason other than he was ineffective, tired, or in trouble.

# TEN

## Slow-Walking Integration

After Brooklyn brought up Jackie Robinson, it was no longer unthinkable for other major-league teams to buck the conservative instinct of the game's ownership powers that be that the time was not right for integration. Of course, when would it ever be right if nobody took the first step? But if it was no longer unthinkable, there was also no rush to follow the Dodgers' lead; there remained significant resistance and a wait-and-see attitude as to whether Robinson would succeed long term. Many—probably most—owners undoubtedly hoped for failure, which would validate long-held prejudicial views against blacks in the big leagues by demonstrating that even Branch Rickey's chosen one could not play at the major-league level and that he was indeed representative of the best the Negro Leagues had to offer.

It didn't work out that way.

By 1952, six years into the Jackie Robinson era, it was surely apparent to every major-league team that there was no going back to segregated baseball. The Brooklyn Dodgers had been competitive every year since breaking the color barrier. They went to the World Series in Robinson's rookie season, finished second in 1948 after adding Campanella, won another pennant in 1949 with Newcombe now an ace on the pitching staff, and finished second in both 1950 and 1951. The Cleveland Indians, meanwhile, would not have won the 1948 American League pennant and the World Series without Larry Doby and Satchel Paige. And with all due respect to Bobby Thomson, the New York Giants would not have won the 1951 pennant without Monte Irvin, Willie Mays, and even Hank Thompson, despite his missing nearly all of the Giants' miraculous come-from-behind drive to overtake the Dodgers because of an ankle injury.

Moreover, black players had proven they could indeed play with the best of the white major leaguers. Robinson was the National League's

123

Most Valuable Player in 1949 and Campanella was the MVP in 1951. Irvin finished third in MVP voting in 1951 and, again with all due respect to Thomson, was the Giants' most indispensible player when it came to winning the pennant that year, hitting .338 in the final two months of the season as New York surged to overtake Brooklyn's big mid-August lead. Irvin led his team with a .312 batting average and led the league in runs batted in with 121.

And beginning with Robinson in 1947, black players monopolized National League Rookie of the Year honors. Newcombe won the award in 1949 (the first year the award was given in each league), Boston Braves outfielder Sam Jethroe in 1950, Mays took the honor in 1951, and Dodgers reliever Joe Black would win in 1952. Newcombe followed his Rookie of the Year Award by winning 19 and 20 games the next two years before being drafted into the army during the Korean War. Jethroe led the National League in stolen bases in 1950 and 1951, his first two big-league seasons. And let's not forget what Willie Mays did with his career.

Meanwhile in the American League, Larry Doby was either the best or second-best offensive player every year from 1950 to 1952, according to the wins-above-replacement metric, and would lead the league in home runs in 1952. Cleveland first baseman Luke Easter was one of the AL's premier home-run hitters after he became a regular in 1950 and, in 1952, would finish one home run behind teammate Doby. As a rookie in 1951, the Cuban-born Minnie Miñoso proved himself an impact player in helping turn around the fortunes of the Chicago White Sox, who had finished sixth the previous year, 34 games below .500. Miñoso hit .324 batting third for Chicago and was the fourth-best position player in the American League, based on his 5.5 wins above replacement, helping the White Sox finish fourth with a winning record for the first time in eight years.

Yet in 1952, despite those players' accomplishments *and* it being six *long* years into the Jackie Robinson era (*long*, because playing careers are so short), only six of the major league's sixteen teams—three in each league—had black players on their rosters. They were the Dodgers and Indians, both at the forefront of integration in 1947; the Giants, who introduced black players in 1949; the Braves, who did so in 1950; the White Sox, who joined Cleveland as the only American League teams with black players in 1951; and the Browns, whose complicated history with integration included being the third big-league team in history to integrate shortly after the Indians in July 1947, releasing their black players—deemed failures—without fanfare in less than two months, and reintegrating with the great Satchel Paige in 1951 after Bill Veeck bought the team. This was the same Veeck who, as Cleveland owner in 1947, followed Branch Rickey's lead when he introduced Larry Doby to the American League.

And six years into the Jackie Robinson era, blacks accounted for only 11 of the 175 players who were regulars on major-league teams in 1952, based on position players starting 100 games and pitchers qualifying for the league's earned run average title with 154 innings pitched or otherwise appearing in 40 games. They were Robinson, Campanella, and rookie reliever Black in Brooklyn; Thompson on the Giants; Jethroe with the Braves; Doby, Easter, and outfielder Harry Simpson in Cleveland; Miñoso and third baseman Hector Rodriguez with the White Sox; and Paige on the Browns. Notably missing were Mays and Newcombe, only because they were draft picks for the U.S. Army, and Irvin, only because a broken ankle suffered in spring training limited him to 46 games.

But while only 6 teams fielded black players in 1952, with blacks accounting for a mere 6 percent of players who were regulars in major-league starting lineups, 6 other teams had blacks playing in their minor-league systems. This meant that 12 of the major league's 16 teams were hedging their bets about the future of blacks in major-league baseball even if they remained opposed to integration at the big-league level. And they included the New York Yankees, one of the 4 teams (the Philadelphia Phillies, Detroit Tigers, and Boston Red Sox were the others) that would be most notorious in holding out against giving black players a chance in the big time.

*  *  *

In the first five years of integration, 1947 to 1951, only 8 of the first 20 black players to don a major-league uniform emerged to become a starting regular on his team for what would become at least five years. In order of their appearance in settling into a starting role to stay, they were Jackie Robinson, Larry Doby, Roy Campanella, Don Newcombe, Hank Thompson, Monte Irvin, Minnie Miñoso, and Willie Mays. Thompson alone among them was not an exceptional player, so good that he could not be denied a starting role. Two others who made their big-league debut within the first five years of integration were regulars for three seasons—Sam Jethroe and Luke Easter, both from 1950 to 1952—but neither was given much opportunity to have a long career because they were in their 30s when they got their big-league shot, and each suffered ailments or injuries that caused their teams to give up on them relatively quickly. And then there was Satchel Paige, one of the greatest pitchers of all time, who did not get his major-league chance until he was at least 42 years old in 1948 and pitched a total of only five big-league seasons, mostly in relief in two acts—one for the Indians (1948–1949) and the second for the Browns (1951–1953).

None of the other nine black players who made their first big-league appearance during these years was given a realistic shot at competing for a regular position or given much chance to succeed in the face of adversity. They were either on the team to be backup players, or they were quickly benched or demoted to the minor leagues—sometimes never to return—if they got hurt or struggled. Two of the nine, however, made comebacks later in the decade.

Going into the 1951 season, the Indians thought so highly of Harry Simpson that they decided to keep him and trade Miñoso, purportedly to avoid any chance of starting three black players in their outfield where Doby was a fixture in center field. Although he played well the following year, Simpson mostly struggled, primarily in a platoon role, and was back in the minor leagues in 1954. He resurfaced with Kansas City in 1955 and was traded to the Yankees in 1957, but most of those years Simpson was a role player. Simpson started as many as a hundred games only twice in his eight-year major-league career and never more than 110.

The Indians also gave up relatively quickly on right-hander Sam Jones, who was a star pitcher for the Negro League team in Cleveland when they signed him. Called up by the Indians at the very end of the 1951 season, Jones made the team out of spring training the next year, but chronic arm problems likely caused by a heavy workload in the Puerto Rican Winter League between seasons undermined his effectiveness and caused Cleveland to give up on him. After two years in the minor leagues, Jones returned to the majors in 1955 in the National League at the age of 29 and proceeded to have a relatively successful career. Pitching for the Cubs, Cardinals, and Giants, Jones averaged 32 starts over the next 6 years with an 88–85 record, led the league in strikeouts 3 times and in walks 4 times, and his 21 wins and 2.83 earned run average for San Francisco in 1959 were the best in the league.

In contrast to Jones and Simpson, who both overcame the adversity of their initial major-league teams' deciding they had limited prospects because of their early struggles, most of the blacks who played in the major leagues in the first six years of the Jackie Robinson era who were not themselves star players did not get second chances. Luke Easter, Sam Jethroe, and Hector Rodriguez were all three cautionary tales of black players who started for their teams but, because they were not elite players, saw their major-league careers arbitrarily cut short or, as in the case of Simpson, not reach the level of success he might have.

First called up by the Indians late in the 1949 season to join Doby and Paige as the only black players not only on their team but also in the entire American League, Easter was Cleveland's regular first baseman the next three years. He became one of baseball's premier sluggers, knocking out 86 home runs and driving in 307 runs between 1950 and 1952. But Easter was also at least 34 years old, and probably older, in his breakout season of 1950, when he hit 28 home runs and had 107 runs batted in, and with chronic knee problems, he was prone to injury. A broken toe suffered in the fourth game of the 1953 season marked the beginning of the end of his big-league career. Although he hit .303 with seven home runs, Easter appeared in only 68 games that year, and his defensive deficiencies became more pronounced because of his more limited mobility after his return to action. This proved most unfortunate for Easter given that excellent defense to back up Cleveland's superior pitching was a very high priority for his manager, Al Lopez. Easter was demoted to the minor leagues in 1954, where he spent the remainder of his career as a potent offensive force hitting 193 home runs in six years as a regular. Back in Cleveland, Easter's replacement at first base was Vic Wertz, another power hitter, who was eight years younger but hardly a defensive upgrade.

Like Easter, the Braves' Sam Jethroe—called "Jet" because he was really fast—had been a star player in the Negro Leagues and had excelled with a .326 batting average, .403 on base percentage, and 89 steals for the Dodgers' top minor-league affiliate in Montreal in 1949 when he got his chance at a big-league career. Not playing off the same page as the American League team in Boston, whose ostensible tryout for three Negro League stars, including Jackie Robinson and Jethroe in 1945, was a sham, the Braves became the third National League team to integrate when they opened the 1950 season with Jethroe in center field.

The Braves were probably motivated to acquire Jethroe by their failure to even compete for the National League pennant the previous year, after having gone to the World Series in 1948. The outfield was the Braves' biggest problem in 1949. Their four principal outfielders combined for only five wins above replacement; five wins above replacement is defined for a *single* player as an All-Star level of performance. Jethroe's acquisition was part of the Braves' wholesale revamping of their outfield, which also involved trading with the Giants for outfielders Sid Gordon and Willard Marshall. That deal cost the Braves their highly regarded double-play combination of Al Dark and Eddie Stanky.

The Braves were able to acquire Jethroe from Brooklyn at the relative discount of three career minor-league players with limited big-league potential because the Dodgers had decided there was no room for him at Ebbets Field despite his outstanding performance at Triple-A Montreal and their own outfield needs. Notwithstanding the success of their three black stars, Dodger executives, including Branch Rickey who was still in Brooklyn, understood that integration was still on trial and they had best be careful not to push the envelope beyond the limit of tolerance of most of the rest of major-league baseball. Moreover, looking ahead to 1950, the Dodgers also had to consider that pitching prospect Dan Bankhead, another African American, was slated to pitch in Brooklyn that year. Whether Jethroe would have been the answer, the Dodgers ironically were nearly always looking for a third starting outfielder during their heyday of winning five pennants in eight years between 1949 and 1956.

Jethroe was the National League Rookie of the Year in 1950 when he hit .273 and led the league in stolen bases, which he did again the next year. By the time the Braves moved to Milwaukee in 1953, however, he was back in the minor leagues and would play only two more games in the Bigs, for Pittsburgh in 1954. Jethroe's three brave years in Boston were fraught with frustration and misunderstanding. Part of his failure to last with the Braves was attributable to Jethroe actually being four years older than he claimed in order to get the chance to play in the major leagues, and much was attributable to defensive deficiencies and vision problems that undermined his performance both in the field and at bat.

Starting 108 games at third base for the White Sox, Cuban-born Hector Rodriguez was also one of the eleven black players who were regulars in 1952, but that turned out to be his *only* major-league season. Originally signed by the Dodgers in 1951 out of the independent Mexican Leagues at the "veteran" age of 31, Rodriguez epitomized the black player not given a chance to recover from struggling performance. The White Sox traded for Rodriguez to play third base—an unsettled position for them since 1946—following his excellent 1951 season in Montreal. Rodriguez got off to a strong start, batting .330 in Chicago's first 27 games, but hurt his foot early in the season and, playing through the injury, went into a prolonged slump that ultimately led to his being benched in September. Rather than being given another chance the next year, Rodriguez was released and signed on to play at the Triple-A level in the Yankees' farm system in 1953.

Given their entrenched unenlightened attitude about blacks in baseball, and the fact that he was approaching his mid-30s, the Yankee organization was not the best place for Hector Rodriguez to be in terms of resuming a major-league career. Rodriguez had nine productive years as a regular on Triple-A teams before finishing his career back in Mexico in the early 1960s. The White Sox, meanwhile, continued on with a different third baseman every year for the rest of the decade.

\* \* \*

The slow pace of integration was also because most teams were in no hurry to promote the black players they had signed and begun developing in their minor-league systems. Major-league teams, if they were thinking at all about integration, were giving priority to scouting and signing young and inexperienced black players who required seasoning in the minor leagues, rather than established Negro League players who were more-or-less major-league ready. This was certainly defensible if the intent was to build for the future, since most of the Negro League stars thought capable of playing in the major leagues—which was by no means a universal sentiment—were already in their 30s and presumed on the downside of their baseball skills and ability.

But, as Easter and Jethroe showed, even 30-something, veteran Negro League players were capable of valuable contributions as starting players at the major-league level for at least a few years. Their presence would have given credibility to individual teams' integration efforts—(these guys can play)—*and* eased the way for young black prospects in their minor-league systems. In the three years each played as a regular, Easter and Jethroe both averaged about three wins above replacement, typical for starting position players in the major leagues.

While few of the black players in their minor-league affiliates were budding superstars, the teams that were at the forefront of integration—the Dodgers, Indians, Giants, and Braves—had the most genuine prospects in their player-development pipeline. Because they were the most committed to the principle of integration, not least for the competitive advantage of moving quickly to secure the best talent before other clubs that were merely hedging their bets became serious about doing so themselves, these four teams aggressively scouted and signed black players and rewarded their development by promotion to the big-league club to compete for starting roles. All four had at least three blacks who were regulars in their starting lineup for at least three years during the length of Jackie Robinson's career. Their commitment to integration also made them the earliest teams to give black players with more average major-league ability the opportunity to realistically compete for starting positions.

For the teams not at the forefront of integration, which is to say most major-league teams, signing black players for their minor-league affiliates was mostly to answer critics accusing them of racism and discrimination even while they held off on integrating their big-league rosters. The historian Jules Tygiel observes in his landmark study on integration, *Baseball's Great Experiment: Jackie Robinson and His Legacy*, that most teams at this time, if they were thinking at all about integration, were giving priority to scouting young and inexperienced black players who required seasoning in the minor leagues rather than players who might make the grade quickly. Just like young white players at the beginning of their professional careers, unformed and in need of experience, black players had to work their way through their teams' minor-league affiliates, often starting in or close to the lowest classification level. Lukewarm at best about seeing black players succeed, they could legitimately argue they did not have many, if any, blacks capable of competing for a regular position at the major-league level.

The upshot of this ultimately self-defeating strategy was that as the pace of integration stepped up in the early to mid-1950s because of growing pressure to concede the obvious—there was no going back to segregated major-league baseball—most of the black players breaking the color barrier on their teams were not ready for prime time. In 1953, the number of integrated major-league teams increased to nine with the Pirates, at the beginning of the season, and the Cubs and Athletics in September. The Cardinals, Reds, and Senators made it 12 of 16 major-league teams in 1954, and the Yankees made it 13 the year after. Most of the 31 black players who made their major-league debut on these seven teams between 1953 and 1956 failed in their bids to become core regulars on their teams, and many of them were gone from the big leagues within three years. If most were marginal big leaguers at best, their being rushed to major-league dugouts, more for appearances sake than because they were major-league ready, was both a disservice to them and a consequence of their teams' scouting philosophies.

Another crucial factor limiting opportunities for black players well into the 1950s was that major-league teams adhered to an implicit quota while owners, managers, and—importantly—white players gradually warmed to the idea of integration. Just as during the days of Commissioner Landis, when there was no explicit rule prohibiting black players from organized (white) baseball, the quota was understood and the owners self-policing. The unspoken rationalization was that more than a handful of black players on a major-league roster, and certainly on the field of play in any one game, would alienate the white fan base. As with their willingness to part with Jethroe, who could have helped in the outfield, even the trailblazing Dodgers took the better part of Robinson's career to buck this underlying reality. With the exception of pitcher Dan Bankhead, who became the Dodgers' and the National League's second black player in August 1947 and, failing to meet expectations, spent only one full season with Brooklyn (in 1950), the Dodgers through 1951 limited the number of blacks on their roster to their three superior players—Robinson, Campanella, and Newcombe.

\* \* \*

By 1956, Jackie Robinson's last big-league season, integration in the literal sense was a fait accompli. Only three teams—the hard-line holdouts in Philadelphia, Detroit, and Boston—did not have at least one black player in their dugout that season. But opportunity for black players, especially to realistically compete for starting roles, was still very limited. Many of the 51 black players who put on a major-league uniform that year also spent time in the minor leagues. Of greater significance, only 21 of the 181 players who were regulars on major-league teams in 1956 were black. This was nearly double the number from four years before, but still just 12 percent of the total.

# ELEVEN
## Exit the Grandmaster

It wasn't until 1954 that the Yankees were a team Stengel could truly call his own. Nearly all the core members of his five-and-five-in-five team whom he inherited from previous winning Yankee teams—DiMaggio and Rizzuto, who dated back to McCarthy, Reynolds, Raschi, and Lopat—were either gone or, in the case of Rizzuto and Lopat, near the end of the road. Mickey Mantle, Yogi Berra, and Whitey Ford were the new marquee players defining Yankee dominance.

While 103 wins in 1954 was not enough to extend their pennant streak to six years, the Yankees reeled off four straight pennants from 1955 to 1958, only the first of which—not cinching until the 152nd game of the season—was a close thing. Their next three in a row were won by margins of nine, eight, and ten games, consistent with the old-fashioned Yankee way of taking a commanding lead by midsummer and not allowing anyone to draw close in September. In none of those years were the Yankees seriously threatened after July, even in 1958 when they did no better than a losing 27–28 record in the last two months of the season.

For all their dominance of the American League, however, the Yankees were less successful in the World Series than the franchise had grown accustomed. "Next year" finally came to Brooklyn in 1955, and the Milwaukee Braves took out the Yankees in 1957. The Yankees avenged both losses in the World Series immediately following, beating the Dodgers in 1956 and the Braves in 1958. All four World Series were exciting seven-game affairs.

After slipping badly and finishing third in 1959, they won big again for Stengel in 1960, although it took winning the last 15 games of the season to obliterate what had been a tight pennant race in mid-September. That turned out to be the second-longest winning streak in Stengel's managerial career—his 1953 Yankees had an 18-game streak—and it ended the season on the high note of a pennant. That was not enough to save the Ole Perfessor's tenure once his contract ran out when the baseball year was over. Even had the Yankees won the 1960 World Series, the 70-year-old Stengel was almost certainly out anyway.

\* \* \*

Mantle was *the* superstar. As vital as Berra and Ford were to their success, the Yankees of these years are justifiably identified with the Mick. From 1954 to 1958, Mickey Mantle had five of the six best years of his career. With an average annual player value of 9.5 wins above replacement, those five years for Mantle rate among the best of any player ever, whether Babe Ruth or Ty Cobb, Honus Wagner or Willie Mays, Barry Bonds or Alex Rodriguez. And this despite Mantle having already endured a horrific knee injury in the 1951 World Series, in only his 98th major-league game, which robbed him of some of his blazing speed and would trouble him the rest of his 18-year career.

Taken in context and considering the totality of his skills—speed, hitting prowess, power, and defense—Mantle for those five years may have been the best player ever. Number 7, Mickey Mantle, alone accounted for nearly one-fifth of the combined wins above replacement on the Yankees from 1952, the first year he was a regular all season, to Stengel's last year in pinstripes in 1960. DiMaggio, by contrast, by far the American League's most dominant player in the first seven years of his career, accounted for only 14 percent of the collective player value of the 1936–1942 Yankees. And yet, Mantle was always perceived as failing to measure up to the Yankee icon who preceded him in center field. Even Casey Stengel was disappointed that Mickey Mantle wasn't somehow better than he was.

Besides Mantle in center field, the only constants in Stengel's starting lineups after 1953 were Yogi Berra behind the plate and Gil McDougald somewhere in the infield. All three were among the American League's 10-best position players during those years, based on their cumulative wins above replacement. Mantle's 52 home runs, 130 RBIs, and .353 average in 1956 were the most in baseball, made him the American League's first Triple Crown hitter since Ted Williams in 1947, and earned him the first of his three Most Valuable Player Awards. The next year, Mantle reached base more than half the time he stepped up to the plate, hit for an even higher average—.365, not even close, it turned out, to Williams's .388—and was again the MVP. Berra was the MVP in both 1954 and 1955 and finished second to his teammate, "the Mick," in 1956. And McDougald was consistently reliable, one of those players indisputably better than his traditional baseball stats. He hit .300 only once in his career— .311 in 1956—and hit only 112 home runs in 10 major-league seasons, but from 1954 to 1958, when the Yankees won four pennants, his player value based on the WAR metric was the sixth best in the league.

Right fielder Hank Bauer was arguably the Tommy Henrich of the second Stengel edition of the New York Yankees—an "old reliable" who could always be counted on. As during the five-and-five-in-five years, when he was famously paired in the outfield with Gene Woodling, the right-handed-batting Bauer was often platooned, a paradoxical role given that Stengel started him so often against right-handed pitchers. By the end of the decade, age had made Bauer expendable, and he was part of a multiplayer trade with Kansas City after the 1959 season that brought Roger Maris to New York. The Yankee infield, meanwhile, was in a state of perpetual change, although Stengel always had a place for McDougald.

Even with them as anchors, however, Stengel was constantly reinventing his team, using multiple players as regulars or in platoons in both the outfield and infield. He wanted redundancy at every position, and he was a master at juggling players in the lineup from game to game and even within games in a sort of controlled creative chaos that effectively recast the concept of platooning.

\* \* \*

As for the pitching, by 1953, age was catching up with the dependable stalwarts of the five-and-five-in-five years, diminishing their starts and innings if not necessarily their effectiveness. Allie Reynolds, who turned 36 before the start of that season, made only 15 starts and became the Yankees' de facto relief ace. He was 6–6 as a starter for the 1953 Yankees and had a 7–1 record with 13 saves that secured the final outs of New York victories. Eddie Lopat turned 35 during the season and started only 24 games but led the league with a 2.42 earned run average and in winning percentage with a 16–4 record. Vic Raschi, who celebrated his 34th birthday in spring training, made only 26 starts and had a 13–6 record. By 1954, Raschi had been sold to the Cardinals, Reynolds retired before the 1955 season, and Lopat was traded to Baltimore later that year.

But along came Whitey Ford, who won his first nine major-league starts for the 1950 Yankees, back from two years in the armed forces during the Korean War. At only 24 years old, Ford led the 1953 Yankees with an 18–6 record. Ford and Bob Turley, acquired from Baltimore after the 1954 season in a trade that ultimately involved 17 players, were the only certainties in Stengel's starting rotation for the last 5 of his 10 pennants.

While Ford was relentlessly effective and twice led the league in ERA, he did not once win 20 games when Stengel was his manager. Because the Ole Perfessor was very much an outlier among managers in not being wedded to starting his best pitchers every fourth day with three days of rest, which was the norm, Ford almost always had many fewer starts than other top-tier pitchers. During his last six years at the Yankee helm, five of which led to the World Series, Stengel started pitchers on three days of rest a total of only 118 times, compared to an average of 223 times by the managers of the seven other American League teams. Ford's pattern of starts, particularly after 1954, was predominantly every fifth day.

Once Stengel was gone, Ford became much more of a workhorse on the Yankee staff, befitting the typical major-league ace. After starting more than 30 games only once in the 9 years he pitched for Stengel, Ford started at least 36 games each of the next 5 years before arm problems sidelined him in 1966 and ended his career in 1967. When the Yankees started the post-Stengel era with four straight pennants to give them a second stretch (including 1960) of five in a row, 64 percent of Ford's starts were on three days of rest. They included the only two 20-win seasons of his career, including 25–4 in 1961 and 24–7 in 1963.

Hard-throwing right-hander Bob Turley, as notorious for walking batters as for striking them out, was the other mainstay in Stengel's rotation during those years, except for when dealing with arm problems or an occasional exile to the bullpen. His 21–7 record in 1958, which led the major leagues in winning percentage, made Turley a Cy Young winner and the only Yankee pitcher to win 20 games in Stengel's last six years in the Bronx.

The Yankees would not have won the 1958 World Series against the Braves, which they trailed three games to one going into Game 5, without Turley's tireless pitching. Only one other team had ever come back from such a deficit to win the World Series and not since 1925. Turley had contributed to the Yankees' being in such a hole by being blown out in the very first inning of Game 2 but redeemed himself by pitching a shutout in Game 5 to keep the Yankees alive, getting the final out and the save in the Yankees' 10-inning 4–3 victory in Game 6 in Milwaukee to force a Game 7, and then giving up only 2 hits and 1 run in 6⅔ innings of relief to win the final game and the Yankees' 18th world championship.

Other than Ford and Turley, Stengel's was typically a makeshift rotation. But, like almost everything the madcap Perfessor did, it worked. Yankee starters during these years included a series of pitchers with unexceptional historical legacies who came through when they were needed. Bob Grim (61–41 in his career) won 20 in 1954. Tommy Byrne (85–69 lifetime), who never lived up to his promise, had 16 wins in 1955. The next year, Johnny Kucks (54–56) won 18 games and then pitched a 3-hit shutout in Game 7 of the World Series as the Yankees snatched the championship back from the Dodgers. Tom Sturdivant (59–51 lifetime) had 16 wins in both 1956 and 1957. Art Ditmar had a lifetime losing record (72–77) but won 13 for the Yankees in 1959 and led the team with 15 wins in 1960.

Then there were the likes of Don Larsen and Bobby Shantz to provide the necessary ballast. Larsen (81–91 lifetime) pitched for the Yankees from 1955 to 1959 and staked his claim to fame with his 1956 Game 5 World Series perfect game. Shantz started 38 games for the Yankees in 1957 and 1958 before being used by Stengel almost exclusively in relief in 1959 and 1960. Notwithstanding Larsen's one shining moment, Shantz (119–99 in his career) was the only player in this group who could be said to have had a quality career.

* * *

To an extent unprecedented in baseball history, relief pitching was a key factor in the Yankees' continuing dominance of the baseball world. Consistent with the constant maneuvering for advantage that characterized his platooning and substitutions among position players, Casey Stengel had a reputation for being quick with the hook if he perceived his starter to be tiring or struggling and more ready to pinch hit for the pitcher—even if he was pitching well—in close games. The Yankees bullpen led the league in saves eight times in Stengel's twelve years as manager, including when winning seven of his ten pennants, three of them in the five-and-five-in-five years.

What was unusual was the percentage of victories that Stengel had relief pitchers "save"—35 percent—for a team that consistently had one of the best starting staffs in the American League. Unlike during the McCarthy years of Yankee dominance, when their starting pitchers led the league in complete games in six of the eight years they won the pennant and once when they did not go to the World Series, none of Stengel's AL-winning teams were better than third in complete games. And only six of his starters—Raschi three times, Turley twice, and Ford once—were ever in the league's top five in innings pitched. The Yankees led the league in ERA in three of Stengel's last five years as manager, but the 29 percent complete games by his starting pitchers was below the league average, which included teams whose starters were roughed up far more frequently. Ford twice, when he was 19–6 in 30 starts in 1956 and 14–7 in 29 starts in 1958, Shantz in 1957 with a 10–5 record in only 21 starts, and Turley in 1958 when he was 21–7 in 31 starts were the only Yankee pitchers who completed more than 40 percent of their starts in any single season.

When it came to starting pitchers, Stengel was clearly of the opinion it was better to replace them too early—specifically, when his team had the lead—than too late, when fatigue or the opposing lineup's familiarity with his pitcher's pattern might betray his starter. In every year he managed the Yankees, Stengel was substantially more likely to bring in a reliever with his team in the lead than other managers. More than a third of Stengel's pitching changes were made when his team was ahead in the game. This was true even when the formidable trio of Reynolds, Raschi, and Lopat were the centerpiece of his pitching staff in the five-and-five-in-five years. Their passing into historical lore left Casey with a less-proven core of starting pitchers, causing him to use his relievers for substantially more innings than the league average.

Stengel, however, was judicious in his overall use of the bullpen. Except for his last season in pinstripes in 1960, when he made more pitching changes than any other manager in the majors, the Yankees were rarely one of the teams among the top teams in relief appearances. Less inclined than other American League managers to replace pitchers in mid-inning, Stengel went to his bullpen less for situational purposes than to manage the outcome of the game.

Like most other American League teams in the 1950s, the Yankees did not use the same pitcher as their relief ace over multiple seasons. Stengel inherited Joe Page when he took over as Yankee manager in 1949, and used him often enough that year for Page to set the new major-league record for saves in a season with 27. Stengel turned to Tom Ferrick as his ace reliever in midseason the next year when Page became ineffective and more trouble in the clubhouse than he was worth.

Allie Reynolds might have been the Yankees' indisputable relief ace the next three seasons had it not been for Whitey Ford being a U.S. Army draft pick in 1951 and 1952. David Halberstam relates in his book, *Summer of '49*, that after the Yankees won the first of their five straight World Series in 1949, Stengel approached Reynolds during the clubhouse celebration and confided that he wanted to make him his relief ace the next year. But starting the 1950 season with only three other reliable starters—Raschi, Lopat, and Tommy Byrne—forced Stengel to keep Reynolds in the rotation, and the absence of Ford delayed the move for two more years. Even while starting 55 games in 1951 and 1952, however, Reynolds was in Stengel's mix to close out victories, leading the Yankees with seven saves in 1951 and earning a save in each of his six relief appearances in 1952. With Ford back in 1953, Reynolds made only 15 starts and pitched 26 times in relief getting 13 saves—third-most in the league.

In 1954, it was Johnny Sain—he of "Spahn and Sain" fame—who took over as the Yankees' relief ace. By now 36 years old, Sain was in the traditional mold of an aging veteran starter converted to relief ace in the latter years of his career. The two previous years, Stengel had used Sain as both a starter (35 games) and reliever (40 games). Sain saved seven in 1952 to lead the team, and his nine saves in 1953 were good for fifth in the league. Used exclusively as a reliever in 1954, his 22 saves were the most in the league.

After Sain, it was Jim Konstanty, the former Phillies relief ace, and Tom Morgan who were Stengel's primary relievers in 1955, Morgan again in 1956, and Bob Grim (who had been so great in the starting rotation only three years before) in 1957. Stengel used flamethrower Ryne

Duren in that role the next two years, but in 1960, he was forced to turn to veteran Bobby Shantz and newcomer Luis Arroyo when Duren's lack of control had gotten out of hand. Duren walked as many batters as the 49 innings he pitched—hardly what a manager wants in his relief ace.

\* \* \*

The end of Stengel's career with the Yankees was hardly the graceful exit it should have been, especially after the Perfessor gave another virtuoso performance as manager in 1960. Facing unexpectedly tough competition from the Baltimore Orioles, the Yankees were two games behind in early September, setting the stage for a hectic finish. It didn't turn out quite that way. With the two teams tied for first and only two weeks left in the season, the Yankees burst the Orioles' bubble by sweeping them in a four-game series in mid-September. They did not lose again until the World Series. Their destruction of Baltimore was the beginning of a 15-game winning streak to close out the season, giving Stengel his 10th pennant, this time by an 8-game margin that belied how close the race had really been. The Yankees were 21–15 with first place on the line after July 4, the first time Stengel had to manage with first place at stake at any point in the second half of the season since 1955.

There followed perhaps the most bizarre Fall Classic in history. The Yankees outscored the Pittsburgh Pirates by 28 runs (55–27) but still managed somehow to lose. Stengel's handling of his pitching staff in the World Series—the last seven games he would manage in a Yankee uniform—was controversial, certainly in hindsight but even at the time.

First, there was the matter of his choosing to start Art Ditmar in the opening game at Forbes Field instead of Whitey Ford. Although Ditmar's 15 wins were the most by a Yankee pitcher, Ford was the undisputed ace despite struggling through shoulder trouble and winning only 12 games. Stengel reasoned that he preferred to have the southpaw Ford start Game 3 at Yankee Stadium, where the short distance to the right-field fence tended to favor left-handed power, making it fraught for right-handers like Ditmar and all the other Yankee starters.

Whatever the logic of Stengel's reasoning, however, Ford wasn't going to start more than one game at Yankee Stadium anyway. Had he pitched Game 1 in Pittsburgh, his start in New York would have been Game 4 instead of Game 3. Starting the opening game would also have set up Ford to start three times in the World Series, including Game 7. Instead, because of Stengel's design, Ford could only start twice, which he did with shutouts in the third and sixth games that put him on the path to setting a new World Series record in 1961 with 33⅔ consecutive scoreless innings.

But having made his choice to go with Ditmar in Game 1, Stengel hardly seemed committed to that decision. No sooner had Ditmar allowed four of the first five batters he faced to reach base, three of them scoring to give the Pirates a 3–1 lead, than Stengel took him out of the game. It was only the first inning, and only one of the three hits he allowed went for extra bases. The two others were singles up the middle.

Stengel started Ditmar again in Game 5 at Yankee Stadium, the Series tied at two games apiece. This time he got through the first inning in order, but when Ditmar got into trouble in the second, Stengel again had little patience for his beleaguered pitcher. Ditmar once again faced five batters in the inning, gave up three hits, two of them doubles, and surrendered three runs. Two of the runs, however, were unearned on account of an error, which should have resulted in the second out of the inning. Pittsburgh was on its way to taking the Series lead, and Ditmar would not get another chance to take the mound in 1960.

And then, in the deciding Game 7 with the Yankees leading 7–4 in the eighth inning and just six outs away from what was looking like his eighth World Series championship, Stengel uncharacteristically chose to allow reliever Bobby Shantz to bat for himself rather than pinch hit for him and bring in another reliever to close out the win. Stengel's decision was no doubt motivated by Shantz having pitched so well since entering the game at the start of the third inning. He had faced the minimum fifteen batters in five innings of work, thanks to two double plays. But the first three Pittsburgh hitters reached base on singles in their half of the eighth, narrowing the score to 7–5 with the tying runs on base. One of those hits was a would-be double-play ball that hit a divot (or something) on the infield dirt and took a bad hop right into the throat of shortstop Tony Kubek, knocking him out of the game and into a hospital.

It was at this point, with the left-handed-batting Bob Skinner due up in a sacrifice situation, that Stengel finally decided to make a pitching change. But instead of calling on southpaw Luis Arroyo, who had saved 7 games in 29 relief appearances for the Yankees during the season and who had not pitched since relieving Ditmar in Game 5, Stengel brought in the right-handed Jim Coates. Even though Shantz had already retired Skinner twice, this decision made sense on its merits. Shantz was working now in his sixth inning of relief, the hitters following Skinner—who was expected to bunt—were right-handed, and while the tying runs were on base, the Yankees did have the lead. Skinner did sacrifice, and Coates got the following batter for the second out on a short fly that failed to score a run, but then committed the cardinal sin for a pitcher of neglecting to cover first base on a ball hit too far for the first baseman to make the out himself. Pittsburgh took advantage of that good fortune when Hal Smith immediately followed with a three-run home run to give the Pirates the lead—a lead, it turned out, they could not hold, leaving it to Bill Mazeroski to save the day with his historic home run off Coates's relief, Ralph Terry. And thus came to an end of Casey Stengel's managerial reign in the Bronx.

* * *

The Ole Perfessor was now 70, and there was general sentiment that Stengel mismanaged the World Series and was perhaps too old in clarity of mind and consistency of attention (let alone physically) to continue on as manager of the New York Yankees, notwithstanding his terrific finish to the 1960 season. In any event, the Yankee front office had decided back in 1958, when they re-signed Stengel to a contract through the 1960 season, that there would be no continuance for the Ole Perfessor. And so shortly after Mazeroski's walk-off home run ended the World Series, Casey Stengel was unceremoniously dumped in an awkward "was he fired, or did he retire" press conference—having had greater success as Yankee manager than was envisioned when he was hired to take over in 1949 but leaving with less dignity and appreciation than he deserved after a run of 10 pennants in 12 years that remains unparalleled in baseball history.

# TWELVE

## Consolidating Integration and the Importance of Hank Thompson

The standard narrative on the integration of major-league baseball rightfully celebrates Robinson and great players the likes of Doby, Campanella, Mays, and Aaron who followed in his footsteps to prove there was no doubt about the ability of black players to compete at the major-league level. By the early to mid-1950s, their demonstrated excellence ensured that black players with *superior* talent would henceforth find a place in major-league starting lineups. And, the standard narrative continues, it was the success of the Brooklyn–Los Angeles Dodgers, with seven pennants and winners of two World Series in the thirteen years after Robinson broke into their lineup in 1947, and the New York Giants and Milwaukee Braves, both winning two pennants and one World Series in the 1950s, with blacks as integral members of their teams that consolidated integration as a fact in major-league baseball.

What the standard narrative glosses over, however, is that the 1950s were not an after–Jackie Robinson post-racial era for major-league baseball where black players had as much opportunity as white players to compete for starting positions on big-league teams. Baseball's powers that be could legitimately say segregation was in the past and acknowledge that black players were capable of playing in the major leagues. But they still could only claim there was no discrimination against black players and that there was a level playing field of competition where positions were won on merit not racial considerations.

In 1960, the percentage of core regulars on major-league teams who were black—about 14 percent—was higher than the 10.5 percent of the U.S. population who were African American, according to census data. But the fact that the percentage of black players who were "elite" by major-league standards was far higher than the proportion of elite white players throughout the 1950s (and the 1960s, for that matter) suggests otherwise. Fourteen years after Robinson had made his big-league debut, and four years after he had retired from the game, it was still not a certainty that African American or black Latinos of far more modest abilities than elite black players at the time—like Mays, Aaron, Ernie Banks, or Frank Robinson—had a realistic chance of becoming regulars on major-league teams.

Unlike the difference between the great and the good, the variability of performance among most players who are regulars in the major leagues, while often still distinguishable, is not nearly as obvious. While elite players are those whose performance excellence underwrites the popularity of the game and its success as an industry, it is the legions of players with five to seven years as regulars without whom the major-league business model would not have survived. Nearly all these players are doomed to be forgotten unless, like Bobby Thomson, they played a role in iconic moments. But it is they who provide the critical mass to the nine-man game's coherence. For every Babe Ruth, baseball needed guys like Wally Pipp, Aaron Ward, Roger Peckinpaugh, Bob Meusel, and Bob Shawkey—his teammates on the 1921 the Yankee team that kick-started the forever-dynasty—who are remembered, if remembered at all, only in the reflected glory of the Babe. It is the average, ordinary, everyday players who make the business of major-league baseball even possible.

It was likely necessary for the first wave of integration's trailblazers (Robinson, Doby, Campanella, Newcombe, Irvin, Miñoso, and Mays)—exceptional players all—to prove they could play with the best of the white players in the major leagues before black players of more ordinary major-league ability had a realistic chance of proving they too belonged in a starting lineup. Without in any way diminishing the importance of the black players who were so superb in the 1950s, and especially the importance of Jackie Robinson, because their excellence ensured there was no going back to segregated major-league baseball, integration could not be considered consolidated until *any* black player with major-league ability, not just those with superior talent, could realistically compete with white players of similar major-league ability for big-league starting jobs, may the best player win.

* * *

By the time Jackie Robinson took off his uniform for the last time in 1956, 78 blacks had made it to the big time. But only 20—16 position players and 4 pitchers—could claim to have been a core regular on a big-league team for at least 5 years by the end of the decade in 1960. Five others would become established regulars in the 1960s. Of those 20, however, 11 (55 percent), were elite players, based primarily on the wins-above-replacement metric for measuring comparative player value for their five-best consecutive years in the 1950s or on career arcs that landed them in the Hall of Fame. Indeed, all but 2 of the 11 are enshrined in Cooperstown today (although Monte Irvin was selected for his career in the Negro Leagues, and Roberto Clemente did not become an elite player until the 1960s), and both of those who are not—Don Newcombe and Minnie Miñoso—were good enough to have been reconsidered several times by the Hall of Fame Veterans Committee. By contrast, only 18 percent of white players who were regulars for at least five years between 1947 and 1960 were elite by either standard.

Perhaps not surprisingly, because their excellence guaranteed integration's success, it is nonetheless revealing that between Robinson's rookie season of 1947 and 1960, based on their cumulative WAR for their five best consecutive years, blacks accounted for five of the top-ten position players in the National League, which was far more proactive in integrating blacks onto major-league rosters than the American League. They were Willie Mays (first, ahead of Stan Musial), Robinson (third), Ernie Banks (fourth), Hank Aaron (tied with Duke Snider for fifth), and Frank Robinson (tenth), whose rookie season in 1956 was Jackie's last in the big leagues.

Moreover, black players dominated the top half of that list, accounting for three of the NL's four best position players and four of its top six. All five had an average *annual* player value during their five best years well above the five-wins-above-replacement standard that denotes an All-Star-quality performance. Mays and Robinson had an average annual player value exceeding eight wins above replacement—an MVP-level of play—during their five best years, and Banks and Aaron were just below that. Roy Campanella, meanwhile, was the National League's 14th-best position player during this time based on his five best seasons from 1949 to 1953—far ahead of Ed Bailey in player value as his league's best catcher.

Of the nine blacks who claimed a starting position for at least five years by 1960 *without* being among the major leagues' best players, only one—Giants' infielder Hank Thompson—succeeded in doing so before 1953. Their average WAR for their five best years as big-league regulars was decidedly below the All-Star level of performance of the elite black players who were their contemporaries, but they *did* play at the level of a typical starting player in the major leagues. They were, in short, fully capable major leaguers—just like most who have played in the big time and were not perennial All-Star candidates. In the 1950s, however, they were very few relative to the number of white starting players with average major-league ability, not to mention outnumbered by fellow black players who were among the best in baseball.

Not to excuse the reluctance of most club owners to go down the path of integration, at least not quickly, the lack of opportunity given to most black players with major-league ability to compete for starting positions in the big leagues was almost certainly a practical consideration by the teams that owned their contracts. For most of the 1950s, even the enlightened teams at the forefront of integration—the Dodgers, Giants, and Indians—limited the number of blacks on their rosters, which put a premium on favoring elite black players for big-league jobs. A key reason for doing so was to avoid provoking any more clubhouse dissension than necessary among white players who, because of personal acculturation and historical precedent, were skeptical, wary, or downright hostile to the idea of having black teammates.

* * *

In the beginning phases of integration, most team owners probably understood that for the great majority of white players, accepting a black teammate with superior ability was one thing, a hurdle that could be overcome, because terrific talent cannot be denied. But in the intensely competitive and tenuous world of major-league baseball, having to compete for scarce starting positions with black players of comparable ability, may the best man win, was something else entirely—a far-bigger obstacle to white players' acceptance. Major-league baseball would have to first accept black superstars as worthy of the big leagues before black players of more ordinary talent would be welcome.

For most of Jackie Robinson's career, this dynamic meant that black players who were not themselves exceptionally talented did not, for the most part, get the opportunity to realistically compete against white players of comparable and, quite often, lesser ability, even for starting positions that were a weakness on the major-league team in whose system they belonged. This was despite the fact that blacks were excelling in their teams' minor-league systems, causing the historian Jules Tygiel to conclude in his book, *Baseball's Great Experiment*, that major-league teams deliberately failed to tap some of the best players in their own talent pool to fill their position needs.

Adherence to a system of player development where prospects steadily progressed through their minor-league systems until they proved themselves to be major-league ready in both performance and mastery of fundamentals worked against black prospects. Although players shine or fail on an individual basis, baseball, especially at the major-league level, is a highly disciplined team sport. Players working their way up their teams' ladder of minor-league affiliates were being groomed to be *professional* baseball players. At a time before big contracts for elite amateur players, the few who were able to avoid years of apprenticeship progressing through different levels of the farm system were typically the very best players—those with the potential to be elite players.

Most major-league teams were not receptive to judging black players on their merits as baseball-skilled athletes, especially those from the Negro Leagues, because of prevailing biases in evaluating talent. Moreover, most teams at this time were conservative and generally risk-averse in their style of play. The Negro Leagues, by contrast, which into the early 1950s remained the only talent pool of black players for major-league teams to scout, were more free-wheeling, aggressive, and—yes—flamboyant on the field of play, providing entertainment as much as playing baseball. Even if their skill and athleticism were obvious, Negro League players may have seemed to major-league scouts and coaches to be undisciplined and less than professional in how they played the game.

Jackie Robinson brought that style to the Brooklyn Dodgers. His flair and audacity on the base paths put him in the spotlight for reasons beyond his race, and not only he, but his team, benefited greatly. But if his style of play was seen to be emblematic of black players in general, then how many could actually play at his level was an open question, and those who could not would be a detriment to the team. Consequently, many blacks playing in minor-league systems with demonstrated major-league-level skills, but who were not clearly elite players, may have been dismissed as still not ready for prime time because they were perceived as still too undisciplined.

For most of the 1950s, starting opportunities for black players, especially those who did not have superior innate ability, depended very much on the major-league team in whose system they belonged. Of the 78 black players who had worn a major-league uniform as of when Robinson retired, 29 had been a regular on their team for at least one year as a starting position player, starting pitcher, or the relief ace, and only 7 had been a regular for as many as five years. These 29 black men combined for 109 single-player seasons. They played for 11 of the 16 major-league teams, but nearly three-quarters of those seasons (78 to be precise) were by blacks playing on just four teams—the Dodgers, Indians, Giants, and Braves. These were the first four teams to integrate and not take a step back, as the Browns did in 1947. Their continued commitment to integration also made them the earliest teams to give black players with more-average major-league ability the opportunity to realistically compete for starting positions.

Most teams, however, got on the integration train late, either to first ensure major-league baseball was not going back to being a whites-only enterprise or because of their resistance to the idea and so had few black players who were actually major-league ready to compete for starting positions until the mid-1950s or even later. The reason, ironically, was precisely one of the arguments made in the 1946 MacPhail Report about black players with raw talent lacking mastery of the skills and fundamentals necessary to play major-league baseball, which the report said are "usually acquired only after years of training in the minor leagues." The report even put a timeframe on that point: "The minor league experience of players on the major league rosters, for instance, averages seven years."

The Dodgers with their "big three," the Indians with Doby, and the Giants with Irvin and Mays short-circuited the need for "years of training in the minor leagues" by signing and rapidly promoting exceptional players from the Negro Leagues. And they were patient, even more understanding and forgiving than they might have been with white players when they struggled at the big-league level, such as Cleveland with Doby and the Giants with Mays.

Of the eleven elite black players who made their debut by the end of the 1956 season and were regulars on major-league teams for at least five years by 1960, only two—Doby and Banks—were put directly on their clubs' big-league roster after being signed from Negro League teams. The other eight position players averaged 188 games in the minor leagues before being called up to the majors. Among them, Jackie Robinson played in 124 minor-league games, Aaron in 224, Campanella in 283, Frank Robinson in 292, and Miñoso played in 317 minor-league games before they became regulars on their big-league clubs. Newcombe pitched three full seasons and started 78 games in the minor league before reaching the mound at Ebbets Field. Their minor-league time was consistent with the number of years and games typically played in the minors by the best of contemporary white players before they were promoted to the big leagues as regulars to stay.

Among the black players who were regulars in 1956, but not outstanding players, Cubs second baseman Gene Baker spent four years and played 629 games in the minor leagues, Kansas City first baseman Vic Power four years and 523 games, and his teammate, third baseman Hector Lopez, had five years and 517 games in the minors before getting their chance in the big time. The same as for the black players who were among the best in the game, their minor-league tenures were not out of the ordinary for comparably talented white players, although they were slightly older than white players making the grade with similar minor-league experience because they were not signed at such young ages.

By giving greater emphasis to signing young black players with very little baseball experience, rather than players with meaningful Negro League resumes or with exceptional talent, it was predictable that few black players of average major-league ability were available to compete for starting positions in the beginning years of the Jackie Robinson era. The frustration for the few such players given the chance to be a regular in the major leagues was that there was also less patience than there likely would have been for many white players of average major-league ability if they struggled or were injured, as Luke Easter and Harry Simpson with the Indians and Sam Jethroe with the Braves could attest.

\* \* \*

While it may have been necessary for the first black players to be far better than the typical big leaguer for them to win and hold onto starting roles before blacks became accepted in the major leagues, at some point some team was going to have to step up with its own fairness doctrine to incorporate a black player who did not have either an impressive Negro League resume or superstar potential as a regular in its starting lineup. That team was not the Brooklyn Dodgers but the New York Giants.

His name was Hank Thompson. Unlike Robinson, Doby, Campanella, Newcombe, and Irvin, who starred in the Negro Leagues and quickly showed they would be outstanding in the majors, Thompson's prospects were uncertain at best when he and Irvin together integrated the Giants on July 8, 1949. With his history of alcohol and anger-management problems and having already failed in his first big-league audition of only 27 games with the Browns in 1947, there was no telling whether Thompson would play any better than before. Giants manager Leo Durocher, however, immediately made Thompson his second baseman. Thompson started in 69 of the Giants' remaining 82 games on the 1949 schedule, and the 13 games he missed toward the end of the season were because of an injury.

Monte Irvin, on the other hand, the presumed star of the duo because of his impressive Negro League credentials and his .373 batting average at Triple-A Jersey City when he was called up, found himself relegated primarily to the bench as a pinch hitter for the rest of the season in New York. With Bobby Thomson, Willard Marshall, and Whitey Lockman all hitting over .300 in the Giants' outfield, there was little reason for Durocher to make a change, and Irvin started in only 20 of the 36 games he played.

Unlike the outfield, second base at the time was a position of weakness for the New York Giants. Durocher had already used five different players at second base by the time Thompson was called up from Jersey City, where he was hitting .296. None of the five was hitting better than .252. Thompson hit .280 the rest of the season and was a significant improvement at second base for the Giants, but the two wins above replacement he contributed to the team was no better than the minimum expected of a starting player in the major leagues.

Meanwhile, Boston Braves second baseman Eddie Stanky had a WAR value nearly double Thompson's, which is significant because Durocher acquired Stanky over the winter to become the Giants' new second baseman in 1950. As part of the deal that brought Stanky to New York, third baseman Sid Gordon, who had the second-highest player value (4.6 WAR) among position players on the 1949 Giants, and outfielder Willard Marshall (whose WAR was 4.2) were sent to Boston, making room for Irvin in the outfield. Gordon's departure opened up the third-base job for Thompson, who seamlessly switched positions with Durocher's encour-

agement and support. Thompson remained a regular in the Giants' starting lineup, occasionally in the outfield, until 1956, when Durocher was no
longer manager.

In the seven years he was a regular in the Giants' lineup, most often
hitting third or fourth in Durocher's batting order, Hank Thompson averaged 3.3 wins above replacement, fairly typical for a starting position
player. The only year he played at an All-Star level of performance, based
on his 5.1 WAR, was in 1950. He was never selected to be a National
League All-Star, not even in 1950 when he was the best third baseman in
the league. According to "similarity scores" developed by Bill James to
compare one player to another, the contemporary player whose career
was most similar to Thompson's was Chicago Cubs third baseman
(1951–1955) Randy Jackson, not much remembered (if remembered at all)
today. Hank Thompson did not make James's list of the 100 best third
basemen in major-league history in his 2001 book, *The New Bill James
Historical Baseball Abstract*.

Precisely because Thompson was not an exceptional ball player, the
Giants almost certainly could have settled on a white player of equal or
even less talent than Thompson to play third base had they been so
inclined. Had they decided that Thompson's abilities were not sufficiently impressive to merit competing for a starting job, a potential alternative
infield option could have been Billy Gardner, then a promising prospect
in his early 20s advancing in the Giants' minor-league system. Instead of
demanding that a black player had to be clearly superior to be a regular,
however, the Giants were at the forefront of allowing a black player with
average major-league skills to earn a starting position. Gardner went on
to be a starting second baseman in Baltimore and Washington between
1956 and 1960, but his player value as a regular was typically more that of
a bench player than a starting position player.

And with Puerto Rican–born Ruben Gomez, the Giants were also the
first team to integrate into their starting rotation over successive seasons
a black pitcher who did not have the ability to overpower batters and be a
dominant ace. Prior to Gomez, the only black man to have found sustained success as a big-league starting pitcher was Don Newcombe, the
Dodgers' ace from 1949 to 1956, minus two years in the middle of that
time span when he served in the U.S. Army. As a 25-year-old rookie in
1953, Gomez brought youth to a pitching staff all five of whose principal
starters the previous year were 31 or older. Age and assorted ailments
caught up with staff aces Sal Maglie and Larry Jansen in 1953, diminishing their effectiveness and contributing to the Giants' fifth-place losing
record a year after they had finished second. Gomez, a regular in the
rotation by June, led the staff in wins, earned run average, and innings
pitched. At 13–11, he was the Giants' only starting pitcher with a winning
record in 1953.

While Newcombe could not be denied because he had exceptional stuff that made him a potential 20-game winner every year—he reached that plateau three times and just missed with 19 wins in 1950—Gomez was merely a reliable starting pitcher who never won more than 17 games and had only one other season with as many as 15 wins. Don Newcombe was one of the best pitchers, black or white, of his generation. If not for those two lost seasons in the military when he was still in his prime, Newcombe probably would have received more consideration as a Hall of Fame candidate. Ruben Gomez was never mistaken for a great pitcher, or even for one of the best in the league over successive years, and he was never his team's ace. The arc of his career was most similar to that of Bill Voiselle, who pitched in the 1940s and was best known as the number-three starter on the 1948 pennant-winning Braves behind Spahn and Sain (and pray for . . . Voiselle to maybe win if it doesn't rain?).

On most major-league teams in the 1950s, the merely reliable Gomez would likely have been displaced by a white pitcher after having back-to-back mediocre seasons in 1955 and 1956 when he went a combined 16–27 with an unenviable 4.58 earned run average. Up until the mid-1950s, teams were especially quick to give up on black pitchers who did not have superstar potential if they struggled in a regular role, even if they had already had some success. Former Negro League star Connie Johnson, for example, was not invited back on the big-league roster by the White Sox after going 4–4 with a 3.93 ERA in 10 starts for Chicago in 1953, although he would later pitch three years for the Orioles.

Gomez, however, was a workhorse on the Giants' staff, starting at least 30 games every year from 1954 to 1958. His best season was when he went 17–9 in 1954 to help the Giants reach and then win the World Series, in which he became the second black pitcher—after Brooklyn's Joe Black in 1952—to start and win on baseball's ultimate stage. Newcombe in five starts never won a World Series game.

\* \* \*

The Brooklyn Dodgers, meanwhile, were careful not to push the envelope on integration too far beyond the discomfort level of most major-league teams in the first half-decade after Jackie's 1947 debut. While Robinson, Campanella, and Newcombe remained cornerstone players on Brooklyn's four pennant-winning teams in the early and mid-1950s, the Dodgers did not have another black player of comparable potential talent until Brooklyn-born Tommy Davis burst onto the scene in Los Angeles in 1960. The Dodgers, probably calculating that the social experiment they unleashed on organized (white) baseball was most likely to be accepted sooner if there were no doubts about the major-league ability of the black players they presented at big-league ballparks, appear to have been risk-averse to giving an opportunity to a black player of far more pedestrian major-league ability—someone like the Giants' Hank Thompson—than their trio of black stars. It was not until 1952 that the Dodgers began to expand their horizons about which black players would be given a chance in the major leagues.

While not predisposed until now to help institutionalize integration by taking a chance on less talented black players at the major-league level, the Dodgers were nonetheless aggressive in acquiring and grooming black talent in their farm system. By spring training of 1952, the Dodgers had a pipeline of black players, some of whom were ready to play in the big leagues but none as obviously talented as their "big three" when they were given their chance. It was also apparent by now that integration was not going to be rolled back, even though only three teams in each league had integrated rosters at the time.

Looking at their needs after having endured an epic collapse in 1951 that ended with Bobby Thomson's home run and with Newcombe, their best and most intimidating pitcher, now in the army, the Dodgers concluded they needed to upgrade their bullpen. Having lacked a true relief ace since Hugh Casey's meltdown in 1948, the Dodgers were sufficiently impressed by Joe Black that they made him that man in 1952 after only one year in their farm system at the Triple-A level, where he had mostly started. The 28-year-old Black, who also had a six-year Negro League resume, delivered with a superb 15–4 record and 15 saves in 56 appearances, all but two in relief, and was the National League Rookie of the Year, becoming the fourth consecutive black player to be so honored.

Just as Phillies' manager Eddie Sawyer decided his Game 1 starting pitcher in the 1950 World Series against the Yankees would be his relief ace, Jim Konstanty, despite his not having started at all during the regular season, so too did Dodger manager Charlie Dressen choose his relief ace—Joe Black—to pitch the opening game of the 1952 Series. Black not only came through with a complete-game victory, but also he started Games 4 and 7, losing both.

Perhaps due to the stress of starting three games and pitching 21⅓ innings in 7 days in the World Series, after having averaged only 2⅓ innings per game as a reliever during the season, Joe Black never again approached the level of excellence of his rookie year. Arm troubles and ineffectiveness the next year put him in Dressen's doghouse. Walt Alston's replacing Dressen did not change Black's standing in Brooklyn. He was demoted to the minor leagues in 1954, traded to Cincinnati in 1955, and pitched his last big-league game for Washington in 1957, where he was the first African American to play for the major-league team in the nation's capital.

In 1953, it was third base that Dressen believed needed an upgrade. The popular Billy Cox dazzled defensively but was marginal as a hitter, and Dressen's plan was to replace Cox in the starting lineup with second baseman Jim Gilliam, shifting Robinson over to third. Gilliam signed with the Dodgers in 1951 after playing five years of Negro League ball and had played two years and 303 games for Brooklyn's top farm team in Montreal. While he was not an elite prospect reminiscent of Robinson or Campanella, the Dodgers deemed the time right to give Gilliam the opportunity to compete for a starting position on the major-league team in 1953, particularly since he was the International League MVP the previous year.

Despite Gilliam's outstanding spring training and the Dodgers' culture of accepting black players, New York baseball writer Roger Kahn observed at the time that there was anger among white players—All-Star southpaw Preacher Roe, from Arkansas, foremost among them—about Cox being downgraded to an off-the-bench role to make room specifically for a black player. His teammates understood, however, that competing for starting positions was part of the game, particularly when an incumbent left something to be desired. Because Cox was barely above a replacement-level player most of the years he started at third base for the Dodgers, according to the WAR metric, they did not show the level of resentment there was about Gilliam toward utility-infielder Bobby Morgan and rookie-aspirant Don Hoak, both white players, who were also getting serious looks at third base in spring training.

Robinson spent the remainder of his career playing third base and left field, while Gilliam embarked on a 14-year odyssey with the Dodgers that began with his becoming the fifth-consecutive black player to win National League Rookie of the Year honors in 1953. Willing to play wherever he was needed, Gilliam was a key contributor to seven Dodger pennants but averaged less than three wins above replacement over his career and was a National League All-Star only twice. The contemporary white player whose career was most similar to Gilliam's was Pete Runnels, another versatile infielder with a 14-year career.

The Dodgers kept incrementally adding blacks to their roster in their remaining years at Ebbets Field, but none proved to be more than marginal players, and all had relatively short big-league careers. The best remembered among them is Sandy Amorós, a Cuban-born black Latino, and he only because of the spectacular run-and-catch in the left-field corner at Yankee Stadium, which he then turned into a double play, to rob Yogi Berra and preserve a slim lead in Game 7 of the 1955 World Series—the only one the Dodgers won in Brooklyn.

Quickly exposed as overmatched by southpaws once he made it to Brooklyn to stay in 1954, the left-handed-batting Amorós was a platoon player throughout his brief major-league career. In 418 games for Brooklyn between 1954 and 1957, Amorós started only seven times against southpaws, and 94 percent of his plate appearances were against righties. By the WAR metric, Sandy Amorós was a marginal major-league player. The Dodgers surely could have replaced him with a white player in a similar role, but Amorós was given the opportunity to compete each year for a shot at playing left field—even if as a platoon player—and four times earned his spot on the roster.

*  *  *

Jackie Robinson's retirement after the 1956 season signaled the beginning of the end of the first wave of blacks in the major leagues. It was also the last year for both Monte Irvin and Hank Thompson. Newcombe, despite his 27 wins, was nearing the end of the road, as were Doby and Campanella. Miñoso played at a high level for another three years. With Mays in his prime, however, and Aaron, Banks, Clemente, and Frank Robinson— the National League Rookie of the Year—just getting started, blacks continued to be among the most outstanding players in the game.

Nearly all of the 21 blacks out of the 181 players who were regulars in 1956—position players starting 100 games or pitchers qualifying for the ERA title or otherwise appearing in 40 games—were either established veterans on the Dodgers, Giants, and Indians, the three teams historically most committed to integration; among the league leaders in baseball's vital statistics; or one of the best players on very bad teams, as was the case with Vic Power, Hector Lopez, and Harry Simpson on the Kansas City Athletics, which had the worst record in baseball. And 10 years into the Jackie Robinson era, unlike among white players, there remained a gross disparity in numbers between elite black players and those whose performance was about average for a player who was a regular on a major-league team.

It is, however, legitimately debatable even by the mid-1950s how many blacks in organized baseball were actually major-league ready. The disproportionate number of elite players among blacks in the big leagues may in fact have reflected a reality that was a consequence of the approach most teams took when they first began scouting black players to hedge their bets about the future of integration in major-league baseball. That reality was that most teams gave emphasis to signing black players who may or may not have been genuine prospects, but in either case required years of minor-league experience—the same as white players of comparable abilities—before being perceived ready to compete as a regular in the major leagues. If so, the disproportionate number of elite black players came down to the selective bias of favoring those with exceptional talent at the big-league level who, because they played as well as the very best white players and could not be denied, clearly gave their teams a competitive boost.

This approach virtually guaranteed that the generation of black players whose careers began during Robinson's time in the big leagues would be predominantly star players. It also virtually assured there would be considerable lag time before blacks of the more average ability typical of major-league players throughout history became more numerous in the big leagues. Regardless, however, of when the cadre of black players in the minor leagues with that level of talent reached sufficient numbers to eliminate any excuse that there were few who could play in the major leagues, the consolidation or integration of major-league baseball could not be considered complete until that happened.

# THIRTEEN

## The Brooks Lawrence Affair

The Cincinnati Reds were among the hard-line teams that held out against integration until it was certain there was no going back to segregated major-league baseball. They did not sign any black player for even their minor-league system until 1952—six years after Jackie Robinson broke the major-league color barrier—and then only after their general manager, Warren Giles, left to become National League president. Giles had taken the position that the Reds could find no black players outstanding enough to play for Cincinnati, a city of Southern sensibilities just across the Ohio River from Kentucky, even though the franchise had not had a winning record since 1944 during World War II.

Giles's replacement, Gabe Paul, took a more enlightened view, and in his first year as GM, the Reds became the 12th of the 16 major-league teams to sign black players. The next year, in 1953, the Reds signed a 17-year-old African American outfielder by name of Frank Robinson. Opening the 1954 season with infielder Chuck Harmon and outfielder Nino Escalera, both of whom they signed to minor-league contracts two years before, the Reds became the next-to-last of the eight National League teams to field a black player. Neither was a regular in the Cincinnati lineup, however, and Escalera did not play another season in the big leagues.

Harmon was still in Cincinnati in 1955 and was joined on the roster all season by outfielder Bob Thurman, but once again both were off-the-bench players. The same was true of infielder Milt Smith, who was called up in July and, like Escalera, played only one year in the Big Time. Pitcher Joe Black, who arrived in a trade from the Dodgers in early June, got the most consequential playing time of the four blacks who played all or part of the 1955 season in Cincinnati, starting 11 games and relieving in 21 others.

It was not until the arrivals of Frank Robinson and Brooks Lawrence in 1956 that the Reds for the first time had a black player among their core regulars, and both were instrumental that very year in Cincinnati's competing for the National League pennant after more than a decade of wandering in the second-division wilderness. The Reds had in fact endured eleven consecutive losing seasons, during which they finished as high as fifth only three times, including each of the two previous years. They had not won a pennant since 1940 and had not been in the top tier of NL teams since the war years of 1943, when they finished second, and 1944, when they ended up third—but they were not really competitive either season because the St. Louis Cardinals were so dominant as to brook no opposition once the season got past midsummer.

In 1956, however, the Reds were in the race the whole way. The biggest reason was the call-up to major-league duty of Frank Robinson, whose 38 home runs were not only second in the league to Brooklyn's Duke Snider but also tied what was then the major-league record by a rookie set 26 years earlier by Wally Berger. Robinson was the fourth-best player in the National League, based on wins above replacement, and was the NL Rookie of the Year by unanimous vote. Paced by Robinson's 38, the 36 home runs hit by Wally Post, 35 by Ted Kluszewski, 29 by Gus Bell, and 28 by catcher Ed Bailey, Cincinnati's 221 home runs tied the mark set in 1947 by the New York Giants and contributed to their leading the league in scoring.

In only his third big-league season, Brooks Lawrence was both the workhorse and the ace of the Reds' pitching staff in 1956. He had begun his big-league career with St. Louis in June 1954, becoming the third black to play for the Cardinals in the year they first integrated at the major-league level. After a promising start with a 15–6 record in 35 games in his rookie season, including 9–2 in 18 starts, Lawrence's pitching performance in 1955 could only be described as "ugly"—a 3–8 record and atrocious 6.56 earned run average in 46 games, all but 10 in relief. Whether succumbing to the so-called sophomore jinx or pitching through the pain of stomach ailments (probably ulcers), he was sent back to the minor leagues in mid-August and became expendable trade bait. The Lawrence trade paid big dividends for the Reds in 1956. He pitched in 49 games—30 starts and 19 in relief—and finished the season with a 19–10 record, 13–9 as a starting pitcher. In fact, and perhaps surprisingly for a team that competed all season for the pennant, Lawrence was the only Cincinnati pitcher with 20 or more starts to have a winning record as a starting pitcher.

To be sure, the Cincinnati Reds spent relatively few days in first place in 1956 and none after July 12. (It should be noted, by the way, that the Reds were then officially the "Redlegs"— which they would be from 1954 to 1959—because it was politically and culturally unwise to be the "Reds" at a time when the Cold War was raging, America had just fought a horrific war in Korea, and the "red scare" ginned up by Senator McCarthy was still a fresh wound on the American psyche.) Despite not seeing the sunny side of first place the entire second half of the season, the Reds were in the pennant race all the way to the end. Cincinnati wound up third, two games behind Brooklyn and one back of the Milwaukee Braves.

\* \* \*

Many years later surfaced the allegation that the Reds lost the 1956 pennant because their manager, Birdie Tebbetts, did not want a black man—specifically, his best pitcher, Brooks Lawrence—to win 20 games and so limited him to only three starts down the September stretch even as his team was in a tense three-team race for the privilege of facing the Yankees, already certain to win in the American League, in the World Series. This accusation was made not only by Hank Aaron in his autobiography, *I Had a Hammer*, based on a conversation he had with Lawrence, but also by Cincinnati's backup first baseman that year, George Crowe, himself a black man.

The question to be asked, therefore, is: what is the validity of such a damning indictment of Tebbetts? More specifically, what was going on that would explain Tebbetts's decisions concerning how he used Lawrence in the final month of the season?

The presumed evidentiary base for this allegation starts with the fact that Brooks Lawrence began the season by winning his first 13 decisions. When Lawrence ran his record to 13–0 with a complete-game victory over Brooklyn's Sandy Koufax on July 17, the Reds were second, only one game behind the first-place Braves, and the defending World Series–champion Dodgers were five back. By the end of July, Lawrence had made 21 starts—tied with Johnny Klippstein for most on the team—and pitched in relief in 7 other games. He had a 15–2 record with a 3.32 earned run average, including 11–2 as a starting pitcher. Not only did Lawrence have by far the best record among Cincinnati starters, but his 3.63 ERA as a starting pitcher was the best on the team.

After he claimed his 17th victory on September 1 in his 28th start of the season, Cincinnati was now in third, only 3½ out of first and still very much in the race. Lawrence won his 18th game two days later, giving up three runs in seven innings of relief against first-place Milwaukee, who the Reds (along with the Dodgers) were going to have to beat if they were to win the pennant.

The linchpin of the argument that Birdie Tebbetts (allegedly) did not want Brooks Lawrence to win 20 games (supposedly) because he was black is that, with 27 days and 22 games remaining after Lawrence won his 18th on September 3, he could have made at least six more starts on the typical three days of rest that was the norm at the time, and possibly seven, if winning the pennant came down to that. But Lawrence made only two more starts, his last on September 15, when he beat the Pirates for his 19th win. The Reds were still third, but only two games out and very much in the running. With 13 games remaining over two weeks, the pennant very much in play for Cincinnati, Lawrence—whose 19 wins (against only 9 losses) at the time were by far the most on Tebbetts's pitching staff—could still have made at least three more starts pitching on normal rest and four if he pitched once on short rest. Instead, Lawrence pitched only 4⅔ innings in five games the rest of the season, all in relief. Lawrence finished the year with the same 19 wins.

* * *

As to the specific allegation that Tebbetts deliberately limited his best pitcher to only two starts after he won his 18th game because he did not want a black man to win 20, that seems far-fetched if for no other reason than winning the pennant would have been a crowning achievement for Birdie Tebbetts. In only his third season as a major-league manager since taking his place in the Cincinnati dugout in 1954, guiding a team long mired in the second division to a pennant would have been a big boost for his career—including for the presumed inevitable day when he would be looking for another managerial opportunity.

Furthermore, there is absolutely no evidence to suggest Tebbetts was deep down a bigot, let alone that he made any managerial decisions based on racial considerations, including those involving Chuck Harmon and Bob Thurman as regulars in his lineup or not. Frank Robinson, moreover, thought it would have been entirely out of character for Tebbetts to deny Lawrence a shot at 20 wins just because he was black. In any case, it was not as though a black pitcher had not already won 20 games; Don Newcombe had been a 20-game winner in 1951 and 1955, and was on his way to 27 wins in 1956, which his Brooklyn teammates happily rode to the National League pennant.

There is of course another possible explanation with a racial element, and that is that even in the 10th year of Jackie Robinson's career, major-league baseball was still grappling with racial stereotypes and misperceptions. These included the insidious canard, based on either outright prejudice or complete ignorance and too little exposure to blacks at any level of professional competition, that black players—and maybe especially pitchers—did not have what it takes in terms of dedication, discipline, or focus to be counted on in the crucible of high-stakes pressure, like a pennant race.

Now to be sure, no major-league manager would have taken his best starting pitcher during the season out of the rotation in the final weeks with a pennant at stake, unless he was hurt, or in more recent times, because of innings limits on tender and presumably fragile young arms.

Did Tebbetts do so because Lawrence was black? Perhaps Tebbetts did not trust Lawrence's competitiveness with so much on the line, maybe because he was a black man? If his best starting pitcher had *not* been black, would Tebbetts have removed him from the starting rotation because he was 3–9 with a 4.66 earned run average in his 12 starts since starting the season 13–0?

Aye, therein perhaps is the rub. Other researchers and writers have pointed out that because Lawrence had not been pitching particularly well—actually, not well at all—Birdie Tebbetts may have had a very good baseball reason as manager to shy away from Lawrence in his rotation down the September stretch. In fact, after being the Reds' *best* starting pitcher the first four months of the year, Brooks Lawrence—by the numbers at least—was their *least effective* starter in the last two months. In nine starts in August and September, Lawrence had a 2–7 record and an ERA of 5.88 while averaging only 5⅓ innings per start.

When Lawrence shut down the Pirates, 6–1, on July 29, his record stood at 15–2 and his earned run average at 3.32. He had also thrown 151⅔ innings after only 96 innings pitched the previous year, when the Cardinals used him primarily in relief, and was only 7 innings shy of the total he had thrown in his rookie season of 1954. And there were still two months to go. *And* the schedule was heading into the hottest month of the year.

Lawrence lost all six of his starts in August, although he did have back-to-back "quality starts" on August 16 and 20, allowing only three earned runs in eight innings both times. His one victory came in relief against the Cubs on August 9, his record now at 16–4. In his ten appearances in August, four as a reliever, Lawrence had gone 1–6 with a 5.89 ERA—hardly numbers to inspire confidence in his manager as the Reds headed into the September stretch run of a tightly contested three-team race, trailing the Braves by 3½ and the Dodgers by one.

But however badly Lawrence was pitching, he had not missed a turn in Tebbetts's rotation, and he was still in turn when he started against Chicago on September 1 and threw a four-hit masterpiece for his first victory as a starting pitcher in more than a month. Rather than Tebbetts's losing confidence in his best pitcher (though he had been struggling of late), it seems more likely, based on the record of game logs, that Lawrence's disappearance from the rotation for most of the final month was the result of Tebbetts's decision to use him for seven innings in relief in a must-win game against the first-place Braves on September 3 with only one day of rest after his complete-game victory against the Cubs.

The Reds had lost the first game of their doubleheader in Milwaukee that day, putting them temporarily four and a half games behind the Braves, and their 5–2 lead in the bottom of the third seemed in grave jeopardy when Cincinnati starter Larry Jansen loaded the bases with nobody out and Hank Aaron and Eddie Mathews, both dangerous hitters, the next two up for Milwaukee. If Tebbetts did not trust Lawrence's competitiveness and ability to get outs, this would not have been the time or place to bring him into the game, especially on one day of rest. This was, after all, a game that meant the difference between Cincinnati's leaving Milwaukee 3½ games out, but still in the pennant chase, if they could hang onto their lead, or 5½ down—almost certainly too big a difference to make up with only 22 games remaining—if they lost.

And it is not as though Tebbetts did not have other options. Both of Cincinnati's principal relief pitchers that year—Hersh Freeman and Joe Black—were available and well rested. Neither had pitched in a week, not since August 26. Freeman was the team's relief ace, with an 11–4 record and 10 saves so far in 48 games. But he had not been pitching especially well since Tebbetts had used him for eight innings over three consecutive days at the end of July. In only 8⅓ innings pitched, Freeman had a 9.72 earned run average in August. Black had not pitched well since June, giving up 15 runs in 19⅔ innings in July and August. Beset by arms problems, Black would pitch only 10 more games in his big-league career—only three in 1956 for the Reds—while Freeman recovered to finish the season strong, pitching in 16 September games with an outstanding 1.23 ERA. But Freeman's excellent September did not begin this day.

Because it was only the third inning, Tebbetts also could have called on right-hander Art Fowler to try to get Cincinnati out of this bases-loaded jam. Fowler had started 20 games through July—one fewer than Lawrence and Klippstein—but had started only twice since then while pitching six times in relief. Having been used as a starter, and also not having pitched in four days since working six shutout innings in long relief on August 29 to beat the Giants, Fowler would have been a prime candidate to come in, minimize the damage, and go the rest of the way to save this crucial game for the Reds.

But instead, Tebbetts went to Brooks Lawrence, only two days after he had pitched a complete-game victory. Lawrence got out of that bases-loaded, no-out situation without giving up a run by getting Aaron on a short fly to left and Mathews to hit into a double play. He finished up by surrendering just three runs over the remaining six innings to win what was to this point—given the two-game swing the outcome of this game would determine—Cincinnati's most important game of the season.

* * *

Trailing by the same 3½ games they brought into the doubleheader, the Reds were still in the hunt, but using Lawrence in that second game threw Tebbetts's starting rotation out of alignment. Having thrown 16 innings in the space of three days, Lawrence needed recovery time. Tebbetts handled Lawrence *exactly* as if he were in the starting rotation; his next start came after four days of rest against the Cardinals. Lawrence pitched badly, however, taking the loss after giving up four runs in two innings.

Although his next start was not until a week later, Lawrence was still in Tebbetts's rotation—the Reds having played only four games between his starts, during which he pitched twice in relief. Lawrence's victory against the Pirates in what turned out to be his final start was not a work of art—he surrendered four runs in 6⅓ innings—but it pulled the Reds to within two games of the Braves and Dodgers, who were tied at the top.

Lawrence did not make another start, but the reason has nothing to do with Tebbetts not wanting him to win 20 games. Instead, the reason was almost certainly because Tebbetts used him in relief each of the next four days—meaning Brooks Lawrence pitched five days in a row beginning with what proved to be his final start of the year in Pittsburgh. And his relief appearances were all in crucial games for the Reds, each of which they had a chance to win—all of which they wound up losing.

After Lawrence's September 15 start in Pittsburgh, the Reds were off to Brooklyn for a two-game showdown with the Dodgers beginning the very next day. Winning both games was a priority for Tebbetts because that would have brought Cincinnati into a tie with Brooklyn; where the two teams would have been in the standings depended on how Milwaukee, also in New York, fared in its two games against the Giants. So when Cincinnati starter Joe Nuxhall gave up a pair of runs in the second inning and had a runner in scoring position, while getting only one out, Tebbetts was quick to remove him from the mound before the Dodgers' 2–0 lead became something worse. Knowing the pitcher's spot was due to lead off in the third, he called on Lawrence to get out of the inning. Lawrence did his job without allowing his inherited runner to score, but the damage was done, and the Reds were now three games behind.

Nuxhall's loss made beating the Dodgers the next day crucial, particularly because it was the last scheduled game of the season between the two teams. After the Reds scored three runs in the top of the ninth to tie the game, it was Brooks Lawrence time once again for manager Birdie Tebbetts. It was now Lawrence's game to win—which would have made it 20 wins for the black man—or lose. Pitching for a third consecutive day, Lawrence gave up a single and walk and had runners on second and third with two outs in the bottom of the ninth but got through the inning. Unfortunately, after Cincinnati failed to score in the top of the 10th, Carl Furillo scorched him for a leadoff, walk-off home run that gave Brooklyn the victory, Lawrence his 10th loss, and dropped the Reds to four games out of first place.

With 11 games left, time was running out, and every game was of crucial importance to the Reds, whose next stop was Philadelphia for a doubleheader the next day, September 18. After losing the first game, the Reds were in danger of being swept when they scored four in the eighth inning of the second game to cut the Phillies' lead to 5–4. In hopes of salvaging a split in the doubleheader to help keep his team relevant in the pennant race, it was Brooks Lawrence who Tebbetts wanted to keep the game in hand. Working for the fourth-straight day, however, Lawrence gave up two runs on a double, two walks (one intentional), and an untimely error on what should have been an inning-ending, no-runs-scoring double play. Cincinnati was now four and a half behind.

Lawrence pitched the day after that, too—September 19—entering the game with the Reds in the lead in the eighth inning with two outs and the Phillies having just scored a pair of runs off starting pitcher Johnny Klippstein to make the score 6–3. Lawrence walked into a situation where there were runners on first and third and he was facing the tying run at the plate in the person of Granny Hamner. Mercifully nearing the end of the worst season of his career, and hardly a power threat with four home runs, Hamner was batting only .224 when Lawrence took the mound to face him. Hamner, however, did have a hot hand, with two hits already in the game, one of them a triple, and two hits against the Reds the previous day. For the fourth day in a row, Tebbetts was asking Lawrence to get outs in a high-stakes situation, but now pitching for a fifth-consecutive day dating back to his last start—which was also the last time the Reds had won—Lawrence walked Hamner. The bases now loaded, Tebbetts replaced the tired Lawrence with Hersh Freeman, who got the final out of the inning and pitched a scoreless ninth to secure the victory and end the Reds' four-game losing streak. Brooks Lawrence got the next five days off.

The Reds' victory that day was the first of seven in a row that improbably brought them back to within striking distance of first-place Milwaukee when the Braves came to town on September 25 for a one-game makeup. With his team one and a half games out of first in a game that had to be won because there would only be two remaining on the schedule after this, Tebbetts had a last opportunity to start Lawrence when it might have made a difference. He chose instead to start Jansen, who imploded in the last major-league game he would ever pitch, giving up three runs in less than two innings. Lawrence did get into the game, pitching two shutout innings of mop-up relief with the Braves sitting on a 6–1 lead behind stingy ace Warren Spahn. The Reds' loss all but officially closed the books on their season. The Braves would have had to lose all three of their remaining games and the Dodgers lose three of their remaining four for Cincinnati to have any hope of the 1956 schedule ending in a playoff-forcing tie.

Why did Tebbetts not start Lawrence, who had not pitched in five days? The answer might be that, notwithstanding his intrepid relief effort against them on September 3, Lawrence had not pitched well against the Braves. He was 2–2 against Milwaukee with a 5.70 ERA—the worst against any team he faced at least 20 innings. Lawrence had lost each of his last two starts against Milwaukee, both in his horrid month of August, in which Braves hitters torched him for nine earned runs in 10⅓ innings. Or Tebbetts might have known or figured that Lawrence was at this point too dogged tired to pitch such an important game; his 217 innings of work were far more than in either of his two previous big-league seasons.

Either way, the bottom line seems clear: Cincinnati manager Birdie Tebbetts did not have an unsavory "racist" agenda for not starting Brooks Lawrence in more than three games down the September stretch. Nor did Tebbetts limit Lawrence's starts because he had not been pitching well of late. Instead, Brooks Lawrence appears to have remained Tebbetts's go-to pitcher when he needed him to be—pitching seven innings in relief on one day of rest to win the most important game of the season for the Reds to keep their pennant hopes alive on September 3 against the first-place Braves, and then four consecutive days in relief in mid-September when Cincinnati was struggling to stay in the pennant race. These actions of Birdie Tebbetts were surely a vote of confidence in Brooks Lawrence, his best pitcher, if ever there was one.

*   *   *

Birdie Tebbetts never again managed a team that came so close to a pennant. Lawrence again led an otherwise mediocre pitching staff in wins with a 16–13 record in 1957, and Frank Robinson had an even better year than in 1956, but the Reds were not in the pennant picture, finishing fourth. Cincinnati fared no better in 1958, causing Tebbetts, said by General Manager Gabe Paul to be a nervous wreck, to step down before the season was over.

Apparently missing the excitement of managing, notwithstanding the stress, Tebbetts descended from a front-office job with the Milwaukee Braves in late 1961 to rescue the team from the ministrations of Charlie Dressen, whose constant need to demonstrate his baseball brilliance and be in control of the action alienated a veteran team. After managing the Braves to a disappointing fifth-place finish the next year, Tebbetts moved on, accepting an offer to manage the struggling Cleveland Indians in 1963. Except for missing nearly half of the 1964 season recovering from a spring-training heart attack (hopefully having nothing to do with the quality of his team), Tebbetts stayed on the job in Cleveland until he was let go late in the 1966 season.

# FOURTEEN

## The Braves' New World

As age caught up with the core players on the Brooklyn Dodgers, the Milwaukee Braves were poised to begin their own extended dominance of the National League. The Braves had three of the greatest players in history in the midst of their best seasons—right fielder Hank Aaron, third baseman Eddie Mathews, and southpaw Warren Spahn as the ace of their pitching staff—and solid major-league players like Joe Adcock at first base, shortstop Johnny Logan, center fielder Bill Bruton, and catcher Del Crandall. Right-handers Lew Burdette and Bob Buhl teamed with Spahn to give Milwaukee the most formidable starting rotation in baseball at the time, and Don McMahon, emerging as a rookie in 1957, quickly became one of the top relievers in the game.

But most significantly, for those who might have argued that the success of the Dodgers, Giants, and even the Indians with integrated teams was almost entirely attributable to their having black players who just happened to be as good as some of the best of the white guys, the Milwaukee Braves had an answer by winning back-to-back National League pennants in 1957 and 1958, and were denied a three-peat only by virtue of losing a playoff to the Dodgers in 1959, with five blacks in key roles, only one of whom—Hank Aaron—was a standout player. Bill Bruton, who replaced the maligned Sam Jethroe in center field when the team moved from Boston to Milwaukee in 1953 and arrived a year before Aaron, had the most successful career of the others.

Although presented as 20 years old when he was being scouted, Bruton was actually four years older when he signed with the Braves in 1950. After three years refining his skills in their farm system, Bruton somewhat unexpectedly won the center-field job in the spring of 1953 over Jethroe, who the Braves had soured on, and Jim Pendleton, another black player acquired from the Dodgers' system who they had expected to take over the position.

Batting mostly leadoff because of his speed, Bruton started all but 10 of the Braves' games in his rookie season. He did lead the league in stolen bases, as he would each of the next two years, but Bruton did not—and never would—have a breakout season. His player value in his rookie year, as measured by wins above replacement, was that of a marginal major-league player, but Bruton remained the Braves' regular center fielder for eight years until he was traded to Detroit in December 1960.

The three most difficult years of Bruton's career with the Braves, ironically, were when they were the most successful. A horrific knee injury sustained in a collision trying to make a play on a bloop hit over the infield cost Bruton the second half of the 1957 season, including the World Series. Although dropped to seventh in manager Fred Haney's batting order, Bruton had started all but five of the Braves' games at the time he was injured—which is significant because when he returned the next year, Haney decided to platoon the left-handed-batting Bruton all the time. Bruton did have a history of struggling against southpaws and had been occasionally platooned before, particularly after Haney assumed Milwaukee's reins of command in June 1956. Haney did not start him in any games against lefty starting pitchers in 1958 and only nine in 1959. After Haney was gone, Bruton returned to the lineup every day in 1960 and batted .289 against left-handers, starters and relievers, who he faced in 68 games. His batting average for the year was .286.

Bill Bruton was never an All-Star. In his eight years with the Braves, 1953 to 1960, he averaged slightly better than two wins above replacement—a player value considered the bottom level of performance for a regular in a major-league lineup. According to similarity scores, Bruton's career arc in contemporary context was most similar to Pirates center fielder Bill Virdon and center fielder Jimmy Piersall over in the American League. Bruton was certainly a capable major leaguer, just like the countless players over the ages who are the backbone of the game. But he was black, and had the Braves so chosen, they probably could have found a white guy to play his position as a regular.

At the time of his injury in 1957, Bruton was one of only five black players who had played even as many as five consecutive years as a core regular on their team without being an elite player on the order of a Mays or Aaron. The other seven blacks who had done so were all elite players.

Wes Covington, in contrast to Bruton, was never more than a journeyman player in his 11 years in the major leagues. As a left-handed-batter, Covington was often platooned in left field, starting mostly against right-handed pitchers. Playing in as many as 100 games only once in his five years with the Braves from 1956 to 1960, Covington contributed a combined six wins above replacement in the two years Milwaukee won the pennant, with 21 home runs in 1957 and in 1958. The white contemporary player to whose career his is most similar was Cincinnati outfielder Jerry Lynch, another left-handed batter in the starting lineup primarily against right-handed pitchers.

The two other blacks on Milwaukee's pennant-winning teams were utility infielder Felix Mantilla, who played seven years for the Braves, but rarely as a regular and was always scuffling, and Juan Pizarro, who proved valuable as a reliever and spot starter for the Braves with a 17–12 record in 69 appearances from 1957 to 1959. Signed as a teenager, Mantilla was in his fifth minor-league season with 547 games of experience when he was called up to Milwaukee as a 21-year-old. During his time in Milwaukee, Mantilla's player value according to the WAR metric was typically below what a replacement-level player would have contributed to his team. His best seasons came later, with the Mets and Red Sox, after he left the Braves.

The Puerto Rican–born Pizarro, on the other hand, was a fast-track prospect who had a 23–6 record at the Single-A level in his first year of professional baseball and was called up to the major-league club after winning his first four decisions with the Braves' Triple-A affiliate in 1957. In his four years with Milwaukee, which also included parts of the 1958 and 1959 seasons in the high minor leagues, Pizarro never lived up to the burden of having been prematurely proclaimed the next Warren Spahn. (Well, they did have being left-handers in common.) Pizarro's pitcher value according to the WAR metric was barely above replacement level in his four years with Milwaukee, after which he went on to greater success and fame with the White Sox in the 1960s before arm injuries derailed his career.

\* \* \*

The Braves were a revelation in 1956, although not an unexpected one. Since moving to Milwaukee in 1953, the Braves had shed their losing ways to finish second, third, and second in their first three years in the Upper Midwest. Eddie Mathews, who broke in as a rookie with the Braves in their last year in Boston, was already making a strong case for being the best all-around third baseman in National League history. He had hit 40 home runs in each of the team's first three years in Milwaukee, including a league-leading 47 in 1953. Once Aaron was called up in 1954, he and Mathews gave the Braves one of the most dangerous middle-of-the-order tandems in major-league baseball. And Spahn was . . . well, Warren Spahn, good for about 33 starts and 20 wins nearly every year.

But the Braves got off to a bad start in 1956 and were barely over .500 and struggling in mid-June. The general consensus in Milwaukee by fans and the front office alike that the Braves were underachieving cost veteran manager Charlie Grimm his job. Grimm was clearly failing to meet expectations that the thirteen years and three pennants on his managerial resume at the time he assumed command of the Braves in Boston in 1952 would be sufficient to lead them to the pennant in their new promised land of Milwaukee. Fred Haney was promoted from the coaching staff to replace Grimm even though he had failed to move the Pirates out of last place in his three years managing in Pittsburgh from 1953 to 1955.

The revelation in 1956 was that the Braves were able to recover from the seemingly death-defying spiral of losing 12 of the 17 games they had played in June up to the time Grimm was let go. Milwaukee had just lost the first two of a four-game series in Brooklyn when Haney took charge, dropping them to 24–22 in fifth place. Even though Milwaukee was only 3½ games out of first, only because the five top teams were closely bunched, their recent struggles did not bode well for the immediate future. Spahn had a losing record at 4–6, Mathews was batting .247 with 10 home runs, and Aaron's average had plummeted from .351 at the end of May to .303 with only one home run so far in June.

In Haney's first day on the job at Ebbets Field, the Braves reversed course with a doubleheader sweep of second-place Brooklyn. These were the first two of eleven consecutive victories to start the Haney regime, and they vaulted Milwaukee into first place. After going 32–10 in Haney's first 40 days as manager, the reenergized Braves in late July held a 5½-game lead over the Cincinnati Reds and were 6 ahead of the Dodgers. On the threshold of taking command in the pennant race, however, they lost three of four to Brooklyn as July turned to August, and by the beginning of September, the Braves' lead had shriveled to 2½ over the Dodgers and 3½ over the Reds.

It was now a three-team race to the finish. Losing three of four at home to Cincinnati in early September reduced their lead to 1½ games, and a two-game split in Brooklyn a week later left the Braves up by one over the Dodgers with fifteen games remaining. They won only eight. The Braves went into St. Louis for their final three games of the season, nursing a one-game lead over the Dodgers. Winning two of three against the Cardinals, who had a losing record, would have clinched at least a tie for the pennant. Instead, they lost the first two games, were now a game behind, and could hope only for the best that a victory in their final game on the schedule would force the Dodgers into a playoff. The Braves did win, but so did Brooklyn, and Milwaukee missed out on the pennant by one game.

The Braves, however, had clearly established that for the foreseeable future they were going to be one of baseball's elite teams. Aaron led the league with 200 hits and a .328 batting average in 1956. Joe Adcock's 38 home runs were tied for second, and Mathews was right behind him with 37. Spahn had another 20-win season, which would be the first of six in a row—something only Ferguson Jenkins has done since—and was second in earned run average to his teammate, Lew Burdette. Both Burdette and Bob Buhl won 18.

The Braves were also a big hit with their fans. It had been four years since they left Boston, and for the fourth straight year in Milwaukee, the Braves led the major leagues in attendance. Two million had come to see them play for the third year in a row. No other National League team had ever broken the two million barrier, and only the Yankees, every year from 1946 to 1950, had done so more often.

\* \* \*

The future came as promised. The Braves won consecutive pennants by identical eight-game margins in 1957 and 1958. Theirs was a relatively soft dominance of the league, however. Milwaukee was the only team in the National League to win 90 games both seasons, and in 1958 there were only three teams—Pittsburgh and San Francisco were the others—that had winning records.

The 1957 pennant was the first for the franchise since 1948, back when they were the Boston Braves, and their 2.2 million fans were by far the most of any in major-league team, by 700,000 over the Yankees. The Braves took control by opening up a tight pennant race in August with a 10-game winning streak, and an 8-game streak with 12 left on the schedule put it away. Aaron had his breakout season, with a league-leading 44 home runs and 132 RBIs, to win the only MVP Award of his career. Mathews's 32 home runs were fifth in the league. Spahn's 21 wins, Buhl's 18, and Burdette's 17 gave the Braves three of the five National League pitchers with the most wins. They went on to stun the Yankees in the World Series that made Burdette and his three victories famous.

August was again the decisive month for the Braves in 1958, when their 23–11 record secured a comfortable 7½-game lead going into September. Mathews hit 31 home runs, third in the league, and Aaron had 30. Spahn won 22 games, Burdette won 20, and the two were third and fourth in ERA. Buhl was on the disabled list from mid-May until September and made only 10 starts all season, but veteran Bob Rush, rookie Carl Willey, and the youngsters Juan Pizarro (21 years old) and 22-year-old Joey Jay picked up the slack. This time, it was the Braves' turn to be stunned in the World Series as the Yankees overcame a three-games-to-one deficit to gain a measure of revenge for what happened to them in the previous Fall Classic.

Milwaukee was the favorite to make it three in a row in 1959. Slow to get untracked, the Braves began September in third place, three games back of the first-place Giants and one behind the unexpectedly competitive Dodgers. Their losing 42–44 record in June, July, and August proved costly in their quest for a return trip to the World Series. From the Fourth of July until one week before the end of the season, Milwaukee was in first place only one day. This time, unlike in 1956, Milwaukee played well in September, going 16–7, to finish the schedule tied with the Dodgers, forcing the National League's third best-of-three playoff to decide the pennant in 14 years.

After losing the first game at home, the Braves had a three-run lead the next day in Los Angeles, needing only three outs in the ninth to force a third, winner-take-all game. Burdette had already given up five runs in eight innings but took the mound to complete the game. That hope ended when the first three Dodgers to bat got hits, loading the bases with nobody out in the last of the ninth. Haney, in the first of two fateful pitching changes that inning, summoned Don McMahon to get the final three outs without giving up any more than two runs.

McMahon might have seemed the obvious choice because he was the Braves' relief ace and his 15 saves were tied for the most in the major leagues. But he had pitched three scoreless innings in relief the day before, had thrown eight innings in four games over the previous week, and was being pushed to the limits. McMahon immediately gave up a single that scored two runs and now the tying run was on third with still nobody out. Haney had seen enough of his relief ace after only one batter and called on the ace of his staff, *southpaw* Warren Spahn, in a rare relief appearance to pitch to *right-handed*-hitting catcher Joe Pignatano, who was due up. Dodger manager Walt Alston countered with another right-handed batter, the more dangerous veteran Carl Furillo, who pinch hit a sacrifice fly to tie the game. Three innings later, it was over for Milwaukee, on a throwing error by Felix Mantilla, who was now playing shortstop because Johnny Logan got hurt turning a double play in the seventh. There would be no three in a row for the Milwaukee Braves.

\* \* \*

Failing to capitalize on their core talent, the Milwaukee Braves in the second half of the 1950s were one of the great underachieving teams in history, notwithstanding consecutive pennants won by eight games each. They had an imposing lineup and probably the most formidable starting rotation in the league. (Warren Spahn, Lew Burdette, and Bob Buhl weren't exactly Greg Maddux, Tom Glavine, and John Smoltz on the end-of-the-20th-century *Atlanta* Braves, but they were tough to beat.) And with three of the greatest players in history—Aaron, Mathews, and Spahn—in the midst of some of their best seasons, it would not be unreasonable to believe the Braves should have won four consecutive pennants. The two they did not win—in 1956 and 1959—they were not eliminated until their last game. The 1959 Dodgers were certainly not as good, let alone better, than the Milwaukee Braves, although it was they who went to, and won, the World Series.

Milwaukee could have—and probably should have—won a third consecutive pennant in 1959. Much of the blame can be laid on the doorstep of manager Fred Haney. In his autobiography, *I Had a Hammer*, Hank

Aaron claimed the Braves might have won the pennant outright in 1959, instead of being forced into the playoff that they lost, had Felix Mantilla (admittedly, a close friend) been given a chance to win the second-base job because, with starting second baseman Red Schoendienst out for the year with tuberculosis, there was nobody better to play the position.

Acquired from the Giants in June 1957, Schoendienst was the final piece the Braves needed to establish themselves as the dominant team in the National League. Moving into the lead-off spot in the batting order and teaming with shortstop Johnny Logan to provide strong infield defense up the middle, his impact on Milwaukee winning the pennant was so significant that Schoendienst finished third in the 1957 MVP voting with eight first-place votes to nine for Aaron, who won the award. But when Schoendienst struggled to gain traction in the summer of 1958 after a good start to the season, a medical exam indicated the reason might be he was afflicted with tuberculosis, still a scourge to the health of the nation.

Schoendienst's continued convalescence in 1959 caused Haney to start seven different players at second base that year. Collectively, they hit a paltry .209. Their combined player value as measured by the WAR metric was more than two games *below* what a replacement-level player would have contributed to the team. Mantilla hit only .215 but started the second-most games at second base—44, one fewer than veteran Bobby Avila. After batting .333 in August, although with only 45 at bats, Mantilla was in Haney's starting lineup for most of September, including substituting at shortstop when Logan was injured late in the season. He batted .239 in the final month as the Braves made their pennant push.

Mantilla claimed in Aaron's book that Haney would not play five blacks at the same time unless he had no choice because of injuries. His accusation, and Aaron's insinuation, reflected the perception among black players that there was still—three years after Jackie Robinson retired—discrimination against blacks on the playing field despite their growing acceptance in the major leagues. When Red Sox manager Billy Jurges sent Pumpsie Green into the game as a pinch runner on July 20, 1959, every team had now integrated at the big-league level—although that did not necessarily mean they always had a black player on their roster. Jurges had replaced Pinky Higgins as manager just before the Fourth of July weekend, which is significant because Higgins had become notorious for his staunch opposition to having any black players on his roster.

Braves manager Haney was certainly not in Higgins's camp, and he did not follow his predecessor Charlie Grimm's inclination to take part in clubhouse banter with white players using belittling stereotypes aimed at black teammates, including even Aaron. The Braves in fact had more blacks on their roster in 1959 than any other major-league team except for the San Francisco Giants. Nonetheless, the issue of how many blacks in the game at any one time was too many, while rarely (if ever) discussed, was still bedeviling major-league baseball in the late 1950s. Five blacks on the field at the same time was an important threshold because it would mean that a *minority* of a team's players in the game were white at a time when segregation was still prevalent in the United States. The implicit quota of no more than four blacks on the field at any one time, said Mantilla, not only limited his own playing time but also meant Haney rarely used talented young pitcher Juan Pizarro when he and outfielders Aaron, Bill Bruton, and Wes Covington were in the game.

Given that Pizarro was sometimes hyped to be the next Warren Spahn, Mantilla's assertion would suggest Haney managed against the best interests of his team. An examination of the Braves' starting lineups does not, in fact, bear out Mantilla's suspicion. Pizarro made fourteen starts for Milwaukee in 1959, and in four of them he took the mound with four black players in the starting lineup behind him—usually Aaron, Bruton, Covington, and Mantilla or Lee Maye, whose big-league debut was in July—including as late in the season as September 10.

Aaron also believed Haney mismanaged his pitching staff that year, including by not giving budding-star pitchers Pizarro and Joey Jay, who would go on to have back-to-back 21-win seasons for Cincinnati in 1961 and 1962, more opportunities down the stretch drive. Because both were young and still learning their craft, Haney apparently preferred to rely on experienced pitchers whom he trusted, even if their arms were tired, rather than young pitchers who had yet to make their mark in the game. Spahn, Burdette, and Buhl accounted for 76 percent of the innings thrown by Milwaukee starting pitchers in the final month of the season and for 71 percent of Braves' starters innings and two-thirds of their team's total victories for the year.

* * *

In his *Bill James Guide to Baseball Managers,* James not only excoriates Haney for never settling on any one player to replace the ill-stricken Schoendienst, although he does not say Mantilla would necessarily have been the best answer, but also accuses Haney of foolishly using slugging Joe Adcock—who had 25 home runs and batted .292 in only 115 games that year—in a first-base platoon with Frank Torre, who hit all of one home run and batted .228. Right-handers started against the Braves in 117 games in 1959, and the left-handed batting Torre was the starting first baseman in 59 of them, even though the right-handed Adcock hit for a much higher average and far more power against righties than Torre. In some of the games Torre started, however, Adcock also started—but in left field after Covington suffered a season-ending injury in August.

Aside from the platooning of Adcock and Torre, Haney's batting or-der in 1959 can only be considered counterproductive. Haney had slugging third baseman Eddie Mathews batting second that year instead of his more logical third or fourth in the batting order, as in previous seasons. Aaron batted third, with Covington, Adcock, or Torre batting fourth and fifth. With Covington, Adcock, and Torre combining to hit a mere 33 home runs (25 by Adcock alone) and drive in only 154 runs in the power slots behind Aaron, second in the order was hardly the most appropriate spot in the lineup for a power hitter like Mathews, particularly since he led the majors in home runs with 46 and was fifth in the league in RBIs with 114. Miller Huggins didn't bat Babe Ruth second. Connie Mack didn't bat Jimmie Foxx second. Joe McCarthy didn't bat Lou Gehrig or Joe DiMaggio second. Leo Durocher didn't bat Willie Mays second. Casey Stengel didn't bat Mickey Mantle second. And Fred Haney should not have batted Eddie Mathews second.

There seems every reason to suppose that the 1959 Braves would have won the pennant without a playoff, even if by only one game, had Mathews batted third in Haney's lineup instead of second. It is not as though the Braves did not already have an accomplished number-two hitter on the team—shortstop Johnny Logan. Logan had batted second for the Braves in 1955 and 1956, hitting .289 in that spot, after which Haney decided he liked Logan better batting much lower in the order. Seventh was his primary spot in 1959, a year in which he hit .291—the second-highest average of his career—and had his career-high in on-base percentage at .369, which was third on the team behind the sluggers Mathews and Aaron. Both of those numbers would have made him very effective batting second, with Mathews and Aaron behind him in the order.

This wasn't the first time Haney had such an unusual batting order. In 1957, after batting third or fourth in Haney's lineup the previous year, Hank Aaron (who had hit 26 home runs in 1956 and would lead the league with 44 in 1957) started the season batting second because, he was told by his manager, the Braves coming out of spring training had no other logical alternative for second in the order. That seemed a somewhat unusual explanation given that Logan had batted .272 hitting second in Milwaukee's lineup the previous year and .306 in the number-two spot the year before that. Haney decided he preferred Logan batting sixth to start the 1957 season, even if he had no other viable number-two hitter other than, apparently, Aaron. It wasn't until after Haney put Aaron back in the clean-up slot in early June for most of the remainder of the season that the Braves made their strong push toward their blowout pennant.

Aside from Haney's questionable decisions, however, the 1959 Braves had a fundamental structural deficiency that magnified his deficiencies as a manager. Their bench lacked depth. Notwithstanding the excellence of Aaron and Mathews and the solid performances of Adcock, Logan, Bruton, and catcher Del Crandall, Milwaukee was a team with largely marginal talent among position players on the bench. The collective player value of the Braves' core position regulars as measured by wins above replacement actually exceeded the team total. Most significantly for a team that finished just a hair's breadth short of the World Series, the Braves' most important role players—Torre (with 64 starts at first base), Covington (who platooned in left field), and Mantilla (whose versatility gave him 71 starts wherever he was needed), with nearly 1,000 plate appearances between them—all performed below the WAR standard for a replacement-level player.

\* \* \*

In 1960, Haney was gone as manager—having resigned shortly after the playoff defeat, never to manage again (although he was hired to be the first general manager of the American League–expansion Los Angeles Angels)—former Brooklyn manager Charlie Dressen was in, Mathews was back to hitting third and Aaron fourth, and Bruton was back to playing every day. But the Pirates got off to a fast start, the Braves to a slow one, and Milwaukee was unable to catch up.

Thus began the Braves' decline into the long-term mediocrity that went with them to Atlanta in 1966. Rather than Milwaukee tiring of the Braves, it was the franchise owners tiring of Milwaukee. Lou Perini, the Boston-based owner who brought the Braves to Milwaukee in the first place, had himself been planning to relocate the team to the South's most up-and-coming commercial metropolis when he sold the team to a new ownership group that followed through on Atlanta's interest in attracting a major-league team.

By bringing the game to the South, the Braves' move to Atlanta was a logical extensive of major-league baseball's expansionist imperative. But it occurred at a time when the states of the former Confederacy that fought to secede from the United States 100 years before over the issue of slavery were now fighting a last-ditch battle pushing back against the civil-rights movement. While the city of Atlanta itself had a sizeable and growing black population, the populous, largely white surrounding area that was expected to contribute the lion's share of the Braves' attendance was staunchly segregationist in their attitudes and lifestyle, and blacks, including in the city, had to contend with the indignities of often-blatant racism. Hank Aaron, as well as most of the other black players on the Braves, had serious misgivings about Atlanta, not the least being how their families would be treated in their day-to-day lives. While the governor of Georgia at the time the Braves made their move had cooperated with President Lyndon Baines Johnson in allowing new federal civil-rights laws to take effect in the state, his successor—Lester Maddox, an unapologetic segregationist—campaigned for governor in the Braves' very first year in Atlanta in 1966 on a platform opposing integration on the constitutional grounds of states' rights. He won the election.

The best years of Hank Aaron's career were in Milwaukee, but playing in Atlanta, he continued on as one of the best in baseball until age caught up with him at 40 in the early 1970s. He led the Braves to the National League Western Division title in 1969, the first year the two major leagues were divided into divisions. (Even though Atlanta and Cincinnati were east of St. Louis and Chicago, they were placed in the Western Division primarily so that the Cardinals–Cubs rivalry could be in the East, since the other great National League rivalry, Dodgers and Giants, was indisputably in the West.) Aaron broke Babe Ruth's career-home-run record in Atlanta.

Although he lacked the vivid intensity of Jackie Robinson on civil-rights issues, Hank Aaron's excellence as a ballplayer and community engagement in Atlanta was possibly just as instrumental in the dismantling of the South's segregationist infrastructure as anything else.

# FIFTEEN

## "Perfessor" Stengel's Controlled Chaos Theory of Platooning

Like the eccentric ole "perfessor" at the prestigious university who writes all over your honors thesis (because anything you say, he can say better), Casey Stengel did not mind messing up his lineup card by crossing out names and penciling in substitutes. He certainly didn't think about what a mess it made of the scorecards for those of us scoring in the bleachers or at home (listening to the sounds-of-summer voices of Mel Allen and Red Barber over the airwaves). Stengel frequently manipulated his lineup during games to get the offensive or defensive advantages he wanted. He was particularly aggressive in going for the jugular if he felt he could break a game open, even in the early or middle innings.

Perhaps most famously, in Game 1 of the 1960 World Series, Stengel pinch hit for his starting third baseman, Clete Boyer, in only the second inning because the Yankees were already losing 3–1, the Yankees' first two batters had both singled, putting the tying runs on base, and with nobody out against Pirates' ace Vern Law, the Ole Perfessor believed this was his first best shot not only at overcoming a very early deficit but also at taking command of the game and even the Series. Pinch hitter Dale Long made out, and Boyer, who would become a terrific defensive third baseman, got to play only one inning in the field—it being this game was in Pittsburgh, meaning the Yankees batted first.

Something like this had not been done in a World Series since way back in 1917 in Game 5 when in the very first inning New York Giants' manager John McGraw sent the left-handed half of his right-field platoon, Dave Robertson, up to pinch hit for the right-handed-batting Jim Thorpe—the former star Olympian—who started against lefties, because Chicago's left-handed starter, failing to get a single out, had already been replaced by a right-handed reliever. Unlike Boyer 43 years later, howev-

177

er, Thorpe did not even get the chance to play in the field since the Giants were the road team and this happened in the top of the first.

* * *

Not for nothing was Casey Stengel known as the "Ole Perfessor" when he was managing the Yankees. Stengel enjoyed giving rambling and often seemingly insensible expositions to the reporters covering the Yankees. If "Stengelese" needed translating, however, his remarks were nonetheless insightful, often with a telling point that he wanted to make. His use of language in this way also played to his image (which he no doubt was proud to cultivate) as a creative genius, not the clown (derived in part from his playing days) he might have seemed when he managed bad teams in the National League or even when he was first selected to manage the Joe DiMaggio–led Yankees in 1949 and was photographed looking into a crystal ball like some deranged seer of the paranormal.

Stengel did many things that seemed unorthodox—but it all worked. Creative genius. Of course, it's easier to be a creative genius when you're given a team with the talent of the New York Yankees in the 1950s than when you're managing the mid-1930s Brooklyn Dodgers or the late-1930s-early-1940s Boston Braves. But perhaps it can be harder, too, because being creative with good talent can be risky if it doesn't work out or (more pointedly) blows up in your face.

One cannot argue with success. Casey Stengel won 10 American League pennants and 7 World Series in his 12 years as Yankee manager. And the first four of those were with a team that was perhaps *not even* the best in the American League in any of those seasons—except, of course, at the end of the year, when it counted the most. A distinguishing characteristic of Stengel's Yankees was how very effective he was in using his entire roster of players, except for third-string catcher Ralph Houk. He was a master at juggling players in and out of the lineup, at substituting for starting position players during games, at finding the right combination of players to win games . . . and pennants, including in down-to-the-wire races . . . and World Series.

Stengel wrote only a handful of names into the lineup on a daily basis during the 1950s—Mickey Mantle in center field, Yogi Berra at catcher, Gil McDougald somewhere in the infield, and Phil Rizzuto at shortstop until 1954. And his regulars, including those he platooned in the starting lineup, did not always know where in the batting order they would hit. Stengel was notoriously fickle in his choice of leadoff and second-place hitters, switching them frequently in his batting order, unlike most managers who preferred more stability from one game to the next at the top of the order.

Call it managing his lineup by controlled chaos. Stengel used many lineup variations, starting different players at any one position on different days in different places in the batting order. And he thought nothing about pinch hitting for his starting position players if he perceived an advantage for doing so. Examining Casey Stengel's lineup card in the 10 World Series he managed against 7 different National League pennant-winning managers—Burt Shotton, Eddie Sawyer, Leo Durocher, Charlie Dressen, Walt Alston, Fred Haney, and Danny Murtaugh—illustrates the point.

Stengel used a different combination of players leading off and batting second in 39 of the 63 World Series games he managed, including a different one-two setup in each of the seven games of the 1960 World Series. His opposing managers used only 16 different pairs leading off and batting second, and in 6 of the 10 World Series, the NL champion's first and second hitters in the lineup batted in exactly the same order in every game. Only Milwaukee Braves manager Haney in both the 1957 and 1958 Series used more than two combinations in the first two spots of the order (he used three), and in 1957, he did so only because of an injury to his leadoff batter and second baseman, Red Schoendienst.

While his National League opponents did not substitute for any starting position player in 31 of those 63 World Series games, Stengel managed only 18 games in which he *did not* replace someone in his starting lineup. In the 1950, 1957, and 1960 Series, there was not a single game in which Stengel did not make at least one position substitution with either a pinch hitter, pinch runner, or defensive replacement, and in two other World Series, there was only one game when he did not substitute for a regular player. Stengel used a pinch hitter for a position player 26 times in the World Series, compared to 20 times by the National League manager.

It wasn't as though Stengel hadn't done all this before in his nine years as a National League manager with the Dodgers and Braves. As he showed abundantly with the Yankees, Stengel even then valued versatile players who could play different positions because of the flexibility they gave him in setting his lineup and making player substitutions during games. Stengel rarely employed a lefty–righty platoon at any one position, but he made significantly more position-player substitutions during games than other managers. Now, it might be said that Stengel made as many position substitutions as he did back then because his teams were so bad—desperate ploys by a desperate manager, please work, please! But since this same strategy worked so well for him as manager of the far-more-talented 1950s Yankees—notwithstanding the hard feelings he often caused among his players—it would be better to say that Stengel was always looking for an advantage by playing the percentages, or playing hunches.

\* \* \*

The most important master narrative of Casey Stengel's place in history is arguably that his ever-changing starting lineups and batting orders brought back the art of platooning from some sort of baseball-strategy purgatory. In fact, however, platooning had already regained credibility with major-league managers by the time Stengel first set foot in the Yankee dugout. What he did was akin to the role of a radical revolutionary, or at least a "mad scientist" (to stick with the persona that baseball writers loved about him), by taking the concept of platooning to unprecedented extremes. In so doing, Casey Stengel gave the practice a visibility unmatched since Boston Braves manager George Stalling introduced the concept in 1914. In both cases, it was the drama of their success—the compelling narrative of the 1914 "Miracle" Braves, last on the Fourth of July to improbable World Series sweep, and the Stengel Yankees winning year after year after year—that ratified platooning as a strategy for winning.

At the beginning of the 20th century, managers rarely replaced anyone in the starting lineup during a game. The players rounding out the roster who sat on the bench were there more for emergencies—to substitute for an injured regular, to give a regular an occasional day of rest, or to take over if the incumbent was ineffective—than for inclusion in the game at crucial moments. Even pinch hitting was rare because pitchers for the most part finished what they started and typically would not be taken out of close ball games in the late innings even if they were losing. Teams that were generally favored by the baseball gods with good health and few injuries would rely on no more than ten or eleven position players who would receive nearly all of the playing time—the four regular infielders, three regular outfielders, typically two catchers, and one or two bench players to fill in where necessary. The wear and tear inherent in playing the position made catcher the *only* position on the field that managers routinely shared between two men.

Many teams, however, had one versatile player—like Honus Wagner in Pittsburgh, before he became the regular shortstop, or Roger Bresnahan in New York with the Giants—who could adeptly play multiple positions in the infield and outfield (or even catcher, in the case of Bresnahan) and were in the starting lineup on a daily basis, though not necessarily at the same position. If a team was truly blessed, its bench players might see hardly any action at all. The 1906 Chicago Cubs, who set the record for regular-season wins with 116, had only three position players aside from their eight starting regulars appear in more than five games, including their second-string catcher, just two of whom had more than 100 plate appearances.

John McGraw was ahead of his time in using his bench strategically in games. From almost as soon as he took over as Giants manager in July 1902, McGraw began pinch hitting and pinch running for selected position players at a key moment in the game, even if it meant he would need a defensive replacement in the field for subsequent innings. Other managers were slow to follow his lead, but by the early to mid-1910s, position substitutions had gained currency among managers as a strategy to help win games. But even McGraw at this point in his managerial career was unwilling to take the tactical "platoon" advantage he often sought during a game to the next step—"platooning" in his starting lineup. McGraw still preferred a set daily lineup regardless of who was pitching for the other side. Platooning position players was virtually nonexistent at the time, even for catchers, most of whom did not play every day.

It was George Stallings who took the tactical advantages of position-player substitutions to their logical conclusion. If replacing a position player was a savvy managerial move to gain a "platoon" advantage against the opposing pitcher (whether the starter or a reliever) in the course of a game, then it made sense to seek such an advantage at a position of weakness—which, for Stallings, was his entire outfield—in the starting lineup by platooning a left-handed with a right-handed batter, depending on from which side the starting pitcher threw. Stallings's adoption of the strategy at the start of the 1914 season was almost certainly making a virtue out of a necessity because nearly all of the Braves' outfielders were marginal major-league players. His master manipulation of all the Braves' outfielders helped his team rise from the ashes of last place in July to not only steal the pennant decisively from McGraw's three-time defending National League champion Giants but also stun Connie Mack's powerful Philadelphia Athletics in a World Series sweep, and other managers took notice.

Platooning was an obvious strategy for mediocre or bad teams trying to compensate for the weaknesses of individual players. But while it was not intuitively obvious that managers of very good teams would find much merit in platooning, every team, even the good ones, had at least one position of relative weakness in their lineup. Managers with much stronger cohorts of players than Stallings had with the Braves were quick to see the value of platooning to take advantage of their comparative strengths and, perhaps more importantly, to mitigate batters' weaknesses, such as an inability to hit southpaws. Starting with Stallings's 1914 Braves, either one or both teams in every World Series until 1926 had at least one position-player platoon during the regular season. They included all four of McGraw's pennant-winning teams from 1921 to 1924. Casey Stengel was platooned in the outfield on three of those World Series teams—the 1916 Dodgers and 1922 and 1923 Giants.

Platooning was widespread in the major leagues in the 1920s with half of all the teams that took the field that decade having at least one position-player platoon. The overwhelming majority of lefty–righty position platoons were in the outfield. With the exception of first base, platooning in the infield was relatively uncommon—and very rare in the middle infield positions—both because most infielders in that era were right-handed batters and because managers desired daily stability at such premium defensive-skill positions. But unlike Stallings, who had more of an inchoate mix-and-match philosophy for platooning in his outfield, most managers relied on a designated tandem pair who split the position between them, which was important not only to provide a semblance of stability in the lineup but also so that players understood their roles in the scheme. Of course, players' understanding their role is not the same as agreeing with such a division of their playing time. Bill James writes in *The Bill James Guide to Baseball Managers* that their understandable resentment about the implication they lacked the ability to be in the lineup every day contributed to platooning's becoming less prevalent by the end of the decade. The same downward trend was also true for in-game position-player substitutions.

The practice did not die out so much as diminish in importance as a strategy for gaining the "platoon" advantage by playing the percentages from the very beginning of every game. American League managers were more disposed toward platooning than their National League counterparts, with one-third of all AL teams taking the field in the 1930s using at least one platoon, compared to only one-fourth of NL teams. While several of the teams that platooned most often—the Washington Senators, St. Louis Browns, and Brooklyn Dodgers—probably used the strategy as a fallback to compensate for their lack of quality players, the 1930s were also notable for the number of pennant-winning teams in each league that did platoon.

Every National League champion from 1930 to 1935 used a position-player platoon—all in the outfield—as did six of the eight American League pennant winners between 1933 and 1940. The Yankees had a traditional lefty–righty platoon in at least one outfield position for all or a significant part of each of their four consecutive pennant-winning seasons from 1936 to 1939.

Even the managers who did platoon backtracked on position-player substitutions in the 1930s. With the qualified exception of Joe McCarthy in his first four years as Yankee manager from 1931 to 1934, "qualified" because he had to accommodate the aging, overweight Babe Ruth's inability to play nine innings day in and day out, managers made the fewest in-game substitutions for starting position players since the beginning years of the 1910s. Part of the decline was attributable to major-league rosters being cut from 25 to 23 players to reduce player-payroll expenditures when the Great Depression was at its worst, which left managers with fewer bench players they could substitute into games. It may also have reflected a change in philosophies, since the 1930s were also a decade when managers became relatively conservative in their approach to the game.

The merits of having a platoon advantage were not lost in the dustbin of the Great Depression, however, particularly at positions where the player most likely to be the full-time regular was an inexperienced rookie or had significant difficulties, most often left-handed batters against southpaws. Position platoons began increasing in number in the late 1930s and early 1940s, a trend that continued through and picked up after World War II. When left-handed-batting Enos Slaughter had difficulty hitting southpaws early in the 1940 season, the Cardinals decided to use him in a platoon, even though "Country" was already an established star. In 1942, they platooned rookie left-handed-batting Stan Musial, who began playing every day with great success the next year and finished his career with a .318 average against southpaws.

Although the two leagues were mostly in sync in their use of position platoons, National League managers in the 1940s were far more inclined to substitute as a strategy during games. In the American League, by contrast, even those managers who used platoons were still apt to stay with their starting position player the whole game despite game situations—such as a pitching change—that might suggest a substitution to gain an advantage in the batter–pitcher matchup.

* * *

By the time Casey Stengel came to New York, neither platooning nor pinch hitting and substituting for position players were strategies in need of rediscovery. Just as "Miracle Manager" Stallings is considered the godfather of platooning, so Casey Stengel is perceived as bringing those strategies back to respectability and the mainstream in a manager's toolkit after a long hiatus. While Stallings's "godfather" role is generally accurate, Stengel's genius about platooning was more unique to how he did so than to his being at the forefront in reviving the practice. Stengel perfected the art of manipulating his roster to win games and brought platooning to a new level of sophistication that, by the end of the decade, was widely employed by other managers.

When the Yankees were winning five-and-five-in-five, Stengel platooned at several positions in his starting lineup, including having an outfield platoon similar to George Stallings's concept of multiple outfielders rotating among the positions. In Stengel's case, center field was the one stable position in the Yankee outfield whenever DiMaggio and his successor Mantle were not injured. Hank Bauer, Gene Woodling, Tommy Henrich, Johnny Lindell, Cliff Mapes, Mantle (in his rookie year of 1951), Jackie Jensen, and Irv Noren shared the corner outfield positions at various times from 1949 to 1953, although Bauer in right and Woodling in left started by far the most often. In the latter half of the decade, with Mantle still the constant in center field, it was Noren, Bob Cerv, Elston Howard, Norm Siebern, Enos Slaughter, and Hector Lopez taking turns in left field for Stengel; some among them also platooned with Bauer in right.

Stengel also began platooning catchers in 1957, starting the right-handed Howard in many games against southpaws to give left-handed-batting Yogi Berra more days off. One of baseball's best clutch hitters and a good defensive catcher, Berra had averaged over 142 games a year behind the plate between 1950 and 1956, a grueling workload in a 154-game season for a catcher, and at 32 years old, Yogi was beginning to wear down. The 121 games he caught in 1957 were the most for Berra from then until the end of his career.

Meanwhile, Stengel was perfectly OK with change—and lots of it—in his infield. Most managers prefer stability in their infield, especially at the high-defensive-skill positions—second base, shortstop, and third base. With the exception of Rizzuto, until Stengel decided by 1953, with evidence from performance, that the Yankees' now 35-year-old diminutive shortstop was losing his edge, the Yankee infield during Stengel's managerial tenure was always unsettled. In any given year, Stengel might decide on someone as his first baseman, second baseman, shortstop, or third baseman for the year—and stay with him (mostly)—but that was no guarantee for the next season, and Yankee infielders often were not on the field at the end of games they started because of Stengel's penchant for pinch hitting and lineup manipulations to take advantage of scoring opportunities or in response to pitching changes.

Stengel never used one player at first base for more than 120 games in a season until 1960, when Bill Skowron played 142 games at the position. Every year before that, two or sometimes three players shared the position, and except for 1954 and 1955 with the left-handed-batting Joe Collins and the right-handed-batting Skowron, they were not part of a traditional platoon. In 1950 and 1951, the Yankees famously employed Collins and the veteran Johnny Mize at first, even though both were left-handed batters, and Stengel often substituted one for the other in games.

The Yankees had a rotating cast at second base during the Stengel era, sometimes because of matters beyond his control—like the draft. Jerry Coleman was Stengel's primary second baseman from 1949 to 1951, until he was drafted during the Korean War. Stengel-favorite Billy Martin claimed the position as his own the next two years, until he too was drafted. Coleman's effort to get his starting job back after two years away in 1954 foundered on a .217 batting average, which led Stengel to shift the versatile Gil McDougald to second base. Unlike Coleman, Martin reclaimed his position upon being mustered out of the army in 1956, but Billy the Kid's after-game escapades with Mantle and Whitey Ford led to his being traded away in early 1957, ostensibly for being a bad influence on them (but mostly to break up the trio, and Mantle and Ford were far too good not to forgive their after-hours foibles). Stengel began easing Bobby Richardson into the position even before Martin was traded, but it was not until June 1959 that Richardson secured his hold on the position. Richardson's light bat, however, made him a prime candidate to be pinch hit for in game-on-the-line circumstances, and he was in at the end of the game in only 100 of the 133 he started at the position in 1960.

The Yankees had a third-base platoon virtually every year of Stengel's tenure. His first two years, Stengel used a traditional platoon with righty Billy Johnson and the young "Doctor" Bobby Brown (who later became a real doctor and, later still, American League president), a left-handed batter, both there when he arrived, sharing the position. After Johnson was traded away and Brown got drafted for the Korean War (which effectively ended Brown's baseball career, especially since his professional track was to be a surgeon), Stengel had a different third baseman seemingly every year, the most notable of whom were Gil McDougald and Andy Carey. His last three years directing the action, Stengel mostly mixed and matched at third with Clete Boyer getting the most starts at the position in 1960.

Because DiMaggio had entered the twilight of his career and was frequently injured and Berra was still proving himself, the only position Stengel did not have to worry about when he took over in the Bronx was shortstop. The incumbent, Phil Rizzuto, was a defensive gem, and after Stengel moved him from the bottom of the order—where Bucky Harris had him—to batting either first or second, he became a cornerstone player on the five-and-five-in-five Yankees. While still the Yankee shortstop in 1953, starting in 132 games, Rizzuto was now 35, and Stengel began to pinch hit for him with some frequency, leaving the "Scooter" on the bench having to watch backup Willy Miranda finish the game at his position.

The end of Rizzuto's playing career came relatively quickly after that. The Scooter lost his starting shortstop job to Miranda in August 1954 because he wasn't hitting, and two years later, seldom used, he was unceremoniously dismissed from the Yankees. After Miranda and Billy Hunter failed to impress, Stengel turned to the all-purpose McDougald to play shortstop in 1956, although his own injuries and Yankee needs at second base limited him to only 88 starts at short. McDougald paved the way for Tony Kubek to ultimately take over as the Yankee shortstop Stengel handed off to his successor.

\* \* \*

Creative, controlled chaos in the infield when the Yankees were winning all those championships worked for Casey Stengel. It was called "platooning," but it was not platooning in the traditional sense because most of Stengel's infielders were, as is typical, right-handed batters. As Stengel moved his infielders in and out of the lineup and around to different positions, he played hunches, played the hot hand, played what he thought would work. And work it did.

It worked in large part because of his genius as a manager in making the most of game situations to exploit scoring opportunities. It worked in some part because of necessity—the U.S. Selective Service, for example, claiming Coleman, Martin, and Brown or age claiming Rizzuto. It worked in part because he had players like McDougald who accepted the merits of being able to play multiple positions, although some were not at all happy about it. It worked in no small measure because the New York Yankees had good enough ballplayers to make it work. And it worked because Stengel had an excellent appreciation of his players' abilities. This last is an important point because Collins, Martin, Coleman, Carey, Richardson, and Kubek were not star players or the best in the league at their positions. They were good, but it was Stengel's genius to know when and where to play them.

Stengel prized redundancy. He liked having a roster of infielders who could play multiple positions and would rotate them according to his needs from year to year, within seasons, even within games. More significant than his willingness to change his starting infielders over the course of a season, which by itself is historically unusual for a highly competitive team, was Stengel's substituting for his starting infielders during games to an extent unprecedented in baseball history. Stengel wanted the flexibility to pinch hit for them whenever the situation called, sometimes even in early innings, while being secure in the knowledge that replacing them in the field would degrade neither his infield defense nor, for that matter, offensive capacity for later in the game. Until the inventive Ole Perfessor upended the equation (and, for the most part, even after), managers had been traditionally loathe to remove their starting infielders from the game, at least not until their expected last at bat in a losing cause, precisely because infielders are the core of a team's defense. Stengel believed such a conservative approach interfered with the task at hand—which was winning games.

Gil McDougald was the model. McDougald could, and did, play anywhere in the field, always fielding his position well and remaining a dangerous hitter all the while. As a rookie in 1951, McDougald alternated between second and third, playing in what was effectively a three-player platoon. Stengel started the right-handed-batting McDougald at second and the left-handed Brown at third when a right-hander took the mound and McDougald at third and the right-handed Coleman at second, with Brown on the bench, when the opposing pitcher was a southpaw. In 10 years and 1,336 major-league games—all with the Yankees and all with Stengel as his manager—McDougald played 599 games at second, 508 at third, and 284 at short; in 55 of those games, he played more than one position.

Coleman, Martin, Kubek, Richardson, and Boyer were capable of playing any infield position. And Stengel always had other versatile players capable of playing multiple positions, including Collins (first base and outfield), Howard (catcher, outfield, and first base), Hector Lopez (third base and outfield), and even Berra, who began playing some outfield in the late 1950s to keep his bat in the lineup when he was given an occasional break from the rigors of constant crouching and being banged up by batted balls as a catcher.

This was not the managerial philosophy of the next two Yankee managers, Ralph Houk from 1961 to 1963 and Yogi Berra in 1964, both of whom got to watch Stengel closely and had observed the disgruntlement of Yankee infielders under the Ole Perfessor's theory of controlled chaos. After more than a decade of seeming instability in the Yankees' infield, there was no doubt about the starting regulars at every infield position for every game from 1961 through 1964, all pennant-winning years— Skowron (1961 and 1962) followed by Joe Pepitone (1963 and 1964) averaged 138 starts at first base, Richardson started a minimum of 150 games each year at second, and Boyer averaged 138 games starting at third. The only infield position that might have seemed unsettled was shortstop; it was Kubek's position, however, and he started 145 games there in 1961 and 132 in 1963, with military service in 1962 and injuries in 1964 limiting his playing time those years. More significantly, neither Houk nor Berra made many infield substitutions. Stability had returned to the Yankees' infield.

\* \* \*

While his constant manipulation of the starting lineup and batting order brought platooning back to prominence, Casey Stengel's greater legacy— because traditional platooning was already making a comeback—was being at the leading edge of a paradigm shift in which position-player substitutions became a new currency in game management. During his 12 years at Yankee Stadium, Stengel substituted for his starting position players with an abandon unprecedented in baseball history.

His first two years at the Yankee helm, Stengel made more than double the league average of position substitutions by the seven other American League teams. By 1951, quite likely influenced by the Ole Perfessor's example, in-game substitutions by the seven other American League clubs increased by nearly 30 percent but were still only half the number made by Stengel—244—the most ever by any manager in either league, breaking Leo Durocher's mark of 229 with the 1946 Dodgers. In 1953, when his Yankees dominated the pennant race from beginning to end, Stengel made 242 position-player substitutions and followed that up with 286—a new record—in 1954.

To personalize the historical in a Yankees context, Joe McCarthy made an average of only 45 position substitutions a year as Yankee manager from 1936 to 1945. Red Rolfe played every single inning of every game at third base for McCarthy in 1939, Joe Gordon did the same at second in

1940, and Nick Etten at first and Snuffy Stirnweiss at second played every inning of every game in 1944. Nobody ever played every single inning of every game for Casey Stengel. In 1949, while Stengel was making a seemingly extreme 197 position substitutions in games, McCarthy as manager of the Red Sox, who lost out to the Yankees by only one game, made only 26 position substitutions all year, and 14 of those were behind the plate. The position players in McCarthy's lineup were in at the end of 98 percent of the games they started, compared to 85 percent for Stengel's starting position players.

It had not always been thus for McCarthy. In each of his first three years in New York, 1931 to 1933, McCarthy substituted more than any other manager, and in 1934, only Brooklyn's rookie manager—Casey Stengel—made more. But close to half of McCarthy's substitutions were because Babe Ruth, although still a great player, was no longer capable of playing nine innings on a daily basis. To keep his power and charismatic presence in the lineup, McCarthy would take the Babe out of many games in the late innings, especially if the Yankees were ahead. In his last four years with the Yankees, which happened to be McCarthy's first four as their manager, Ruth finished only 52 percent of the games he started. Once Ruth was gone, McCarthy rarely made substitutions during games and was soon making significantly fewer than the major-league average.

Phil Rizzuto was Stengel's Ruth, although the circumstances were very different. Notwithstanding Rizzuto's excellence as the best shortstop in the American League when the Yankees won the first four of their pennants for Stengel with his playing nearly every day and rarely being taken out of games, by 1953 the Perfessor determined it was time to account for his shortstop's 35 years on planet Earth by relieving him of the burden of playing complete games. Although he had another very good year and finished sixth in the MVP voting in 1953, Rizzuto was still in the game for the final pitch in only 91 of the 132 games he started, almost always because Stengel chose to pinch hit for him. It was even more frustrating for Rizzuto (not getting any younger) in 1954, when he appeared in 126 games at short, of which he started only 97 and played a complete game only 50 times.

While Willy Miranda is not somebody one thinks of when thinking "1950s New York Yankees," he more than admirably served Stengel's purpose as a defensive replacement when Stengel pinch hit for Rizzuto, usually when he was due up in the last third of the game, for the purpose of getting some (more) runs. Miranda finally got his chance to be the starting Yankee shortstop in mid-August 1954, when the Scooter's batting average stood at .202 and the Yankees were only three games behind the Indians in their quest for a sixth-straight pennant. Rizzuto became *his* defensive replacement, coming into 19 games after Stengel had removed Miranda, himself a weak hitter, for a pinch hitter. Stengel started Rizzuto at shortstop in just three games the entire rest of the season, all three in

September after Cleveland had taken command of the pennant race. The next two years, Rizzuto started in only 58 of the 277 games the Yankees played before he was released in late August 1956 to make room for Enos Slaughter, a veteran claimed off waivers for his hitting prowess.

Unlike Ruth, who knew he was king of the roost and was perfectly OK with enjoying the accolades for two-thirds of a game and retiring for the day to rest his weary legs, Rizzuto resented being pulled for a pinch hitter, as did most of Stengel's Yankees who found themselves similarly afflicted. Casey Stengel no doubt valued and was grateful for Phil Rizzuto's contributions to his five-and-five-in-five Yankees—the Scooter's defense alone made the difference in the outcomes of four pennants that were not won until the final week—but no sentimentalist was the Old Man. The combination of frequently being removed for a pinch hitter and playing 81 games as a defensive replacement limited Rizzuto to an average of only 2.6 plate appearances in the 239 games he played in his last three seasons.

The Ole Perfessor's seemingly magic touch daring to pinch hit so often for selected starting position players—*selected* because you don't pinch hit for DiMaggio, Berra, Mantle, or even McDougald—and substituting for them in the field with highly capable replacements, validated the utility of position-player substitutions as a strategy to gain an advantage that could be instrumental in winning ball games. It wasn't popular with his players and would certainly have provoked more controversy and second-guessing had his pinch hitters not come through so often. Stengel always had a premier veteran left-handed power hitter on the bench to use in a pinch—Charlie Keller in 1949, Tommy Henrich in 1950, Johnny Mize from 1951 to 1953, Eddie Robinson the next two years, and later there were Enos Slaughter (late 1956 to 1959) and Yogi Berra (1960)—all of whom, except for Keller, limited by a back injury, were often in Stengel's starting lineup.

In the first seven years of his Yankee tenure, 1949 to 1955, when Stengel won five close pennant races, the Yankees led the American League in pinch-hit home runs five times and in pinch-hit RBIs four times. Their pinch-hit batting average was substantially better than the league average in four of those years. In 1955, even though Stengel's pinch hitters hit only .202, they still whacked more home runs (5) and drove in more runs (37) than the pinch hitters for any other team in the league—no small thing in a close-fought pennant race the Yankees won by only three games. The Yankees led the league again in pinch-hit home runs (7) and RBIs (31) when they won their last pennant for Stengel in 1960, a close contest until their 15-game winning streak to end of the season left the Orioles choking in the dust.

\* \* \*

By the mid-1950s, Stengel was no longer a radical revolutionary because other managers had caught on, employing their rosters more aggressively than ever before. Rather than the traditional practice of using their reserves primarily as insurance to cover for injuries and slumps by the team's starting position players, or to pinch hit for the pitcher, managers were increasingly using their bench to try to affect the outcome of games. More frequent pitching changes often involved a double-switch with a position player, depending on when the pitcher's spot was due up. Pinch hitting for starting position players, especially those who struggled against a specific pitcher, or even a particular type of pitcher, to gain a favorable matchup became more common at crucial moments in the game—so too did pinch running for slow guys on base in the late innings when runs were needed and putting a better fielder into the game in the late innings as a defensive replacement.

Stengel's lead was followed most avidly, in principle if not quite the seemingly incomprehensible way the Ole Perfessor managed his roster, by the new generation of managers who debuted in the 1950s. They included Al Lopez, Paul Richards, Eddie Stanky, Fred Hutchinson, Bill Rigney, and Walt Alston, all of whom typically exceeded the league average in position-player substitutions. But even as Stengel's influence caught on, managers whose careers dated back to the 1930s were far more traditional—which is to say reluctant—in replacing position players during games than those beginning their managerial careers after 1950. Bucky Harris, who first became a manager in 1924; Charlie Grimm, who first managed in 1932; Jimmy Dykes, who made his managerial debut in 1934; and Steve O'Neill, whose managerial history dated back to 1935 before he found his groove managing the Tigers in the 1940s, all made substantially fewer position-player substitutions in games than the league average as managers in the 1950s.

The one manager who out-Stengeled the madcap Ole Perfessor in crossing out and penciling in names on his lineup card was Paul Richards after he moved from the up-and-coming Chicago White Sox to the dismal Baltimore Orioles in 1955. In his six years in Baltimore, Richards made an astonishing 2.3 position-player substitutions per game as he gradually built the Orioles into a contending team that unexpectedly challenged Stengel's Yankees for the 1960 pennant until the final two weeks of the season. Richards invested heavily in position-player platoons, doing so at two different positions—and twice at three positions—every year from 1956 to 1960.

What was remarkable about Richards's substitutions was the number he made in his outfield. The Orioles never had a settled outfield when Richards was manager. Only two Baltimore outfielders started as many as 120 games for Richards between 1955 and 1960, and one-third of the time his outfielders in the starting lineup were not in the game for the final out. This was understandable when Baltimore had bad teams, but even when the Orioles were a surprise contender in 1960, their starting outfielders completed only 59 percent of their games. Jackie Brandt, for example, started 127 games in center and right for the 1960 Orioles but was in at the end of only 87 of them, and Gene Woodling, who knew all about (and was unhappy with) platooning from his days with Stengel's Yankees, completed only 56 of the 117 games he started in left field.

Just as Stengel was willing to pinch hit for his starting position players in hopes of a scoring payoff, so too was Richards. The difference was that, unlike Stengel's Yankees, who were a formidable offensive team, Richards's Orioles had difficulty scoring runs; until 1960, they had been last in the league in scoring four times in the previous five years and next-to-last once. Exceeding the league-average number of position-player substitutions by 75 percent between 1955 and 1960 was very much indicative of his desperation to generate offense.

* * *

Nobody did it quite the way Casey did, nor could they since major-league managers are rarely willing to risk playing the role of eccentric genius whose ways defy easy explanation, but Stengel gave new vitality and enduring life to the concept of mixing and matching players to game circumstances. Just as relying on a dedicated relief ace to stymie rallies and hold leads became ever more prominent as a strategy as major-league baseball entered the expansion era in the 1960s, there was little if any retrenchment to the parallel strategy of playing the percentages and seeking the platoon advantage, certainly in the late innings with the game on the line. In the 1960s, Phillies manager Gene Mauch followed in the philosophical footsteps of Stengel, but like Richards, Mauch did not have anywhere near the quality of players to be as successful at it as the Ole Perfessor.

It would not be until the 1970s that major-league baseball would see another manager who platooned and substituted players to such great effect as Mr. Stengel. That would be Earl Weaver, manager of the Baltimore Orioles.

# SIXTEEN

## Diversity and the Los Angeles and Chicago Speedways

The combatants facing off in the 1959 World Series were an anomaly compared to the powerhouse teams that had advanced to the Fall Classic in all the previous years of the decade—the Yankees and Indians in the American League, the Giants and Dodgers before they moved to California and the Braves after they moved to Milwaukee in the National League. The Los Angeles Dodgers and Chicago White Sox were not typical of the era. Because neither team had an imposing offense, their style of play gave much greater emphasis to stealing bases, sacrificing, and situational hitting to set up and take advantage of scoring opportunities. They seemed a throwback to the dead-ball era before Babe Ruth demonstrated the offensive advantages of the long ball. And the two teams foreshadowed the changing face of major-league baseball, which in the next decade would see a significant increase in African Americans and players from Latin America, particularly the Caribbean. And finally, both teams had redemption stories. After being punished with a dismal seventh-place ending to their first season out West in 1958, the Dodgers atoned for the sin of breaking the hearts of the Flatbush Faithful by leaving Brooklyn. The White Sox ended 40 years of wandering in the wilderness on account of eight players on the best team in franchise history conspiring to throw the 1919 World Series.

Major-league baseball was at the time a conservative game. But conservative did not mean immune to change, only slow to change. Major League Baseball as an institution embodied the American adherence to tradition, respect for individualism, and willingness to go in directions shown to be productive in terms of winning ways. And in the spirit of America, the game was bankable, as in profitable. Ultimately, baseball

193

embraced the best impulses of America, however much resistance there
was at first to change.

In the 1950s, this dynamic was at work in the response to Branch
Rickey's "great experiment." There was substantial opposition, but by
the early 1950s, even when few teams had any black players on their
rosters, it was clear the national pastime was going forward on integration. The same was true when it came to the superstructure of organized
baseball. There had been half a century of inertia in which the big-league
game did not move to new vistas despite the unprofitability of at least
one franchise in most two-team cities, even as the United States was
gaining in population with some of the biggest gains in the West. And it
was true in how the game was played, where the emphasis remained on
the power game blazed by the Babe and the Bronx Bombers. While the
strategies that dominated the dead-ball era never disappeared, they were
sidelined as tactics to be used for effect rather than a guiding philosophy.

* * *

The Dodgers were still finding their footing after leaving Brooklyn in
1958 for Los Angeles. No disrespect intended to the Flatbush Faithful, the
move had become an economic necessity. Open for baseball business in
1913, Ebbets Field had long since become untenable. The storied ballpark
was too small, outmoded, and at the very least in need of expensive
renovation. Even so, the Dodgers still drew more than one million in
attendance their last year in Brooklyn, despite not competing for the
pennant. The Ebbets gate was less than when they won the 1956 pennant
but virtually the same as when they dominated the National League in
1955 and won the World Series besides.

Meanwhile, location was by now a significant drawback at a time
when the Dodgers' attendance base was no longer as local as it had been,
in large part because urban demographics were changing and the suburbs were growing. There was little room around Ebbets Field to expand
or build new parking lots that would be necessary to accommodate the
growing proportion of Brooklyn fans now in the suburbs. Dodger owner
Walter O'Malley's ambitions for a new, more convenient ballpark to keep
his team in Brooklyn were thwarted by New York City's powerful coor-
dinator for urban planning and construction projects, Robert Moses, who
had other development plans for the prime location O'Malley wanted.
Moses pushed for the Dodgers' new ballpark to be in Queens, at the
location where Shea Stadium was eventually built to house the expansion
New York Mets.

When Moses refused to relent, O'Malley moved his team out West. He
had company in New York Giants owner Horace Stoneham, who was
dealing with his own dilapidated ballpark and deterioration of the neighborhood around the Polo Grounds and moved his team to San Francisco.

Certainly attractive to O'Malley was the fact that Los Angeles was now the third-largest city by population in the United States (or would be in the 1960 census), Pacific Coast League baseball was popular, and he was able to procure an attractive tract of land in Chavez Ravine near downtown L.A. on which he would build Dodger Stadium—the most beautiful ballpark in America when it opened in 1962. Moving at first into the Los Angeles Coliseum, the Dodgers drew 1.8 million fans in their first year in California—the second most in the major leagues in 1958 after the defending World Series–champion Milwaukee Braves—but suffered the consequences of their aging roster from Brooklyn, and perhaps of abandoning the Flatbush Faithful virtually overnight, by finishing a mere two games out of last place.

There was little reason to believe the Dodgers' chances in 1959 would be any better. With most of Brooklyn's "Boys of Summer" either gone or in the twilight of their careers, the Dodgers would not have finished the 1959 scheduled season tied for first with the Braves, and gone on to sweep a best-of-three playoff to win the pennant, without significant contributions from four black players who would never play up to the level of Jackie Robinson, who had retired, Don Newcombe, traded away the previous season, and Roy Campanella, tragically paralyzed in a car accident in the winter before the team moved to L.A. Because black players not of superstar stature had been added seamlessly, although piecemeal, to their roster throughout the 1950s, by the time the Dodgers moved to Los Angeles it was no longer necessary for the blacks they promoted to be great players the caliber of Brooklyn's early trailblazers.

Jim Gilliam, in the middle of his very respectable career with the Dodgers, was now playing third base for L.A. His season-high batting average was .349 at the All-Star break, which was crucial to an inferior Los Angeles team keeping pace with Milwaukee and San Francisco, only a half-game behind both at the break.

Now at second was Charlie Neal, who made the spring-training cut with Brooklyn in 1956 after 6 years and 796 games in the minor leagues—about average for any player with his ability before making it to the majors. After a year of sitting mostly on the bench, Neal replaced Pee Wee Reese at shortstop in 1957, with Reese moving his body of declining skills to third, and the next year the versatile Gilliam played wherever else he was needed so that Neal could become the new Dodger second baseman. Even though he batted second in the order, Neal's 83 runs batted in were second on the team to Snider's 88, he hit 19 home runs, and 1959 was the highpoint of a modest eight-year career that ended just four years later. Charlie Neal's similarity score was most akin to early 1950s Yankee second baseman Billy Martin.

Catcher Johnny Roseboro was in his second year with the Dodgers in 1959, having become their backstop the previous year, after four minor-league seasons, only because of the accident that ended Campanella's career. The left-handed-batting Roseboro was platooned all year, starting only once when a lefty took the mound against L.A. His home run in the sixth inning of the first playoff game against Milwaukee broke a 2–2 tie and proved the difference in the Dodgers' 3–2 victory. Although one of the National League's best catchers in the first half of the 1960s, Johnny Roseboro was no Roy Campanella. Roseboro's career arc was most similar to Johnny Edwards, another National League catcher whose best years were in the first half of the 1960s.

And now playing shortstop for the Dodgers was Maury Wills. Not called to L.A. until June, Wills took a long time getting to the major leagues. He was already 26 years old, in his ninth year, and had played 1,100 games in the minor leagues, mostly at the Single-A level or below, at the time he finally made it to the big leagues. Wills hit .260 in 88 games, but his .345 batting average in September was indispensable to the Dodgers' winning the pennant in a tight three-team race that also involved the Giants until the final week of the season. Of the four black regulars on the 1959 Dodgers, only Wills received any Hall of Fame votes by the Baseball Writers' Association of America, and though he was on the ballot all 15 years of eligibility, he never came close to the threshold for Cooperstown immortality.

All four were productive players through most of their big-league careers. While Neal's career fizzled, Wills and Roseboro were core regulars and Gilliam a significant role player in the Dodgers' winning three more pennants in the 1960s, as well as ending the 1962 season in a first-place tie with the Giants, resulting in their losing another three-game playoff to their arch-nemesis—seemingly a Cosmic predestination for the Dodgers. But none of the four was so good that had he come along in the first years of integration he would necessarily have been given a realistic opportunity to compete for a position as a regular on a major-league team at the expense of a white player. According to the WAR metric, in their collective 50 years in the big leagues, only Gilliam (in 1956 and 1963) and Wills (1962 and 1965) played at or close to All-Star level in any given year, contributing at least five wins above what would be expected of a replacement player. Any of the trailblazing teams might have allowed for one such player to compete for a position, but it was not until the end of the decade—once black superstar players had made integration a fait accompli—that it was possible for four blacks, none of whom were superior major-league players, to be regulars on one team without thought to the color of their skin.

\* \* \*

If 1959 was the foundation year for the Dodgers winning four pennants and three World Series in Los Angeles by 1966, it was the capstone year for the decade-long resurrection of the Chicago White Sox. The ignominy of the eight Black Sox—including superstar Shoeless Joe Jackson and Eddie Cicotte, one of the best pitchers in baseball—conspiring with gamblers to lose the 1919 World Series condemned the American League team in Chicago to decades in baseball purgatory, mostly in the nether regions of the standings. All that began to change with the arrivals of southpaw Billy Pierce in 1949, in what turned out to be a steal of a trade from Detroit; second baseman Nellie Fox in 1950 from Philadelphia, an even bigger lopsided deal favoring Chicago; and a dynamic new manager and new outfielder—Paul Richards and Minnie Miñoso—in 1951. Although Fox was alone among them in having a starring role when the White Sox broke their 40-year drought by winning the 1959 pennant, and Richards and Miñoso were no longer in Chicago, all four were instrumental to their ultimate success.

Al Lopez may have been the manager who took them to the promised land of the World Series, after leaving Cleveland for Chicago in 1957, but it was Paul Richards who was the most responsible for turning around White Sox fortunes. When Richards took the managerial reins in 1951, the White Sox had endured three straight years of at least 90 losses to cap seven consecutive losing seasons. A former catcher whose big breaks in making it to the majors were the depletion of rosters due to World War II and previous injuries that made him, at 34 years old, unsuitable for military service, Richards gave emphasis to improving Chicago's pitching and defense. He was one of the first American League managers in the 1950s to prioritize the importance of a strong bullpen. The White Sox immediately became one of the stingiest teams in baseball and would remain so for nearly two decades.

Richards was also the mastermind of the "Go Go Sox" speed-based offense that became identifiable with the 1950s White Sox, energizing their fan base and boosting attendance at Comiskey Park to consistently over one million for the first time in team history. It was not so much that the White Sox, who were one of the worst offensive teams before Richards took charge, did not have power—first baseman Eddie Robinson's 29 home runs were third in the league in 1951—as much as Richards's calculating that a multifaceted offense that emphasized situational hitting and at least the threat of the stolen base would be more productive.

Unusual for the era, and particularly in the American League, the White Sox became arguably the most aggressive team on the bases in baseball, the possible exception being the Dodgers. The "Go Go Sox" philosophy carried beyond Richards, who left Chicago at the end of the 1954 season to take on the seemingly hopeless challenge of building the former St. Louis Browns, now the Baltimore Orioles, into a contending team. The speed game was more of a necessity in the years leading up to 1959 because the overall offense of the White Sox became weaker.

Billy Pierce was the cornerstone to Richards's and then Lopez's building a first-rate pitching staff. With all due respect to Whitey Ford, Pierce was probably the best southpaw in the American League in the 1950s. His 1.97 earned run average to lead the league in 1955 was not only far better than runner-up Ford's 2.63 but two full runs lower than the league ERA. Pierce also had back-to-back 20-win seasons in 1956 and 1957. Having piled up close to 2,400 innings in 12 major-league seasons, however, Pierce had a less-than-robust 14–15 record when the White Sox finally reached the top in 1959 and did not get a start in the World Series. Chicago's best pitcher when they won the pennant was 39-year-old Early Wynn, picked up from Cleveland the previous year, who resuscitated his flagging career with a 22–10 record that made him the major-league Cy Young winner. Bob Shaw, in his first full season in the big leagues, had the league's best winning percentage with an 18–6 record.

Even if not the most dynamic of stars, Nellie Fox was the center of gravity for the 1959 White Sox—a fact recognized when he was named the American League's Most Valuable Player, as much for his leadership role in helping his team to the pennant as for his specific performance. In addition to being a defensive standout at second base, Fox was a craftsman with the bat. Batting second, Fox excelled at the hit-and-run and putting the ball in play; he struck out only 13 times in his league-leading 717 plate appearances. He finished the year second in the league in hits and fourth in batting with a .306 batting average. His six wins above replacement were exceeded only by Mickey Mantle among AL position players in 1959 and matched by Tigers star Al Kaline.

* * *

But the player who arguably had the biggest impact in turning around White Sox fortunes was Cuban-native Minnie Miñoso, one of only five black players making their major-league debut before Jackie Robinson retired in 1956 to have been a core regular on an American League team for as many as five years as of 1960. Originally signed by Cleveland out of the Negro Leagues in 1948, Miñoso played a handful of games for the Indians in 1949, excelled in the Pacific Coast League in 1950, and came to the White Sox ten games into the 1951 season in a three-team, multiplayer, round-robin trade on the last day of April. The White Sox put him into the starting lineup the very next day, where he stayed the rest of the season. Miñoso was only the third black player in the league's history, after Larry Doby in 1948 and Luke Easter in 1950, to be in his team's starting lineup on a daily basis. The only American League team at the time to have an integrated roster was the team that traded him, the Cleveland Indians.

Miñoso immediately made his impact felt in Chicago. His .359 average in his first two months with the White Sox was instrumental in their reaching and staying in first place for virtually all of June and staying competitive until August. While they could not ultimately keep up with the far-superior Yankees and Indians and finished the season in fourth place, the White Sox had a winning record for the first time in eight years. Miñoso hit .347 in the final month to finish the year second in the league in batting average (.326) and second in runs scored (112, one behind Boston's Dom DiMaggio).

Showing off his speed, he led the league in triples with 14 and in stolen bases with 31. Befitting his batting third in the order, Miñoso had the third-most extra-base hits, of which his 34 doubles were 2 short of the league lead, and his player value of 5.5 wins above replacement was fourth-best among position players. Minnie Miñoso was better in all these categories than any other rookie in baseball, including Willie Mays, but it was the pennant-winning Yankees' versatile infielder Gil McDougald who spent the winter polishing the AL's 1951 Rookie of the Year award.

With Miñoso at the heart of the batting order and playing more in the style of Jackie Robinson than Larry Doby, the White Sox continued to improve and became a competitive team. They were still not ready for prime time against the Yankees and Indians, however, and beginning in 1952, finished third behind those two teams for five consecutive years before finally displacing Cleveland in second place in 1957.

The best year of Miñoso's career came in 1954. Batting .320, scoring 119 runs, and driving in 116, Miñoso was the best player in the American League based on his player value of 8.2 wins above replacement—the standard for an MVP-kind-of-year. He finished fourth in the MVP voting, however, behind Yogi Berra, Doby, and Cleveland second baseman Bobby Avila. More importantly, Miñoso helped the White Sox to win 94 games—their most since 1920, when the Black Sox scandal broke at the end of the season—although that was far too few to keep pace with the Indians and Yankees, both with over 100 wins. They finished third.

When the White Sox finally did escape from under the weight of the Yankees and Indians, Miñoso was no longer in Chicago to enjoy the World Series they finally made it to in 1959. He had another typical Miñoso season in 1957, batting over .300 with on-base percentage exceeding .400 for the fifth time in seven years, but perhaps because he turned 32 shortly after the season ended, Miñoso was traded back to Cleveland for Early Wynn and outfielder Al Smith. Ironically, he was traded back to Chicago in 1960 and had another strong year for a team that ultimately could not keep pace with the Yankees in September. The defending AL-champion Sox finished third.

\* \* \*

The significance of Minnie Miñoso was not only that he was an elite player who was among the first blacks to integrate the major leagues but also that he was from Cuba and at the leading edge of the first wave of both black Latinos and white Hispanics from Latin America to play in the United States. Although non-black Hispanic players were never excluded from organized (white) baseball, major-league teams did not invest in seeking out talent in the region despite being well aware of the passion for baseball in Caribbean countries, particularly Cuba and Venezuela (where the game was inculcated by the presence of Americans working the oilfields) and knowing that the quality of play in their leagues was often quite high. Indeed, Cuba in particular had a long history of highly competitive leagues dating to the early 20th century that produced out-standing players clearly capable of playing at the major-league level.

Unlike in the United States, neither the Cuban leagues nor those else-where in baseball-crazed Caribbean countries were segregated, and the fact that many of the best players in those leagues were black Latinos put the region largely off the map as far as major-league scouts were con-cerned. The original Washington Senators beginning in the mid-1930s were the only team to take meaningful interest in Caribbean players, primarily because their most valued scout had good contacts in Cuban baseball.

Of the nearly 6,400 players who appeared in major-league games in the first half of the 20th century, fewer than 60 were born south of the border. Almost all were Cuban and, of course, none were black. Or, there were none who could not at least pass for white. Born into a society where interracial couplings were neither unusual nor ostracized, howev-er, some must have been at least partially black. Major-league teams may have been willing to overlook the "swarthy" complexions of those Latin players, but also gave them relatively short shrift in their opportunities to make good.

The most prominent player from the region before Miñoso was Cu-ban-born Dolf Luque, celebrated as the "Pride of Havana," who had a 20-year big-league career that ended in 1935. In the first half of the 1920s, Luque was one of the best pitchers in the National League, including a 27–8 record and 1.93 ERA for second-place Cincinnati in 1923. The num-ber of Latin-born Hispanics prior to the integration era reached its peak during the war years when so many major leaguers were in the service. While on the side of the Allies against Nazi Germany, Cuba did not institute a draft to support the war effort.

But once the color barrier was broken, and certainly once Miñoso became a star, the Caribbean Basin quickly emerged as a new talent pool for the major leagues. In the decade after Miñoso broke in, close to a hundred players from the Caribbean and Latin America played in the majors, nearly double the total that had appeared in the big leagues be-fore 1950. While a significant number were black Latinos like Miñoso, the majority were white Hispanics like Mexican-born Cleveland second base-man Bobby Avila. By the end of the decade, the Senators—the one club with a modest scouting effort in Cuba before integration—were ahead of the field in recruiting talented, mostly Hispanic, players from the island nation. None of the Cubans who were important players for Washington in the 1950s—pitchers Connie Marrero, Pedro Ramos, and Camilo Pascual—were black.

* * *

The Chicago White Sox were at the forefront of teams integrating Latin players into their starting lineup, both black and Hispanic. The year before Miñoso had his outstanding rookie season, the White Sox introduced as their new shortstop, Chico Carrasquel, who became the first Hispanic Venezuelan player of consequence in the major leagues. (Carrasquel was a nephew of Alex Carrasquel, who was one of the Senators' Latin signings and had pitched credibly, without much acclaim, in Washington in the first half of the 1940s before returning veteran ballplayers from World War II cost him his job.) In the last two months of the 1952 season, Chicago regularly had four Latin players in their starting lineup—Miñoso, Carrasquel, Hector Rodriguez at third base, and Jim Rivera, acquired in a trade at the end of July, who was born in New York to Puerto Rican parents. And when Carrasquel missed nearly two months with an injury, his replacement at shortstop was Cuban-born white-Hispanic Willy Miranda.

Chico Carrasquel set the template of the athletic, nimble, great-glove, dynamic-arm major-league shortstops from Venezuela. For six years he paired with Nellie Fox as the best defensive double-play combination in baseball. The White Sox, however, had not scouted Carrasquel in Venezuela; they had purchased his contract from the Brooklyn Dodgers, who had. Similarly, they did not scout the next standout defensive shortstop from Venezuela but took Carrasquel at his word when he insisted that Luis Aparicio was someone they should sign.

Luis Aparicio had a famous-in-Venezuela pedigree. His father, Luis Aparicio Ortega, was a legendary shortstop in Venezuelan baseball history but did not get a shot at playing in the United States, first because his country was off the map as far as major-league teams were concerned and then because injury forced him to turn down an offer extended by the Senators in 1939. The junior Aparicio was only 19 when he was signed before spring training in 1954 and spent just two years in the minor leagues before his quick development made Carrasquel expendable as trade bait for Cleveland slugger Larry Doby after the 1955 season.

Dazzling in the field and on the base paths, Aparicio came just two votes shy of being the unanimous selection for 1956 American League Rookie of the Year. He led the league with 21 steals in 25 attempts. This was the first of nine consecutive years Aparicio led the league in steals—something no other player has ever done, not Ty Cobb, not Maury Wills, not Lou Brock, and not even Rickey Henderson. With Rivera second in steals and Miñoso fourth, Aparicio helped cement the team's moniker as the "Go Go Sox."

Defensively up the middle and batting first and second in Lopez's lineup, Aparicio and Nellie Fox teamed to become the dynamic duo that ultimately led the White Sox to their first pennant in 40 years. While it was Fox who won the 1959 MVP award, Aparicio was second in the voting. His 56 steals not only led the league for the fourth-straight year but also were the most since Washington's George Case stole 61 in 1943—when offense was down significantly because wartime exigencies led to the manufacture of lesser-quality baseballs—or, discounting the war year, since the Yankees' Ben Chapman stole 61 in 1931.

The exceptional defensive prowess of the acrobatic Aparicio and sure-handed Fox around second base was especially important because the offensively challenged White Sox, although perhaps not quite the "hitless wonders" of 1906, had to rely on defense and pitching for success. Only two American League teams scored fewer runs in 1959 than the White Sox, who compensated with by far the best team ERA and the best defense in the league, according to several metrics, which made them the stingiest of all major-league teams in giving up runs.

* * *

The offensive philosophy of both 1959 pennant winners was different from the prevailing approach of most major-league teams. Since neither team was an offensive powerhouse, both emphasized situational strategies to advance base runners and set up scoring opportunities. The Dodgers, who had the third-fewest extra-base hits in the National League despite hitting 148 home runs, led their league in both stolen bases with 84 and sacrifice bunts with 100.

The White Sox—the only major-league team with fewer than 100 home runs (they hit 97) and sixth in AL batting average—led the majors in stolen bases with 113, the most of any team since the 1949 Dodgers. It was the third-straight year they had stolen over a hundred bases, the first time any team had done that since the late 1920s, and the ninth-straight year they led the league in steals. To put their "Go Go" philosophy in perspective, the White Sox accounted for nearly a quarter of the league's total stolen bases from 1951 to 1959 and averaged more than twice as many steals as any one of the seven other American League teams.

Baseball in the 1950s is often characterized as a relatively unimaginative era in which runs were scored by advancing one base at a time, with home runs powering big innings. While total runs scored in the decade were up only marginally from the 1940s—which included three anomalous years during World War II when so many veteran players were in the service—far fewer runs crossed the plate in the 1950s than during the 1930s. Home runs, however, were being blasted at unprecedented rates.

The two leagues combined for nearly 21,000 big blasts from 1951 to 1960, an increase more than half again as large as the approximately 13,400 homers hit in each of the two previous decades. The ratio of home runs to runs scored rose from 11 percent in the 1930s to 19 percent in the 1950s, even though 10 percent more runs were scored in the Depression years.

Indicative of baseball's power surge in the 1950s, strategies to advance runners diminished in importance. But they did not uniformly move to the back of the bus in favor of the long ball as much as the two leagues emphasized different approaches to put runners into scoring position, although each league had several teams in the other direction. AL teams relied much more on sacrifice bunts than stolen bases to advance runners than they had in the 1930s. It was the other way around in the NL, where sacrifice bunts were down substantially but stolen bases only marginally from 1930s totals. The diminishing of importance of the sacrifice in the National League may have been because the NL, which had a larger number of premier sluggers, hit many more home runs than the AL.

Widespread in practice throughout the game's history in the never-ending quest to set up runs, especially by teams not blessed with offensive firepower, the value of sacrifice bunting as a strategy had its critics long before advanced metrics grounded in probabilities demonstrated that in most cases sacrificing outs also sacrifices possible runs. Even in the dead-ball era, when teams worked hard to create scoring opportunities because pitching was dominant and home runs rare, no less a master strategist than John McGraw, true believer in what he called "scientific baseball" though he was, did not look favorably on the sacrifice as a means to set up runs. Rather than wasting outs with sacrifice bunts, McGraw emphasized the hit-and-run and stolen bases as the best ways to advance runners. The risk of both those strategies however—particularly stolen-base attempts—is that failure could cost the team both an out and a valuable runner on base.

The fact of integration presents a more nuanced picture because National League teams were more proactive in giving black players major-league opportunities. It wasn't necessarily that black players had greater speed than white players, but the fact that many of the blacks who starred in the 1950s—foremost among them Jackie Robinson and Willie Mays, but also lesser lights like Sam Jethroe and Bill Bruton—played in the daring style of the Negro Leagues may have made their teams much more open to the running game. Beginning with Robinson in 1949, a black player led the major leagues in stolen bases every year except for one until 1959, including Bruton three consecutive years from 1953 to 1955 and Mays the next three years.

The exception was in 1952, when Jackie's teammate Pee Wee Reese stole the most bases. Reese, starting at age 29 in 1948, stole 20 or more bases 5 times in 6 years—the only times in his career he had so many steals. As suggested by Reese's sudden turn to becoming a base-stealing threat, the advantages of Robinson's dazzling base running were not lost on Brooklyn managers, even though they had a formidable power-driven offense led by sluggers Duke Snider, Gil Hodges, Roy Campanella, and Carl Furillo. With Robinson as a fearless (and peerless) threat whenever he got on base, the Dodgers led the league in stolen bases in each of Robinson's first seven years and in all but two of his ten-year career, even while they were also the most prolific home-run-hitting team in the league for seven consecutive years between 1949 and 1955.

* * *

The Dodgers were a hybrid team in transition from the dangerous offensive club they were in Brooklyn to their 1960s teams in Los Angeles that were distinguished by superior pitching, excellent team speed, and a reliance on small-ball strategies to score runs—especially after the spacious, very-favorable-to-pitching Dodger Stadium opened in 1962. Back when the Boys of Summer were in their prime and playing in Brooklyn's relatively cozy Ebbets Field, the Dodgers were capable of scoring runs, and lots of them, because they had a lineup of power hitters.

When they won the 1955 pennant by a decisive 13½ games and finally beat the Yankees in the World Series, the Dodgers, aided by their league-best 201 home runs, scored 857 runs, also the most in the major leagues. And, with Jim Gilliam, Robinson, and Sandy Amorós—all black players—leading the team, the Dodgers also had the most stolen bases in baseball with 79. As important as speed was to Brooklyn's offense, however, it was the power game that made the Dodgers so dominant; their 201 blasts alone brought home 337 runs, accounting for nearly 40 percent of their scoring. In the National League, home runs accounted for, on average, 30 percent of total runs.

By 1959, the Dodgers were not only in California, but also sluggers Hodges, Furillo, and Snider had grown older and slowed down, and Campanella's paralyzing accident kept him from ending his career out West. To make matters more interesting, the Dodgers played in a stadium, the Los Angeles Memorial Coliseum, built for track and field and football, not baseball. The field had to fit into the dimensions of an elongated oval, meaning it was just 301 feet down the right-field line, there was a vast expanse in right and right-center, and it was extraordinarily confined on the left side—just 320 feet to the fence in the left-field power alley and only 251 feet down the left-field line. While the advantage would seem to be for right-handed sluggers like Hodges and young center fielder Dom Demeter, with five left-handed batters and two switch-hitters getting at least 250 plate appearances for the 1959 Dodgers, the majority of Dodger at bats at the Coliseum were from the left side of the plate. Left-handed-batting outfielder Wally Moon, who was the Dodgers' most valuable player in 1959 based on the WAR metric, led the team in going deep at the Coliseum, hitting 14 of his 19 home runs at home.

With a less powerful lineup, Walt Alston began using run-creation strategies more frequently on his way to becoming celebrated as a manager who won games the dead-ball way—with speed, situational hitting, and superior pitching. Given, however, that they won the pennant with only 88 wins, and that it took the Dodgers 156 games to do so, including their playoff with the Braves, Alston's greater emphasis on small-ball strategies may well have been self-defeating and kept his team from winning the pennant outright. Despite leading the league in stolen bases, the Dodgers were successful only 62 percent of the time, no better than the league average. And their 57 percent success rate in sacrifice-bunt attempts was the worst among the 16 major-league teams.

Too often—51 times—a Los Angeles base runner was thrown out trying to steal, and too often—74 times—the Dodgers sacrificed an out without the dividend of advancing whoever was on base. This was significant because, even though the Dodgers' power was not what it was when they were winning pennants in Brooklyn, home runs were directly responsible for 31 percent of the runs they scored in 1959, which was appreciably better than the 28 percent league average. Moreover, more than a third of the Dodgers' sacrifice bunts were by position players or pinch hitters batting in the third through sixth spots in the batting order, where batters are expected to drive in runs, not move them over, substantially higher than the major-league average of 22 percent.

As for the White Sox, saddled by their sixth-in-the-league .250 team batting average, they were also no better than sixth in scoring. They won the pennant anyway without being seriously threatened down the September stretch because a 41–16 record in July and August had them ahead by five and a half games going into the final month. Unlike the Dodgers, nearly a third of whose runs were driven home by the long ball, less than a quarter of Chicago's runs trotted home on the strength of a home run, far below the American League average of 32 percent. Having to rely of necessity on small-ball strategies, the White Sox were by far the most proficient team in the major leagues in advancing base runners on outs, and they stole 45 more bases than any other team in the American League. Aparicio was successful on 81 percent of his stolen-base attempts.

But the White Sox were not as efficient scoring runs in the dead-ball-era way as their "Go Go" offense might suggest. Without much of a power game, the White Sox needed more than three base runners for every run they scored, whereas the league average was just under three. While Aparicio's stolen-base success rate was individually impressive, his Chicago teammates—who combined for 57 steals, just 1 more than Aparicio alone—failed in 41 percent of their attempts, costing the Sox 40 base runners.

Moreover, the theoretically ideal scenario of the speedy Aparicio lead-ing off and Fox, a master at putting the ball in play, batting behind him did not yield the scoring dividends that might be expected, although this may not have been realized so much at the time. While Fox was excep-tional in his role, hitting .367 and striking out only four times when he came to bat with runners on base, Aparicio was much less of a table setter than top-of-the-order batters are supposed to be. His .254 average in the 141 games he batted first was not as much the problem as that fact that he got on base in less than 31 percent of his plate appearances, a rate far below the league average on-base percentage of .340 for leadoff hitters. Aparicio particularly struggled as Chicago's first batter in the game, bat-ting less than .200 and getting on base only 26 percent of the time. With Aparicio kept off base far more often than not to start the game, the White Sox were rarely able to capitalize on his speed and disruptive influence on the bases to take a first-inning lead. Aparicio got on base and scored in the first inning in only 20 of the 141 games he batted leadoff.

Aparicio and Fox combined for 17 hits and both hit over .300 in the World Series, which proved to be more dominated by the long ball than by speed and dead-ball-era strategies. The Dodgers won the Series in six games and hit seven home runs. The White Sox hit four, three by Ted Kluszewski, one of baseball's premier power hitters in the mid-1950s when he was with Cincinnati. With the World Series in view, Chicago traded for Big Klu in late August to boost their anemic offense for base-ball's biggest stage. The two teams combined for seven stolen bases—five by L.A.—none of which resulted in a run. Aparicio, who attempted only two steals and was thrown out once, scored just once.

* * *

Nonetheless, the aggressive, situational, and speed-based style of play of both 1959 pennant winners heralded the beginning of an era when major-league teams adopted a more multidimensional approach to scoring. In particular, stealing bases was back in vogue and brought new excitement to the game. Luis Aparicio and Maury Wills were avatars of the return to prominence of the stolen base, even while the long ball remained the most formidable and desirable of offensive weapons. Aparicio led the AL in steals every year through 1964, when he stole a career-high 57, while Wills led the NL six straight years beginning in 1960, including 102 in 1962 to break Ty Cobb's imposing record of 96 set nearly half a century before in the dead-ball era. Wills was more of the prototypical leadoff batter than Aparicio because he worked his way on base much more often. By the end of the 1960s, Bert Campaneris in the American League and Lou Brock in the National had taken over as baseball's preeminent threats to run.

Ultimately, however, even as a new pitcher's era emerged in the 1960s, the offensive strategies most identifiable with the bygone dead-ball era could not, by themselves, be all that productive. The teams that relied on them the most were typically the teams that had difficulty scoring runs, usually because they lacked a potent lineup.

The Los Angeles Dodgers were the only team to be successful with a weak offense that emphasized speed, situational hitting, and sacrificing for the cause. They won consecutive pennants by close margins in 1965 and 1966 despite finishing eighth in scoring in the now ten-team league both years and having the second-lowest slugging percentage in the league, behind the lowly Mets who lost as many games (97 and 95) as the Dodgers won in each of those years. The Dodgers, however, had the best pitching in baseball and played in the vast expanse of Dodger Stadium, which played to their strength in pitching and style of offense.

At the other end of the spectrum, the St. Louis Cardinals with pennants in 1964, 1967, and 1968 were the poster team for success with a multifaceted offense that combined speed—Brock batting leadoff and a leading base stealer—and a potent lineup.

# SEVENTEEN

## Coming to Terms with Integration

As the 1960s began, black players were among the best in the game. It was certainly true there was no going back on integration, but that was probably true as early as 1950 when the total number of blacks who had ever worn a big-league uniform was twelve, eight of whom were regulars in their team's starting lineup for at least one season. More importantly, black players of varying abilities were more prevalent on major-league rosters and accepted as teammates in mostly white big-league clubhouses, even if still not necessarily welcomed by some players.

An important validation of integration's success was that every pennant-winning team in the National League beginning with the 1951 Giants included blacks as core regulars who were *not* elite players. A strong argument can be made that it was the 1959 Los Angeles Dodgers' winning the pennant and the World Series with Robinson, Campanella, and Newcombe no longer in Dodger blue but four blacks in their starting lineup—Jim Gilliam, Charlie Neal, Johnny Roseboro, and Maury Wills— who were not close to being elite players that paved the way for major-league baseball's broader acceptance of African American and black Latino players of more modest abilities to realistically compete for starting positions.

If integration could not be considered fully consolidated until black players who were not of superstar stature could compete for starting positions in the major leagues, may the best player win, it was still an open question how close major-league baseball was to that ideal. Of the generation of players whose careers began between 1958 and 1962, it was a certainty only that black players with exceptional ability like Orlando Cepeda, Vada Pinson, Willie McCovey, Juan Marichal, Bob Gibson, and Billy Williams would be starting lineup regulars in the 1960s. It was still not certain that players with more modest abilities who also began their big-league careers during those years—the likes of Tony Taylor, Earl Wilson, Leon Wagner, Ed Charles, John Wyatt, and perhaps even Curt Flood—could make a career as starting players in major-league lineups, as they in fact did. In their first five full seasons as regulars on major-league teams, those players' average annual player value was about two wins above replacement, the bottom of the range of performance expected of a starting player at the big-league level. Precedent from the 1950s suggested that such a level of performance over any consecutive-year period would likely have short-circuited their careers on most teams.

Black players still counted for only 23 of the 183 players who were regulars on major-league teams in 1960, based on starting 100 games as a position player or throwing enough innings to qualify for the ERA title or otherwise appearing in 40 games as a pitcher. Of those 23, seven played on just two teams—Gilliam, Neal, and Wills in Los Angeles and Mays, Cepeda, Willie Kirkland, and pitcher "Toothpick" Sam Jones in San Francisco. With Roseboro in a catchers' platoon and Tommy Davis replacing the aging Duke Snider as a regular in the outfield at the end of July, the Dodgers closed the season with five black players as position regulars.

While every National League team had at least one black player who was a core regular based on those criteria, the same was true for only four American League teams, although all eight had blacks on their big-league roster at some point in the season. Only 6 of the 23 blacks who were regulars in 1960 played in the American League, none on the pennant-winning Yankees and four of them on just two teams—Minnie Miñoso and Al Smith in Chicago, and Vic Power and Jim (Mudcat) Grant in Cleveland. As for the Yankees' black players, Hector Lopez started 98 games in the outfield and Elston Howard 79 behind the plate.

Because the percentage of blacks among all players who were regulars on major-league teams incrementally increased from 6 percent in 1952 (6 years into the Jackie Robinson era) to 12 percent in 1956 (Jackie's last major-league season) to still barely 13 percent in 1960 (14 years after Robinson broke in with the Dodgers and 4 years after he retired), it might appear that, aside from the vitally important fact of integration itself, progress had been slow in benefiting any number of black players who had the talent, skills, and ability to play in the major leagues but were not elite players.

\* \* \*

Progress may have been slow, but the powers that be in major-league baseball surely noticed the competitive advantages of integration enjoyed by the Dodgers, Giants, Indians, and Braves in the 1950s. Perhaps even more important, however, was the fiscal bottom line. Contrary to assertions in the 1946 MacPhail Report that black players attracting black fans to the ballpark "could conceivably threaten the value of the Major League franchises owned by these Clubs," overall attendance did not suffer because of integration, except insofar as a team's competitiveness—or lack thereof—was concerned.

From the end of World War II until 1952, AL teams had attracted more fans to their ballparks than did NL teams every year except for Jackie Robinson's 1947 rookie season. But beginning in 1953, the National League, with its greater preponderance of black stars, outpaced the junior circuit in attendance every year until 1977 with the exception of only 1955 and 1961, and 1961 was an anomaly because the American League had expanded to 10 teams that year while the National remained at 8 before it followed suit the next year.

The MacPhail Report had singled out the Giants, Yankees, and White Sox as franchises whose value might decline if integration resulted in a boost of blacks in attendance at their stadiums, presumably causing many whites to stay away. The Giants and White Sox were both early to integrate, became much better teams competitively as a result, and did not suffer at the gate. The figures show that the cardinal determinant in their attendance fluctuations was competitiveness, as well as the increasing physical deterioration of stadiums approaching 50 years old and with limited parking options at a time when Americans were falling in love with their cars and suburban lifestyles. Similarly, the Yankees' attendance did not suffer after they integrated with Elston Howard in 1955, nor would it when they were winning pennants in the early 1960s with Howard, Hector Lopez, and Al Downing as key players. Not until the Yankees plunged into the depths of the second division in the second half of the 1960s did their attendance plunge as well.

Even for an ownership group that in general was not enlightened about racial diversity, still less about equality, winning and its attendance dividend was the bottom line. The 1960s, a decade of agitation for fundamental civil rights and economic opportunity for black Americans, saw African Americans and black Latinos become established and accepted as integral members of major-league baseball teams. By 1964, 21 percent of the 247 players who were regulars on now-20 major-league teams were blacks.

Suggesting that integration was now institutionalized in major-league baseball, blacks accounted for 34 percent of the position players who were regularly in the starting lineup for at least five seasons between 1961 and 1970, a substantial improvement over 14 percent in the years between Jackie Robinson's 1947 debut and 1960. As a carryover from the National League being out front on integration, NL teams in the 1960s were far more likely to have blacks as core regulars than the historically more-resistant-to-integration American League; 70 percent of the black position players who were big-league regulars in the 1960s played in the National League, and blacks accounted for close to half (46 percent) of the total position players who were starting regulars in the NL for at least five years that decade, compared to only 22 percent in the American League. The percentage of blacks among pitchers who were settled in starting rotations or as their team's bullpen ace for at least 5 years in the 1960s remained disappointingly small at 14 percent, which was nonetheless orders of magnitude better than only four black pitchers (all in the National League) who met the 5-year standard in the first 14 years of integration.

An unprecedented influx of players from Caribbean Basin countries, which began in the 1950s, was a key contributing factor to the increase in black players as major-league regulars during the 1960s. The Latin wave picked up steam in the 1960s, particularly from the Dominican Republic and Puerto Rico, with more than 150 players from Caribbean Basin countries appearing in the major leagues, and the number would have been much higher if not for Fidel Castro's clampdown preventing Cubans from fleeing his oppressive Communist regime. Reflecting the changing demographics in major-league baseball, 17 of the 56 black players who were starting position players, starting pitchers, or the relief ace on their teams for at least five years between 1961 and 1970 were from Latin America. And they do not include Tony Perez (Cuban) or Rod Carew (from Panama, but whose family moved to the United States when he was a teenager), who failed to meet the five-year standard only because they did not become regulars on their teams until late in the decade.

* * *

Despite undeniable progress as measured by the number of African American and black Latino players who were regulars on major-league teams, a social-science researcher published a study in September 1967 with two broad conclusions: first, that "the Negro ball player may have to be better qualified than a white player to win the same position," and second, that "such discrimination places little handicap on the outstanding Negro, because he is too valuable a property to exclude." This is a basic summation of the black experience in the major leagues during Jackie Robinson's entire career but made long after there was no longer any doubt about blacks playing in the major leagues. Ironically, the study by Aaron Rosenblatt, "Negroes in Baseball: The Failure of Success," was published in the journal *TransAction: Social Science and Modern Society* just before the 1967 World Series, which featured ten black starting players on the two teams—the most in any Fall Classic until then—Bob Gibson, Orlando Cepeda, Julian Javier, Lou Brock, and Curt Flood on the Cardinals, and Elston Howard, George Scott, Joe Foy, Reggie Smith, and José Tartabull on the Red Sox, whose relief ace, John Wyatt, was also black.

It is not obvious, however, that the researcher's data set substantiates his conclusions, which were based on findings that black players hit for higher averages than whites every year between 1953 and 1965 and that the number of blacks who hit better than .270 in 1964 and 1965—when the major-league batting average was about .250—accounted for more than a third of total black position players. Rosenblatt wrote that it was not possible to compare the performance of black versus white pitchers because there were so few blacks who had pitched in the major leagues by 1965. His data does not necessarily say anything meaningful about the realistic opportunities for blacks to win major-league jobs because it could indicate nothing more than that the generation of black players he examined was, in general, better than their white counterparts.

What more persuasively substantiates his conclusion is that the percentage of *elite* players who were core regulars was substantially higher among black major leaguers than white. More than a third of the black position players who were starting regulars for at least five years in the 1960s were exceptional at the time—among the 10 best in their league for the decade based on their player value as measured by the wins-above-replacement metric—or had a career arc that led them ultimately to the Hall of Fame. While this was a far more appropriate proportion between players with superior talent and those with more pedestrian major-league abilities than in the 1950s, when nearly two-thirds of the black position players who were core regulars were elite players, it was still far higher than only 16 percent of white position players in the 1960s who could be considered elite based on the WAR metric or who were on their way to Cooperstown.

Twenty years after Jackie Robinson broke the color barrier, the integration of African American and black Latinos in major-league baseball had been consolidated, with significant progress in terms of more open competition for starting positions between black and white players capable of playing at the major-league level. But the large disparity in the relative proportion of elite players suggests the odds still favored the white player with average major-league ability, unless the "typical" black player was demonstrably better. Based on the evidence, it would not be until the *next* decade that major-league baseball, most likely because of competitive imperatives, became more colorblind to the principle of players earning their positions based on their merits in a fair competition without regard to racial considerations.

* * *

By the time Jackie Robinson died at the age of 53 in 1972, his health and longevity almost certainly compromised by the stresses of both the challenges and the responsibilities of breaking the color barrier, black players falling within the full range of major-league abilities were competing on the playing field as big-league regulars, from marginal to elite and superstars about whom there was no doubt. But the question must still be asked, when exactly—if at all—did major-league baseball put the issue of integration behind it? *On the field of play*, integration may have become a dead letter by the end of Jackie Robinson's lifetime because talent, of whatever color or nationality, was now (mostly) decisive when it came to opportunity and has remained so. If you can play, we're gonna pay, and if you can play better than the other guy, then you're the man.

This does not mean, however, that major-league baseball did not continue to grapple with the issue of race. Hank Aaron, on the threshold of passing Babe Ruth's 714 career home runs, received vitriolic hate mail because an icon's hallowed record was about to be broken by a black man. Until nearly the turn of the 21st century, Boston and Philadelphia, ironically both in the Northeast, continued to have bad reputations among black players as cities whose civic cultures had a persistent undertone of racism, subtle or otherwise, that was unsparing toward blacks. Many black players in those cities felt unwelcome or personally isolated. And even long after Robinson's death, black players continued to be dogged by racial stereotypes whose characteristics were rarely impugned on white players who failed to meet expectations or had personal issues outside of the game. And these stereotypes were brought into the cultural realm when it came to Latino players from the Caribbean Basin, most of whom were black, as they became much more prevalent on big-league rosters.

That the issue of race was most assuredly *not* behind major-league baseball was made embarrassingly clear on the 40th anniversary of Jackie Robinson's big-league debut when Dodgers general manager Al Campanis, appearing on the popular *Nightline* TV program on April 15, 1987, answered a question on why there were no black managers, general managers, or owners in major-league baseball by suggesting, first, that they had not paid their dues by managing in the minor leagues and then saying blacks "may not have some of the necessities to be, let's say, a field manager."

At the time there had been exactly three black managers in major-league history and just one black man who had served as a senior executive on a major-league team. The Cleveland Indians made Frank Robinson the majors' first black manager in 1975. He was fired in 1977. The Chicago White Sox made Larry Doby the second black manager in 1978, and the Seattle Mariners made Maury Wills the third in 1980.

Frank Robinson got a second chance with the San Francisco Giants in 1981, lasting until 1984. None of the three was successful by winning standards of division titles, pennants, or World Series championships. None of the three even had a winning record as manager. With five full seasons and parts of two others, Robinson was the only black manager who had any longevity in the dugout; neither Doby nor Wills managed more than 87 games. On the executive side, the Atlanta Braves made Bill Lucas, who had been their minor-league director since 1973, their de facto general manager in time for baseball's winter meetings in 1976, a position he held until his sudden death less than three years later when he was only 43 years old.

From the time Frank Robinson integrated the major leagues' managerial ranks in 1975 until Campanis appeared on *Nightline*, there were 140 managerial changes in the two leagues, not including interim managers who kept the manager's spot on the dugout bench warm for a handful of games. Including Doby, Wills, and Robinson for his second go-around, only three openings went to black men. More significantly, however, all 29 of the managers named to their position *after* Robinson became the first black manager who went on to win division titles between 1975 and 1986 were white. The teams they took over were either already contenders or had sufficient talent that they were poised to contend.

This was in stark contrast to the opportunities given to baseball's first black managers, none of whose teams had a realistic chance to contend. Neither the Indians in 1975 nor Giants in 1981 were very good when Robinson took charge of them, and although he had both teams play above their collective abilities at the beginning of his tenure, their reversion to their true talent level cost him his job both times. The White Sox were a bad team when they were handed over to Doby for the second half of the 1978 season, and the Mariners were a terrible team, only four years into their history, when Wills was named manager late in the 1980 season. Notwithstanding the expansion quality of his team, however, Wills proved himself to be unquestionably in over his head as a big-league manager.

Just as the major-league validation of black players was in large part attributable to Jackie Robinson's playing on a winning team—the Brooklyn Dodgers were one of the best teams in baseball at the time he was promoted to Ebbets Field and then won the pennant with him as a core regular in his very first season—Campanis's remarks suggested that, for major-league owners and executives, the validation of blacks as managers could only come, at least at first, from what a black manager did with a competitive team. After all, had Robinson played for a bad team, as did Hank Thompson and Willard Brown when they debuted later in the 1947 season with the awful St. Louis Browns, his breakthrough more likely would have been perceived as a sideshow and his excellence more easily dismissed.

Campanis, who had many black players during his tenure with superior baseball intelligence, should certainly have known better, particularly given his long history with the Dodgers. Perhaps indicative of the times in American political and cultural history in the 1980s, when there was significant backlash against some legacies of the civil-rights movement—affirmative action, in particular—Campanis's choice of words were likely meant to emphasize that managers were chosen based on their merits, not entitlement. His words instead betrayed a pervasive but subtle discrimination in providing opportunity for blacks. Frank Robinson, who was not managing at the time, believed Campanis was accurately reflecting the "ugly prejudice" of major-league front-office executives about blacks lacking the skills and ability to be managerial candidates.

The firestorm raised by Campanis, especially because it came on a day of such significance, not only in baseball but also in American social and ultimately political history, forced Major League Baseball institutionally to take action to ensure that teams looked at minority candidates as they considered managerial and front-office executive changes. Within a year, Frank Robinson was back in a major-league dugout but with the flailing Baltimore Orioles rather than a competitive team.

It would fall on Clarence "Cito" Gaston to be the first black man to be given charge of a team with realistic potential to compete for a championship when he was named manager of the Toronto Blue Jays early in the 1989 season. The Jays had been in the pennant chase each of the two previous years after having already won a division title in 1985. In his first year as their manager, Gaston led Toronto back to the top of the American League's Eastern Division standings. They won their division again two years later. And the year after that, in 1992, Cito Gaston became the first black not only to manage in a World Series but also to win the World Series, which his Blue Jays did again in 1993.

Meanwhile, on the executive side, when former Cardinals' star first baseman Bill White was named president of the National League in 1989, he became the first black man to serve at such a high executive level in major-league baseball. As for the 28 big-league franchises, it wasn't until the Houston Astros made Bob Watson, a star player for them in the 1970s, their general manager following the 1993 season that another black man (only the second in history) held a senior front-office position, a gap of 14 years since Bill Lucas had served in that role with the Braves. Three years later, now in New York, Watson became the first black general manager of a championship team—the 1996 Yankees.

Campanis's remarks ensured that the rarity of blacks managing major-league teams would end, at least for appearances sake. While it was inevitable that sooner or later blacks would be successful in managing competitive teams, a case can be made for Gaston's back-to-back World Series triumphs being what truly broke the color barrier for managers. Gaston proved a black man had the "necessities," to use Campanis's word, to manage a team that was legitimately competitive to the promised land of championships. More than 20 years later, Gaston remains the only black manager to win a World Series—he won two—although Dusty Baker, with the 2002 San Francisco Giants, and Ron Washington, with the 2010 and 2011 Texas Rangers, also successfully brought teams to the Fall Classic. As of 2015, five other black men have had managerial careers lasting at least five years since *Nightline* in 1987, including Frank

Robinson returning to the dugout at Major League Baseball's behest to take charge of the financially struggling Montreal Expos in 2002.

* * *

Jackie Robinson's 1947 entrance with the Brooklyn Dodgers was the beginning of a continuing process for major-league baseball in dealing with race and, more broadly, diversity. What began as an imposing challenge—accepting any black player in the formerly all-white world of the clubhouse and the field of play—because of strong institutional resistance, ultimately required black players with all levels of major-league ability being given a fair chance to compete for starting positions before integration could be considered consolidated. If integration is thus no longer an issue, diversity is, especially as American society has become more diverse and the talent pool for major-league baseball more global. While one-fifth of all those who played in the major leagues during the 2013 season were born in the Dominican Republic, Venezuela, Cuba, or Puerto Rico, less than 8 percent of the players on opening day rosters in 2013 were African American—a monumental drop from 27 percent in 1975, according to a survey by *USA Today*.

With players from the Caribbean Basin becoming dominant among minorities in the big leagues, the issues of race and diversity have taken on a new angle. Dominicans, Venezuelans, and a second wave of Cubans who had to defect to play in America have assumed star-studded prominence on major-league teams. Not only are African Americans now significantly outnumbered by players from Latin America, but there are substantially fewer young black Americans even interested in baseball as a sport in their formative years. Commissioner Bud Selig was spurred in 2013 to organize a task force to examine the reasons why and to propose initiatives to reverse the decline of African Americans in major-league baseball.

Reflecting the better nature of American society—and validating the legacy of Jackie Robinson beyond honoring his eternally retired number 42 every year on the anniversary of his first big-league game—Major League Baseball is as attentive today as it has ever been to the issues of race and diversity. The process continues.

# Bibliography

Aaron, Hank. *I Had a Hammer: The Hank Aaron Story*. With Lonnie Wheeler. New York: HarperCollins, 1991.

Anderson, Dave. *Pennant Races: Baseball at Its Best*. New York: Main Street Books, 1994.

Appel, Marty. *Pinstripe Empire: The New York Yankees from before the Babe to after the Boss*. New York: Bloomsbury, 2012.

Barber, Red. *1947: When All Hell Broke Loose in Baseball*. New York: Da Capo, 1982.

Barra, Allen. *Yogi Berra: Eternal Yankee*. New York: Norton, 2009.

Bryant, Howard. *The Last Hero: A Life of Henry Aaron*. New York: Anchor Books, 2011.

———. *Shut Out: A Story of Race and Baseball in Boston*. Boston: Beacon, 2002.

Cohen, Stanley. *Dodgers! The First 100 Years*. New York: Birch Lane, 1990.

Cramer, Richard Ben. *Joe DiMaggio: The Hero's Life*. New York: Simon and Schuster, 2000.

Creamer, Robert W. *Stengel: His Life and Times*. New York: Simon and Schuster, 1984.

D'Antonio, Michael. *Forever Blue: The True Story of Walter O'Malley*. New York: Riverhead Books. 2009.

Davenport, Clay. "Durocher's Obsession: Static versus Dynamic Offenses." In *It Ain't over 'til It's Over*, edited by Steven Goldman, 266–72. New York: Basic Books, 2007.

Deane, Bill. *Baseball Myths: Debating, Debunking, and Disproving Tales from the Diamond*. Lanham, MD: Scarecrow, 2012.

Dickson, Paul. *Bill Veeck: Baseball's Greatest Maverick*. New York: Walker, 2012.

Durocher, Leo. *Nice Guys Finish Last*. With Ed Linn. New York: Simon and Schuster, 1975.

Fetter, Henry D. *Taking on the Yankees: Winning and Losing in the Business of Baseball*. New York: Norton, 2003.

Frommer, Harvey. *New York City Baseball: The Last Golden Age, 1947–1957*. Lanham, MD: Taylor Trade, 2013.

Fussman, Cal. *After Jackie: Pride, Prejudice, and Baseball's Forgotten Heroes*. New York: ESPN Books, 2007.

Goldman, Steven. "Tyranicide," In *It Ain't over 'til It's Over*, edited by Steven Goldman, 58–82. New York: Basic Books, 2007.

Goldstein, Richard. *Superstars and Screwballs: 100 Years of Brooklyn Baseball*. New York: Dutton, 1991.

Golenbock, Peter. *Bums: An Oral History of the Brooklyn Dodgers*. New York: G. P. Putnam's Sons, 1984.

———. *Dynasty: The New York Yankees, 1949–1964*. New York: McGraw-Hill, 2000.

Halberstam, David. *Summer of '49*. New York: Harper Perennial Modern Classics, 2006.

Helyar, John. *Lords of the Realm: The Real History of Baseball*. New York: Villard Books, 1994.

Hirsch, James S. *Willie Mays: The Life, the Legend*. New York: Scribner, 2010.

Jaffe, Chris. *Evaluating Baseball's Managers: A History and Analysis of Performance in the Major Leagues, 1876–2008*. Jefferson, NC: McFarland, 2010.

Jaffe, Jay. "Alston's L.A. Confidential." In *It Ain't over 'til It's Over*, edited by Steven Goldman, 30–45. New York: Basic Books, 2007.

James, Bill. *The Bill James Guide to Baseball Managers: From 1870 to Today*. New York: Scribner, 1997.

———. *The New Bill James Historical Baseball Abstract*. New York: Free Press, 2001.

James, Robert A. "Field of Liens: Real-Property Development in Baseball." *Baseball Research Journal* 39, no. 2 (Fall 2010).

Jordan, David M. *The Athletics of Philadelphia: Connie Mack's White Elephants, 1901–1954.* Jefferson, NC: McFarland, 1999.

Kaese, Harold. *The Boston Braves, 1871–1953.* Boston: Northeastern, 2004.

Kahn, Roger. *The Boys of Summer.* New York: Harper Perennial Modern Classic, 2006.

———. *The Era: 1947–1957: When the Yankees, the Giants, and the Dodgers Ruled the World.* Lincoln: University of Nebraska Press, 1993.

Kaiser, David. *Epic Season: The 1948 American League Pennant Race.* Amherst: University of Massachusetts Press, 1998.

Kiernan, Thomas. *The Miracle at Coogan's Bluff.* New York: Crowell, 1975.

Lamb, Chris. *Conspiracy of Silence: Sportswriters and the Long Campaign to Desegregate Baseball.* Lincoln: University of Nebraska Press, 2012.

Lanctot, Neil. *Campy: The Two Lives of Roy Campanella.* New York: Simon and Schuster, 2011.

Leavengood, Ted. *Clark Griffith: The Old Fox of Washington Baseball.* Jefferson, NC: McFarland, 2011.

Leavy, Jane. *The Last Boy: Mickey Mantle and the End of America's Childhood.* New York: HarperCollins, 2010.

Levy, Alan H. *Joe McCarthy: Architect of the Yankee Dynasty.* Jefferson, NC: McFarland, 2005.

Lowenfish, Lee. *Branch Rickey: Baseball's Ferocious Gentleman.* Lincoln: University of Nebraska Press, 2009.

Maraniss, David. *Clemente: The Passion and Grace of Baseball's Last Hero.* New York: Simon and Schuster, 2006.

Marshall, William. *Baseball's Pivotal Era, 1945–1951.* Lexington: University of Kentucky Press, 1999.

McCue, Andy. "Allan Roth: The First Front Office Statistician." *Baseball Research Journal* 43, no. 1 (Spring 2014).

Moffi, Larry. *This Side of Cooperstown: An Oral History of Major League Baseball in the 1950s.* Iowa City: University of Iowa Press, 1996.

Montville, Leigh. *Ted Williams: The Biography of an American Hero.* New York: Anchor Books, 2004.

Paper, Lew. *Perfect: Don Larsen's Miraculous World Series Game and the Men Who Made It Happen.* New York: New American Library, 2009.

Pietrusza, David. *Judge and Jury: The Life and Times of Judge Kenesaw Mountain Landis.* South Bend, IN: Diamond Communications, 1998.

Prager, Joshua. *The Echoing Green: The Untold Story of Bobby Thomson, Ralph Branca and the Shot Heard Round the World.* New York: Vintage Books, 2008.

Rampersad, Arnold. *Jackie Robinson: A Biography.* New York: Ballantine, 1997.

Reisler, Jim. *The Best Game Ever: Pirates vs. Yankees, October 13, 1960.* Cambridge, MA: Da Capo, 2009.

*Report for Submission to National and American Leagues on 27 August, 1946* (The MacPhail Report), Box 162, A. B. Chandler Papers, Special Collections Research Center, University of Kentucky Libraries. file:///C:/Users/owner/Downloads/HDFS-3042-1946+leaguereport.pdf.

Ribowsky, Mark. *The Complete History of the Home Run.* New York: Citadel Press, 2003.

Rosenblatt, Aaron. "Negroes in Baseball: The Failure of Success." *Trans-action* 4, no. 9 (September 1967) 51–53.

Shapiro, Michael. *Bottom of the Ninth: Branch Rickey, Casey Stengel, and the Daring Scheme to Save Baseball from Itself.* New York: Times Books, 2009.

———. *The Last Good Season: Brooklyn, the Dodgers, and Their Last Pennant Race Together.* New York: Doubleday, 2003.

Swaine, Rick. *The Black Stars Who Made Baseball Whole.* Jefferson, NC: McFarland, 2006.

———. *The Integration of Major League Baseball: A Team by Team History.* Jefferson, NC: McFarland, 2009.

Tebbetts, George "Birdie." *Birdie: Confessions of a Baseball Nomad*. With James Morrison. Chicago: Triumph Books, 2002.

Turbow, Jason. *The Baseball Codes: The Unwritten Rules of Baseball*. With Michael Duca. New York: Pantheon, 2010.

Tygiel, Jules. *Baseball's Great Experiment: Jackie Robinson and His Legacy*. New York: Oxford University Press, 1983.

———. *Past Time: Baseball as History*. New York: Oxford University Press, 2000.

Vecsey, George. *Stan Musial: An American Life*. New York: Ballantine, 2001.

Veeck, Bill. *Veeck as in Wreck: The Autobiography of Bill Veeck*. With Ed Linn. Chicago: University of Chicago Press, 2011.

Ward, Geoffrey C., and Ken Burns. *Baseball: An Illustrated History*. New York: Alfred A. Knopf, 2001.

Warrington, Robert D. "Departure without Dignity: The Athletics Leave Philadelphia." *Baseball Research Journal*, 39, no. 2 (Fall 2010).

Weintraub, Robert. *The Victory Season: The End of World War II and the Birth of Baseball's Golden Age*. New York: Back Bay Books, 2014.

White, Bill. *Uppity: My Untold Story about the Games People Play*. With Gordon Dillow. New York: Grand Central, 2011.

Zimbalist, Andrew. *May the Best Team Win: Baseball Economics and Public Policy*. Washington, DC: Brookings Institution, 2003.

The following websites were also consulted:

www.baseball-reference.com

www.census.gov — population of the 100 largest cities/decade

www.retrosheet.org

www.sabr.org/bioproject

# Index

# About the Author

For the love of the game and its history, Bryan Soderholm-Difatte is a member of the Society for American Baseball Research. He has no favorite team but grew up in New York, went to college in Los Angeles and graduate school in Boston, lived and worked in the Washington, DC, area—which is also easily within distance of Baltimore—and has a girlfriend from Colorado, which should provide a fair indication of the teams he follows most closely. Soderholm-Difatte is a former senior analyst at the Central Intelligence Agency and the National Counterterrorism Center. He is a regular contributor in SABR publications, including the *Baseball Research Journal*, and writes the blog *Baseball Historical Insight*.